Nigel Pickford read English at Cambridge University, and is a professional maritime historian who has made documentaries for Channel 4 and has published books with Dorling Kindersley and National Geographic.

LADY BETTE

AND THE

MURDER

OF

MR THYNN

NIGEL PICKFORD

WEIDENFELD & NICOLSON

A W&N PAPERBACK

First published in Great Britain in 2014
by Weidenfeld & Nicolson
This paperback edition published in 2015
by Weidenfeld & Nicolson,
an imprint of Orion Books Ltd,
Orion House, 5 Upper St Martin's Lane,
London WC2H 9EA

An Hachette UK company

1 3 5 7 9 10 8 6 4 2

A CIP catalogue record for this book
is available from the British Library.

ISBN 978-1-7802-2654-5

Typeset by Input Data Services Ltd, Bridgwater, Somerset

Printed and bound by CPI Group (UK) Ltd, Croydon, CR0 4YY

The Orion Publishing Group's policy is to use papers that
are natural, renewable and recyclable products and made
from wood grown in sustainable forests. The logging and
manufacturing processes are expected to conform to the
environmental regulations of the country of origin.

www.orionbooks.co.uk

For Rosamund

Contents

Author's Note on
Dates, Spellings and Names

During the period of this book, the late seventeenth century, the New Year in England did not start officially until 25 March, even though in the popular mind it had already begun on 1 January. In response to the confusion this caused, many wrote the date during the first three months of the year using both numbers such as in the lettering 1681/2 used on Thynn's tomb. There was also a ten-day difference between the date in England, following the Julian calendar, and the date on the Continent, following the newer Gregorian calendar.

Many of the characters in this book were happy to spell their own names in several different ways. For the sake of reader clarity I have standardised the many variant spellings. In the case of Bette, her name was pronounced Betty, but I have preferred to follow the Bette style of spelling.

When quoting original source material I have tried as far as possible to use the original spellings, except where clarity of meaning has become hopelessly jeopardised.

Thomas Thynn's Memorial

PROLOGUE ⁓
1682
WESTMINSTER ABBEY

As through the Abbey wondring strangers pass,
To view the Fabrick, Tombs and painted glasse,
When the Great Thynn's Rich monumental shrine
(Which like the Moon, 'mong lesser Stars doth shine,)
Containing Sacred Relics, Dust Divine;
They see, and by the epitaph certified
How that by murder he untimely dye'd:
Desire to know, who was the Cause; the Clarke
With Truth shall soon reply, Count Konigsmark.

– Anonymous poem published as a broadsheet 1682[1]

Arnold Quillan[2] lies on his back upon the ancient and uneven paving stones of the Abbey, tapping with mallet, gouge and chisel at a block of the finest white Italian marble. His eyes grow dim with the strain of constantly gauging the exactness of the line. It is difficult working in such sepulchral gloom. His apprentice Jan Ost stands over him with a lantern, but the flickering light can prove deceptive. One slip now and the work of months would be ruined. He is putting the finishing touches to the tomb of Thomas Thynn. Most of the carving has been completed in the workshop on Ludgate Hill, the 'Belle Sauvage', but there is always some last-minute pointing and polishing after the slabs have been hoisted and swung into their final positions.

It had been a troublesome commission from the outset. Quillan had spent long weeks on the lettering of a convoluted inscription that had been stipulated by the executors, only for Dean Thomas Sprat of the Abbey to intervene at the last moment and insist on its immediate and total removal. The words may have been in Latin, and so understood only by the few, but they were still an insult to Count Konigsmark, a libel upon Lady Bette, a slur upon the English justice system, and, above all else, they were defamatory of King Charles himself. So the slab had been removed in its entirety and smashed into pieces and a new monument has been lowered solemnly into its place which reads simply:

THOMAS THYNN of LONG LEATE in Com. WILTS Esqr.
Who was barbarously murdered on Sunday the 12th February 1681/2

No fingers pointed. No explanations offered. Below is just a large and empty space.[3]

Quillan gets to his feet, brushes the dust from his shirt and stretches his cramped legs. He is a tall, well-shaped man, not yet thirty years old, an immigrant from Holland. He stands back a couple of paces and views his handiwork. His own name is already being spoken of in the same breath as the great Grinling Gibbons.[4] There are those who are saying he may soon surpass him.

Quillan is well enough pleased with the top section. He has embellished it with the required paraphernalia of swagged curtains, pediments and urns. Thynn is shown reclining with a cupid at his feet. He is gazing heavenwards, his lips slightly parted, a limpid expression on his face, indicative of his saintliness. Neither the executors nor the Dean could surely quarrel with any of that. But it is the scene depicted below upon which Quillan has lavished his greatest care.

It records the moment of Mr Thynn's brutal murder. Three horsemen are shown attacking a fashionable coach. One of the assassins, with elaborately coiffeured hair, which falls forward in two lustrous locks, catches hold of the carriage harness. A second, wearing a small three-cornered hat, threatens the two footmen travelling pillion. The central figure of the three shoulders a musquetoon and discharges its fatal contents through the coach window. Thynn throws his hands into the air in a gesture of horror and despair.

The Abbey, as always, is busy with tourists and pilgrims, antiquarians and beggars, the idle and the curious. Once they have finished viewing the main attractions, Elizabeth's tomb or the painting of Richard the Lion Heart, the more adventurous wander off towards the South Choir Aisle to gaze upon the newcomer who has just taken up residence there. Everyone of course has their opinion about the murder. Some say the young and handsome foreign Count, Karl Konigsmark, who was quite the talk of the town, commissioned it for love of Lady Bette. Others think it was the fourteen-year-old girl herself who was behind the killing, and if Konigsmark was involved at all, it was only out of gallantry. Then there are those who whisper that Thynn's death was nothing to do with love or honour, that there are many in high places who are glad to see him dead, especially the Catholic conspirators.[5]

Quillan professes no opinions. He is not paid to profess opinions. He is paid to raise monuments to the dead, magnificent shrines to embellish the memory and to immortalise the names of the departed.

PART ONE

1681

Soldier and Girl in a Brothel by Frans Van Mieris

1

THE AMSTERDAM ORDINARY

He's well acquainted with the ostlers about Bishopsgate Street
and Smithfield, and gains from them intelligence of what booties
go out that are worth attempting. He pretends to be a disbanded
officer, and reflects very feelingly upon the hard usage 'we poor
gentlemen meet with, who have hazarded our lives and fortunes
for the honour of our Prince, the defence of the Country, and
the safety of religion . . .' At such sort of cant he is excellent.

— Ned Ward, *London Spy*[1]

In August 1681 Lieutenant John Stern, forty-two years old, a soldier
by trade, washed up in London. Like Quillan, he was an immigrant,
one of the thousands constantly deposited by the tide on
the muddy shores of the Thames. Unlike Quillan he didn't have a job or
a network of contacts. He arrived wearing a small three-cornered hat and
among his meagre possessions he carried a single book, *Dilheren's Way to
Eternal Happiness*, a self-help guide to getting into heaven. He had been

kicking around northern Europe for the previous twenty-three years, enlisting in whichever army would have him. His only marketable skill was killing people.

In his *Last Confession*, hastily scribbled in Newgate Gaol, Stern claimed to have been born of Swedish nobility, a son 'by the left hand' as he put it. It may have been true but his failure to name his father does not inspire confidence. There is not much about Stern to inspire confidence. There must have been some family money, because after he left his native Sweden at the age of fifteen he spent two years at school in Germany. This smattering of education, however, just made his present reduced circumstances that much more galling. He clearly saw himself as a cut above the general run of illiterate cannon fodder.

At the age of nineteen he travelled to Pomerania, where he entered the military service of the Elector of Brandenburg. Within three months he had quit that employment and was on the road again, heading south this time through Poland and into Bohemia. From there he went to the Netherlands and then to France. After that it was back into Bohemia, followed by Austria and Hungary, and ending up with a longer stay than usual in the Netherlands, now fighting for Louis XIV, the most powerful Catholic king in Europe, against the Protestant Dutch. When things finally got too difficult for him in Holland, he once again upped and left, this time for Denmark and finally Holstein.

'I have ever had a great fancy to travel, and from a Child have had inclination to be a soldier,'[2] he confided. This desire to travel was often cited as the reason for enlisting by both soldiers and sailors, but it was also the last resort of miscreants fleeing from their murky pasts. Ned Ward, that sharp observer of London low life around this period, certainly made the connection between out-of-work soldiers bewailing their misfortunes and the criminal fraternity looking to pick up useful information for their next big haul.

By 1681 times were hard for the average mercenary like Stern. The Treaty of Nymegen three years earlier had put an end to the wars between Holland and France, and so drastically reduced demand for the professional soldier. It was while he was in Holstein that he decided to try his luck on the other side of the North Sea. He must have heard the common rumour that London was the place to go if you wanted to make a quick fortune. There was some truth to it. London was the fastest-growing city in Europe, with over half a million inhabitants. It was shortly to become the largest metropolis in the world, overtaking Paris. Metropolis was the new fashionable word to use when trying to communicate the wondrous seething monstrosity of it all.[3]

Stern took a room in the Amsterdam Tavern, or Ordinary, as pubs were then called. It was situated in Broad Street close to the Royal Exchange in the commercial heart of the city. It was an odd choice. If he had been serious about enlisting in the King's Life Guards, as he claimed in his *Confession*, he would have been better advised to go to Westminster, where most of the soldiery lived. Alternatively he might have found a welcome in the Swedish quarter around Well Street, near Wapping Docks. Instead he gravitated towards the Dutch financial centre, the home of diamond dealers, insurance brokers and bankers.[4]

Whatever Stern's reasons for choosing the Amsterdam, one thing was quickly evident. By the time he arrived in London the allure of travel was long over. As he himself put it, the desire to travel had 'much decreased with time'.[5] At forty-two he was, by the standards of the age, an old man. He was almost out of money. His boots were worn down. His clothes were shabby. He had a string of broken relationships behind him and he was fond of fulminating about the inconstancy of women. He preferred horses. Horses were creatures you could rely on.

There is a painting, from around the middle of the seventeenth century, by Frans van Mieris that hangs in the Mauritshuis in The Hague. It shows a leering officer holding out his glass, waiting for it to be filled with ale by a pretty young serving maid. They may be in an inn or possibly a brothel. In the background a man and a woman are embracing in a doorway. Two dogs are depicted in the act of copulation. Used bedclothes have been slung over a railed gallery to air. Another soldier slumps in a dead-drunk stupor with his head on a table. It is impossible to look at this painting and not think of Lieutenant Stern drowning his sorrows.

Then a miracle happened. Stern was a man who believed in miracles as well as visions, apparitions and the mysterious power of dreams. The miracle was the arrival of a man called Vollichs. Except Vollichs wasn't his real name. His real name was Vratz, Captain Christopher Vratz. He moved into the big room next to the one that Stern was quartered in.

The two men struck up an immediate friendship. It wasn't surprising. They were both professional soldiers who had seen something of the world. Vratz was a little younger, but only by four years. They both spoke High Dutch.[6] They both had a contempt for the established order of things. The big difference between them was that Vratz was flush with money, and Stern wasn't. Vratz had four servants and a shiny new pair of leather boots.

It was the boots that most impressed Stern. The possession of a stout pair of boots was high up on any poor soldier's wish list.

Drinking quarts of ale together soon bred intimacy. It wasn't long before Vratz confided to Stern that he had an important request to make. Stern answered promptly that he would do whatever he was commanded, 'to the utmost of my power'.[7] He was a natural follower, eager to assume the deferential role in this relationship right from the outset. Vratz was obviously impressed by Stern's enthusiasm to serve. He decided to take him into his confidence a little further. He explained that he 'had a quarrel with a gentleman'.[8] He was proposing to challenge him to a duel. He wanted Stern to act as his second. Duels were illegal, but they were also commonplace, and the authorities largely turned a blind eye. Vratz told Stern that if he would like to stay on in London, 'during the four weeks he should stay, then he [Vratz] would pay for everything'.[9] Stern accepted. The fatal pact was sealed.

But talk of the proposed duel was soon dropped. When the subject of the quarrel was next raised it was in the context of 'fighting' rather than duelling, a subtle but important shift of emphasis. November came. It was a month for conspiracy and cheap taverns were seductive places for the imparting of secrets. Customers sat in closely panelled booths almost as if they were in a private room. The constant fug of sulphurous smoke from an ill-functioning chimney combined with the sweeter smell of tobacco and the meaty tang of tallow candles. Smoke and beer fumes mingling created a convenient cloak of obscurity, blurring a man's breath, clouding his words. It was in such fuddled circumstances that Vratz, a man not much given to idle chatter, came across with one all-important further piece of information. He told Stern the name of the man who was his intended victim. It was a 'Mr Thynn'. 'Mr Thomas Thynn of Longleat'. Not only did Stern learn the name of the enemy, but the nature of Vratz's ambitions underwent a further and critical evolution. There was no longer talk of duelling or even of fighting. Instead, Vratz was much more interested in the hiring of a professional assassin. He told Stern that if he could find him someone 'who would kill the gentleman, . . . he would give him 200, nay 300 Dollars'.[10] For Stern this was a mouth-watering, beer-dribbling, sum of money.

Then quite suddenly, around the middle of the month, Vratz left their lodgings early and didn't come back. 'The Captain went out one morning, saying he would return in the afternoon, but . . . came not again,'[11] Stern explained during his cross-examination. A tailor, who had been previously employed by Vratz to work on his plum-coloured velvet coat and white lace shirts, came round and paid for the cost of lodgings to date. He also collected Vratz's boots which Stern so admired, and which Vratz had left behind in his haste to depart. Although Stern knew that Vratz was only intending to stop in England for around four weeks, he had not expected the leave-taking to be quite so abrupt. There was no message. No arrangements had been made for his future maintenance. He felt profoundly let down. He hung around for a few more days and then decided to cut his losses and head back to the Continent. London was just one more place that wasn't working out for him.

The Royal Exchange in 1681

2

THE ROYAL EXCHANGE

**Husbands are very bad, and scarce any good ones . . . Ungrateful
and vile age!**

– Charles Bertie, in a letter to his niece,
the Countess of Rutland, 8 September 1681[1]

aptain Vratz was not the only one leaving London for the
Continent in a hurry during that November. Lady Bette also
had plans to flee. She had been married to Mr Thynn on 14 July
of the previous summer. At the time of the ceremony it had all seemed
rather like a game. A coterie of admiring and laughing friends had egged
her on. But within just a few hours of the marriage she was bitterly regretting the rashness of her actions. She was also very angry. She had been
misled by those who were closest to her, those whom she had believed
she could rely on and trust, including her own grandmother, the Dowager
Countess of Northumberland. She had quickly come to learn certain particulars about Thynn's character and, still worse, his person, which made

her blood congeal. She now dreaded the thought of him touching her with his poisonous lips. He was everything that was most loathsome in the world.[2]

It had been a specific requirement on Bette's part that the marriage would not be consummated until the year of mourning for her first husband, Henry Ogle, had been completed. For this reason the marriage was also to be kept a secret. Thynn had complied with these requests. She was, after all, still only fourteen. There was plenty of time. He was content that the contracts had been signed, the marriage solemnised, and he was now in possession of Bette's immense property empire. The rest could wait. His friend Major Brett[3] had badgered him about the importance of bedding Bette at the first opportunity, as if his own gratification depended on it, but Thynn was happy to delay. Delaying had certain advantages. It gave him a few more months to attend to some pressing private matters of his own.

The year of mourning expired on 1 November 1681. Thynn communicated to Bette, from his bachelor lodgings in Canon Row, Westminster, that he would shortly be taking up residence with her in her home, the stately and sprawling Northumberland House.[4] It was an imposing property and it was now legally his to do with as he wanted. Rather more to the point, she too was his to do with as he wanted. He told her that he desired that they should now live as man and wife. The consequences of her summer madness were fast closing in on her.

On the morning of Monday, 7 November, she rose early, dressed in her outdoor clothing and ordered her carriage to be prepared, stating that she wished to go shopping in Lombard Street in order to buy some silver plate and other items of value at a particular goldsmith's she was fond of patronising. She departed the house at 9 a.m. with no trunks, portmanteaux or baggage, merely the clothes she stood up in, her purse and her servants.[5] It was a cold brisk morning. The coach rattled through the great iron gates onto the street already choking with chairmen and carmen, hansom cabs and carriages, horses, pigs, cattle, dogs, street purveyors of every imaginable form of comestible from oyster pies to lemon tansies. Bette was impatient. She wished they could move faster through the pressing crowds. The flags flapping loosely from the highest turrets of the grand houses along the northern bank of the Thames confirmed her great fear, that the wind was blowing from the east.[6] That was most unfortunate. An easterly wind could trap shipping in the river for days, sometimes weeks, and completely destroy her hopes of escaping. She prayed that the breeze might shift towards the west.

She left her carriage and servants outside the goldsmith's, telling them she would return shortly. She first wished to visit the Royal Exchange,[7] which was close by and could be easily reached on foot down Exchange Alley. She set off with only her page in attendance. The Exchange had been severely burnt in the Great Fire of 1666, but since then, like much of the old city, it had been magnificently reconstructed. At ground level there was now a colonnaded walkway, with a black and white tessellated marble floor, running around the fronts of the new emporiums. The central area was open to the sky and the ground sparkled with 'Turkey stones',[8] the size of small chicken's eggs. It was here that merchants and lawyers, bankers and brokers, stock holders and underwriters, flocked each day to pick up vital news on shipping arrivals, imports and exports, fluctuations in insurance rates, price movements, bankruptcies. It was a place for meeting, gossiping and making deals. At each corner there were spacious flights of black marble stairs that led up to a higher gallery where a further 190 shops were situated. The rent for a unit was very high, £20 per annum, but they were all taken. London was riding the crest of a trade boom and was awash with easy money and luxury goods. There was plenty here to make a young girl's mouth water, and Bette was a keen shopper, but on this particular morning her mind was running on more urgent matters.

On arrival at the Exchange, she promptly sent her page on an errand, commanding him to return to where she was waiting when he had finished. When he came back she was no longer to be seen. After some period of procrastination, the page started to look for her in her favourite haunts, the bookshops and the tea emporiums, but she was nowhere to be discovered. He returned to the coach thinking he must have misunderstood her instructions, but she was not to be found there either. A wholesale search was now commenced. The fear was that she had been abducted. The abduction of heiresses was a frequent occurrence and there had been much talk of such plots in relation to Bette all through the preceding summer.[9] Now Bette was legally married there would be nothing to be gained from kidnapping her, but as the marriage had been kept secret, a fortune hunter might well be ignorant of her married status.

Anxious servants remained at the Exchange until after dark, still hoping their young mistress would put in an appearance. They were terrified that if they went back to Northumberland House without Bette they would get the blame. The Dowager Countess was notorious for her short temper. She was fond of flaying the naked backs of her female maids with her own hand for the most minor of indiscretions.[10] For a misdemeanour of this magnitude, who could say what kind of rage she might fall into? But eventually there was no avoiding it. Return empty-handed they must.

On learning of her granddaughter's disappearance, the Dowager Countess promptly dispatched messengers scurrying this way and that to every house in the neighbourhood where something might be learnt. They called on Lady Wriothesley, Bette's estranged mother, and also on Lady Rachel Russell, her aunt. Thomas Thynn was notified and Major Brett, as were all those of importance with whom the family was involved – the Powerscourts, the Orrerys, the Longfords and the Albemarles, the Newcastles and the Sunderlands. The word went rapidly round the great houses of London. Bette was missing. But all enquiries drew a blank. If anyone knew anything, they weren't saying.

The following morning, in spite of the frantic searching that the Countess had ordered, there was still no clue to Bette's whereabouts. The situation was considered to be so serious that Major Brett was prevailed upon to go to the King and enquire directly of him whether he knew of any plot to steal Bette away. It was an unenviable task. He first had to confess that his good friend Thomas Thynn had married the young heiress in secret several months ago, even though Brett had given the King repeated assurances that this was not in fact the case. It was hardly going to be welcome news at Westminster, particularly as Charles had always hoped to secure Bette for one of his own tumultuous and impecunious brood, preferably his favoured bastard son George Fitzroy.[11] Only the King was likely to know whether or not the ruthless and reckless Barbara Palmer, Duchess of Cleveland, Fitzroy's mother, had commissioned some wild scheme to kidnap Bette.

The King's reaction was as Brett had feared it might be. He told Brett bluntly that if Bette was married to Thynn then 'she had been betrayed by those who pretended and ought to have been her best friends'.[12] He went on, in his sardonic manner, to thank Brett, 'for having played the knave', but explained that he declined to play the role of fool, as it appeared Brett wished him to do. There was clearly no assistance forthcoming from that quarter, and it was a sign of Brett's desperation that he had gone to him in the first place.

The mystery of Bette's disappearance was partially solved later that same day when her personal chambermaid handed the Dowager Countess a letter written in Bette's own hand. The contents were brief and to the point: 'she did own her marriage in some measure to Mr Thynn, but not fully, and that now she could not endure him, and therefore could not think of living with him, and therefore was gone away, but would not let her [the Dowager Countess] know where nor with whom'.[13] In the letter was enclosed the ring that Thynn had given her which she asked to be returned to him. Bette had accomplished her departure with careful planning and admirable coolness of head.

When Thynn learnt that Bette had run off, he was furious. At this stage he wasn't particularly concerned that his possession of her property might be challenged. Indeed her absenting herself made his administering her estate to his own advantage even easier. What riled him was that he had been made to look a complete fool before the entire world. 'Mr Thynn storms and rages to extravagancy in his passion,'[14] wrote the Duke of Newcastle to the Duke of Albemarle. 'She has left in her lover no other passion but that of indignation against the sexe,'[15] concurred Charles Bertie. The main reaction, however, to the news of Thynn's discomfiture was, predictably enough, one of amusement. Chaloner Chute thought the whole story was all rather more fun than a fashionable comical novel.[16] The Viscountess Campden took it as an opportunity for a weak quip: 'My Lady Ogle's great fortune has brought her to a great deal of ill-fortune.'[17] Charles Bertie was probably the most sympathetic of the town's gossips to Bette's feelings. He described how 'the contract she lately signed rises in her stomach', and 'she shows all manner of aversion to the match with Thynn'. He concluded on a note of caution: 'Wee must be allowed a little more time to learn the reason for this so surprising an action.'[18]

What everyone wanted to know was not only where she had gone, but even more importantly, who she had gone with. According to the Duke of Newcastle ''twas said she was gone along with the Count Konigsmark, but that is only a report'.[19]

Anti-Catholic Propaganda 1681

3

THE DUTCH LUTHERAN
CHURCH, BROAD STREET

**The Fire in the City was begun and carried on by the Treachery
and malice of the Papists.**

– New inscription ordered 5 August 1681 by the Corporation of London
for the Monument commemorating the Great Fire of 1666[1]

L ondon was a filthy, dark, noisy and overcrowded place. A contemporary *Guide for Foreigners* warned of 'the thick air proceed-
ing from the moisture of the weather and the smoak' as well as
the night being made 'incommodious by the rattling of the coaches, hurry
of chairs, and the great crowd of people, and the streets being not so well
lighted as so Great a City ought'.[2] All these disadvantages could be supported easily enough with money in the pocket, but without Captain Vratz
around, Lieutenant Stern was critically low on funds. He stowed his few
meagre belongings on an outward-bound ship lying in the Thames which

was ready to sail in just a few days and set about finalising his affairs. At this point he was staying in lodgings at Bock's Place in Nicholas Lane. He and Vratz had transferred there shortly before Vratz had disappeared. It was cheaper than the Amsterdam Tavern.

One of Stern's last ports of call before he was due to leave was the Dutch Lutheran church in Broad Street.[3] There he found a letter waiting for him. He must have been using the church as a kind of poste restante. The letter was from Vratz, and Stern gives it in full in his *Last Confession*:

> Sir,
> I am sorry I could not have the Honour to take my leave of you; but be it all to your advantage. I am going for France, yet have not as yet a certain Commission. In the meanwhile be pleased to continue, either at Mr Bocks, or in the City of Amsterdam, where I will not fail to pay for all. I am your obliged servant, De Vrats, alias de Vollichs.[4]

It is not clear whether Stern was quoting this letter from memory or whether he still had the original letter in his possession and was transcribing its contents. Either way it must have been through a further translation, because the original, like the *Last Confession* itself, was written in High Dutch. It is oddly formal. One suspects that Stern, who was rather fond of literary flourishes, and who had aspirations towards the gentility of learning, may have embellished it a little. On first glance the content seems straightforward enough. Vratz confirms that he has left the country, but makes it clear that while he is gone he is happy to continue bankrolling Stern's living expenses. However, other parts of it are more opaque. For a start there is the issue of Vratz's alias. It can be presumed that Vratz signed this letter simply Vollichs and that it is Stern who has decided to include his true name of Vratz for the sake of reader clarity. But Stern never explains why Vratz was going under an alias in the first place. It probably had something to do with the fact that Captain Vratz was already infamous in Eastern Germany for several major thefts.[5] If Stern was aware of this he doesn't let on. To admit that he already knew something of Vratz's criminal history would have been to undermine his presentation of himself as an innocent, caught up in a business that he always regarded as honourable.

The phrase 'have not as yet a certain Commission' is intriguing. There can be little doubt that this is an oblique reference to the much-discussed murder plan, but for the first time it is suggested that the final decision lies not with Vratz alone, but is dependent upon authorisation from a higher and more powerful personage as yet unnamed. Vratz is no longer the principal in this quarrel, which is how he had previously presented himself. He is now just an agent, and the trip abroad is a necessary preliminary before Thynn's murder can be given the go-ahead. This is not seen, however, as diminishing the chances of both men receiving rich rewards. The general tone of the letter is breezily optimistic. Vratz is confident that the deal is going to come off and that everyone is going to benefit.

The effect of this letter on Stern was to promptly make him change his mind about leaving. He fetched his belongings from the ship and went not to the Amsterdam Tavern, nor back to Bock's, as suggested, but to a new lodging house in Blackmore Street. It is a characteristic of both Stern and Vratz that neither of them liked to stay in the same place for too long.

The exact chronology of these events is important, particularly the timing of Vratz's sudden return to the Continent, but Stern's grasp of dates is infuriatingly vague. In his *Last Confession* he offers two different time sequences for the same events, and in his cross-examination by Justice Reresby there is a third version.[6] The one that makes most sense has Stern arriving in London in late summer, Vratz turning up in the middle of October, and then leaving again around the middle of November. This places Vratz's departure just a few days after Lady Bette's.

So Stern returns to what he is best at, hanging around in taverns and waiting. He can be pictured easily enough slumped in a drunken haze, clutching his weak beer in a jug decorated with the satirical figure of the fat-bellied, long-bearded Jesuit Cardinal Bellarmine. Even drinking vessels had been co-opted into anti-Catholic propaganda. Hatred of Catholics ran deep through the city and the mood on the streets was increasingly fractious. Stern was not much interested in any of this bitter political and religious factionalism. He never mentions it in his *Confession*. He was far too preoccupied with his own problems and his own dreams. All the same he must have been aware of it swirling around him. Hardly a week went by without a new demonstration by one grouping or another. Windows were stoned, lanterns broken, constables attacked. Legitimate political protest easily turned into alcohol-fuelled rioting. On occasion there were pitched battles between rival gangs of London apprentices or 'crews' as they liked to call themselves. Stabbings were frequent. Some nights great fires lit up the skyline and the rumour went round that the Catholics were burning the city again. Usually it turned out to be nothing more sinister than a neglected candle in a warehouse full of pitch.[7] But the atmosphere was tense and Stern was shortly to find himself in the centre of this maelstrom, whether he wanted to be or not.

Late seventeenth-century royal yacht

4

THE *CLEVELAND* YACHT

**You must confess that I have reason to condemn this senseless
passion, that whereso'ever it comes destroys all that entertain it;
nothing of judgement or discretion can live with it.**

Dorothy Temple to her husband, William Temple,
condemning the folly of elopement.[1]

Within a few minutes of giving her servants the slip Bette met
up with Dorothy Temple, fifty-four years of age, ample-
bosomed, kindly-faced,[2] and an old family friend. Bette, estranged from her own mother, at loggerheads with her grandmother,
betrayed by those she had thought she could trust, had found in Dorothy
a comforting maternal surrogate. For her part, Dorothy regarded Bette
almost as her own. She had given birth to nine children, only two of whom
had survived infancy, and one of those, her only daughter and a playmate
of Bette's, had recently died of smallpox.[3]

Dorothy Temple was a woman of impeccable reputation and her

husband, William, was a much-respected former ambassador to Holland, and close friend to the Percy family. Dorothy was the last person who would ever knowingly have involved herself in a mad escapade or a wild romantic dash. She thoroughly disapproved of unrestrained passion. The fact that she was prepared to aid Bette in her flight from Thynn merely underlines the gravity and urgency of Bette's situation.

While her servants waited patiently in Lombard Street outside the goldsmith's, Bette pulled a hood over her head and hastened into a hired coach waiting in Cornhill. Curtains were hurriedly drawn across the windows and the small party set off. They must have turned right into Birching Lane, crossed over Lombard Street and then gone down St Nicholas Street, where Stern and Vratz were still residing in Bock's lodging house, discussing the different ways in which Thynn might be killed. Bette's carriage passed the Fox Tavern on the right, turned left into Great East Cheap, and then right into Fish Street, heading for London Bridge. Progress was painfully slow, for the streets were narrow and congested. Every time they stopped to allow for the passage of a suicidal pig, or the crossing of a blind water-carrier, Bette must have been terrified that they were being held at gunpoint and that she was about to be seized by some of Thynn's henchmen and dragged back to Northumberland House, where Thynn himself would be waiting for her with his drooping lower lip and his heavily jewelled fingers. But on each occasion it proved a false alarm and the carriage jerked forward again.

They reached New Fish Street with the Sun Inn on the left, where Pepys admired the quality of both the breakfasts and the conversation.[4] They passed the church of St Magnus the Martyr and entered onto London Bridge, seething with people in a perpetual whirl of movement.[5] The river was choked with shipping, wherries, ketches, pinks, galliots, scullers, smacks, hoys, flyboats, doggers and sloops, as well as the great East India Company ships at anchor further down towards Black-wall. Everywhere, jetties, wharves, and wooden bulwarks, were pushing out into the tidal stream, extending rickety walkways for the unload-ing and stowing of barrels, boxes and bales. There were so many new obstructions being built out from the river banks, despite all the ordinances and regulations forbidding it, that the pent-up waters constantly frothed and eddied in frustration at the many obstacles that were put in their way. Once the bridge had been safely traversed, they turned east by St Thomas's Hospital, crossed Horsley Down, passed through Rotherhithe and headed out towards Deptford.

It was at Deptford Royal Docks that the two fleeing women met up with Henry Sidney. He was a cousin of Bette's, in his early forties, a bachelor and a notorious womaniser. He would not have been any-one's first choice to play the role of chivalrous knight, but he was undeniably a useful fixer. He was the current ambassador to Holland and he had a house in The Hague.[6] Even more importantly he had use of a royal yacht, the *Cleveland*, which was at that very moment riding in the Thames, with his own goods and servants on board, waiting to be dispatched to Rotterdam. A royal yacht was the fastest and most conven-ient mode of transport available. It was the perfect solution for a quick getaway.[7]

The sight of the *Cleveland* must have set Bette's heart racing with a mixture of relief and excitement. On the surface it was a shimmering dream. The beauty of its lines and the richness of its decoration sug-gested Cleopatra's barge, or some similarly sumptuous vessel out of the *Arabian Nights*. At the bowsprit was the painted figurehead of a young woman in loose Roman robes with bare breasts. In her left hand she held a sceptre decorated with a lily that quelled a monster which writhed be-neath her. The stern was even more elaborately carved, gilded with the royal arms, the rampant lion and unicorn bearing aloft the crown, and a variety of magical creatures, serpents, birds and flowers, interlaced be-neath. Three massive lanterns surmounted the aft railing. It was only a small ship, some sixty feet long by eighteen feet wide, eight small cannon of the Rupertino design piercing its sides. It was single-masted with a gaff mainsail and a square topsail. A silken pendant hung limply from the truck at the top of the mast. What wind there was still came from the east.[8]

Bette was entered onto the ship's books as 'Madamoiselle Ryswick'. Lady Temple travelled as 'Madame Borlaise'.[9] Both women spoke good French and so the subterfuge was easy to maintain. Henry Sidney handed over one hundred pounds in cash and a bill of credit for one thousand pounds that Bette could draw on once she reached The Hague.[10]

The appearance of the *Cleveland* yacht may have been pretty on the outside but inside the accommodation was cramped in the extreme. At the stern were situated the quarters of Captain John Clements. The rest of the crew of thirty were crowded together in the forepart. Lady Bette and Lady Temple, along with half a dozen or more of Sidney's servants, were squashed into a small cabin towards the stern. Below the waterline the yacht's wormy and barnacle-encrusted timbers creaked and groaned.

That night the wind shifted to the south-west[11] and the yacht got underway on an ebbing tide. Bette's prayers had been partially answered. The candles inside the great stern lanterns sputtered and flickered into life, creating a fretwork of reflections on the water. Sidney stayed with the fugitives until the *Cleveland* was safely below Gravesend. From there he took a horse straight back to Westminster and reported what had taken place to Charles in person. As he later wrote in his diary: 'The great business I had then upon my hands was about my Lady [Bette] ... The 7th of November I went with her aboard the yacht, and conducted her below Gravesend, and came back and told my story to the King, who was very well pleased.'[12] It is clear from this diary entry that Bette's flight from her husband had received a prior nod of royal approval.

When Sidney's role in facilitating Bette's escape became known, it was generally rumoured that he was hoping to marry her himself.[13] Such rumours were inevitable and there is no evidence that there was any truth to them. Sidney's motives were far simpler. Assisting Bette was a way of ingratiating himself with King Charles and furthering his own political career.

When Thynn discovered that Sidney had been instrumental in spiriting Bette out of the country, he promptly sent a servant to Sidney's London house and challenged him to a duel. This message was delivered early on the evening of Sunday 13 November. Sidney sent his answer by return. He remarked on the fineness of the weather and the fullness of the moon and suggested they should settle their differences immediately. Thynn demurred. Sidney had a reputation for being an excellent swordsman. Thynn told him that the following morning would after all be more convenient and he would hear from him further. Sidney waited in all that Monday morning but there was no further message. By three in the afternoon he had grown tired of waiting and so sent a friend of his to Thynn's to remind him of his previous promise. Thynn replied that 'he had since better considered of it, and thought it not proper on that account to quarrel and fight with him so near a relation of his Lady's'.[14] He had no doubt made the pragmatic calculation that apart from the public humiliation involved, Bette's flight hardly mattered. Eventually her head must cool and she would be left with no alternative but to slink back home. Meanwhile, he instructed his steward to start collecting Bette's huge rent roll. All further talk of a duel fizzled out.

London Coffee House

5

PETER'S COFFEE HOUSE

If you see the great Morat
With Shash on's head instead of hat,
Or any Sultan in his dress,
Or picture of a Sultaness, . . .
Or if you see a Coffee–cup
Fil'd from a Turkish pot, hung up
Within the clouds, and round it Pipes,
Wax Candles, Stoppers, these are types
And certain figures . . .
Which plainly do Spectators tell
That in that house they Coffee sell.

– From *The Character of a Coffee House* (London: s.n., 1665)[1]

In the late autumn of 1681 the disappearance of his bride was not Thynn's only problem. He was also seriously out of favour with the King. The reason was his close and longstanding friendship with the Duke of Monmouth, Charles's eldest, illegitimate and trouble-some son. For the previous ten years, Thynn and Monmouth had shared a taste in foppish clothes, fine clarets, fast horses and debauching pretty young women, none of which was likely to upset Charles. But more recently they had turned their attention to an altogether grander prize. Monmouth had started openly canvassing to be named as the Protestant heir to the throne, the popular alternative to the Catholic but legitimate James, Duke of York, Charles's younger brother. Charles was still fond of Monmouth in a doting, fatherly kind of way, admiring of his handsome looks and his expert riding skills, but he was also increasingly annoyed by his unwanted and unhelpful political interventions. In Charles's view it was men like Thynn who were encouraging Monmouth in this ridiculous dream he had of becoming King, and the particular danger with Thynn was that he had the financial resources to bankroll Monmouth's foolish campaigning antics.

By October 1681 the West Country, where Thynn was a powerful land-owner, was in virtual open rebellion. Unemployment in the wool trade had reached alarming levels.[2] Thynn had been named in July by one of Secretary of State Sir Leoline Jenkins's spies as one of 'the greatest countenancers of the disaffected party'.[3] Charles had already made a move against Thynn the previous March, stripping him of his position of Colonel of the Wilt-shire Militia, but Charles's ministers were having difficulty enforcing this humiliation. The office of regimental colonel was technically in the gift of the Earl of Pembroke and Pembroke was one of Thynn's closest cronies and adept at finding reasons to delay. By the beginning of November a new Colonel had still not been put in place.[4]

Thynn and Pembroke and others of their faction felt that they could flout the views of the Court because Protestant opinion in the country was behind them. The succession issue was becoming increasingly urgent because of mounting worries about Charles's state of health. It was this nagging anxiety that fed into the growing movement for an Exclusion Bill to be passed, banning a Catholic from sitting on the throne, which would have the effect of sidelining James and bringing in Monmouth.[5]

It was not very long before the old story of the mysterious 'black box' resurfaced. It supposedly contained documents to prove that the King had been lawfully married to the Duke of Monmouth's mother, Lucy Walter. If true, Monmouth would be legitimised and his path to the throne cleared. A Captain Aldridge appeared before the Privy Council to swear to its existence and he claimed that there were twenty others who would swear likewise.[6] The black box was said to be secreted in a convent in France and access to it was strictly guarded. Lucy Walter herself had died in 1658.

As demonstrations became more frequent, attitudes hardened. On 6 October Lord Mordaunt, another close friend of both Monmouth and Thynn, obtained an interview with the King and 'for two hours was endeavouring to reconcile him [Charles] to the Duke of Monmouth'. Afterwards Charles's Secretary of State, Lord Conway, commented that Mordaunt 'received little satisfaction'.[7] Charles was generally lackadaisical when it came to issues of government, but on some matters he could be stubborn, and he was determined that it was his brother James who would succeed him.

The two sides had some inventive terms of abuse for each other. Monmouth and his supporters were the 'Fanatick Party', the 'Discontented', the 'Mutineers' and the 'Whigs'. The Court Party were 'Yorkists', 'Tantivies', 'Sham plotters', 'Papists' and 'Tories'.[8] The struggle between them took place as much on the streets as in the corridors of Parliament, but it was the columns of the newspapers that fanned the flames.

No one better represented the new breed of newspaper man than Nat Thompson.[9] He was a tough Irish-born journalist, except, of course, the word journalist had not yet been invented. If you'd asked him he would have described himself as a printer. He was in reality a news gatherer, writer, printer, publisher, entrepreneur and political activist all rolled up into one. Like Stern he'd arrived in London more or less penniless. His first job had been as an inky-faced apprentice to the printer Thomas Radcliffe. His first astute career move was to marry his boss's daughter, Mary. When Thomas conveniently died in 1678, son-in-law Nat promptly took over the family firm. He was soon publishing his own weekly paper, *The Loyal Protestant and True Domestick Intelligence, or News from both the City and the Country*. It was not exactly a snappy title, and the use of the word Protestant was something of a smokescreen. Most of his contemporaries considered him to be a closet Catholic. 'Popish Nat', as he came to be known, was certainly a fervent supporter of James, Duke of York, and he missed no opportunity for sniping at the Protestant Whig lobby.

The newspaper business was in its infancy, but growing rapidly. Between 1679 and 1682 no fewer than forty different titles were published, mainly by one-man bands.[10] No wonder John Evelyn, writing to Samuel Pepys on 28 April 1682, referred to 'This diffusive age, greedy of intelligence and public affairs'.[11] There was fierce competition for this new readership and men like Thompson were none too scrupulous about how they got their information or its accuracy, just so long as it caused a sensation and satisfied his clientele. He had a pugilistic way with words and was not averse to a scrap in the gutter.

In early November 1681, Thompson was involved in a very public row over whether or not the Earl of Huntingdon had abandoned the Whigs and joined the Tory loyalists. A rival newspaper called *The True Protestant Mercury*, published by Thompson's great enemy Langley Curtiss, carried a letter, signed by Monmouth and Pembroke, which denied that Huntingdon had defected and called Thompson's reporting 'insolent and injurious'.[12]

As it happened, this particular argument was not just being carried on in the columns of the rival newspapers. It had also spilled over into that latest social phenomenon, the coffee house. Much of the unrest in London around this time was centred on individual coffee houses. Such places were widely regarded as breeding grounds for subversive political opinion. In the popular imagination, drinking the juices of the potent bean was synonymous with intellectual ferment and the brewing up of dissent. Coffee houses were places where newspapers were freely available, broadsheets were pinned to walls, leaflets were left lying around, and even the playing cards were loaded with satirical insults directed at the celebrities of the day. The physical structure of the coffee house, with its long plain wooden tables set in one large room, was much more conducive to open debate and discussion than was the case inside the traditional tavern, where wooden partitions separated off one party from another, and conversations were huddled private affairs.[13]

Sensitive to their troublesome character, in December 1675 Charles had passed a decree banning coffee houses altogether. When this proved impractical he tried to impose a licensing system. When that didn't work either, Charles, with his usual pragmatism, just gave in. By the end of the century it was estimated that there were two thousand coffee houses in London alone. There were still over twice as many taverns, approximately one for every one hundred inhabitants, but considering that fifty years earlier coffee houses were almost unheard of, it was an amazing growth story.

The seventeenth of November 1681 was a big day in the Whig calendar. It was the anniversary of the accession to the throne of Queen Elizabeth, the hero of the Protestant cause. Nonconformist belligerence was all fired up. Nat Thompson might have been well advised to stop indoors, but keeping a low profile wasn't his style. He was out and about early as usual, picking up on rumours about the big march planned for after dark.

He very probably called in at Peter's Coffee House, situated in Covent Garden. He was certainly in the vicinity a little later, on that same morning. Peter's was one of a number of establishments where Monmouth's supporters had put up posters denying Thompson's newspaper story about the Earl of Huntingdon going over to the pro-James lobby. A day or so after the poster had first appeared a Tory loyalist had torn it down. Pembroke himself replaced it with a new version, this time with the postscript: 'the rascal that dares pluck this down I will send his soul to the Devil with a brace of bullets in his head.'[14]

Pembroke was not a man to mess with. He was pathologically violent, but not untypical of the young overprivileged aristocratic thugs that marauded the streets of Restoration London, many of whom were numbered among Monmouth's friends and supporters. The memoirist John Aubrey described Pembroke's grand house at Wilton as being a place you would find '52 mastiffs, 30 greyhounds, some bears and a lion and 60 fellowes more bestial than they'.[15]

At 11 o'clock on the morning of 17 November, Nat Thompson was strolling along the Strand, not very far from Peter's, when he became aware that he was being followed. He continued on his way determined to take no notice. He passed between the two gates of the Temple, leading to the Inns of Court, a quieter area where prostitutes lingered and muggings were frequent. He was in the vicinity of Pissing Alley when a man came from behind and struck him three blows to the head with a cudgel. One of his attackers cried out, 'god damn you . . . I am resolved to be revenged on you, you dog . . .'[16] Thompson fell to the ground. His attackers assaulted him some more, kicking him several times in the stomach, and then ran off leaving him for dead. Thompson, however, was not quite done for. He struggled to his feet, made his way back to Fleet Street and into the nearest shop, to get his breath back and attend to his injuries. He was in the middle of cleaning up his clothes when his attackers, who must have noticed his recovery, came back for a second go. They burst into the same shop, much to the dismay of a bemused assistant. Thompson fled upstairs and locked himself in a storeroom to save his life. Eventually the attackers withdrew before the beadles arrived. There is no conclusive evidence as to who was behind this attack on Thompson, but it was almost certainly organised by those close to Monmouth, and there was no one closer to Monmouth than the likes of Pembroke and Thynn.

Thompson's rough treatment on the morning of 17 November may have prevented him from going out again later that evening and seeing for himself the biggest demonstration the Whigs had got together yet. Some twenty thousand people marched on the streets, shouting, singing songs and hurling abuse. Bonfires were lit, coaches were stopped and drink money demanded, and there was the repeated chant of 'No Popish successor. No York. A Monmouth. A Monmouth. A Monmouth.'[17]

The mob started out at Katherine Wheel Alley in Whitechapel, progressed to Aldgate, turned down Leadenhall Street, then Cornhill and Cheapside, to Temple Bar. From there they turned up Chancery Lane, went down Holborn to Newgate and then on to Smithfield, where a giant effigy of the Pope was ceremoniously burnt. The route mainly passed through those nonconformist areas where sympathy for anti-Catholicism was likely to be at its strongest.[18] Leaflets were handed out with simple messages satirising the Catholic religion. 'For money you may heaven Buy / But those that have no money got / Hell is their Portion and their Lot.'[19] Afterwards you could purchase a cheap print of the entire occasion, to remind you of the good time you had enjoyed, or to give to a friend who had unluckily missed the chance to be there.

At the front of the procession was a bellman, solemnly tolling. There followed, on a white horse, a straw effigy of the dead body of Sir Edmundbury Godfrey, who was believed to have been murdered by Papists in revenge for his role as a judge in a trial of Catholic conspirators. He wore white gloves on his hands and there were spots of blood on his wrists and chest, a visual echo of Christ's crucifixion. Around his neck he wore the cravat which, according to some, had been used to strangle him, before his body had been further mutilated. In the three years since Godfrey had been found dead, he had achieved the status of a martyr among supporters of the Whigs.

Behind their hero came the villains. The Pope was pre-eminent, of course. He was depicted seated on his gaudy throne, a triple crown upon his head, a sceptre in one hand and a cross in the other, a fawning spaniel on his lap, a pen in his ear, a fiddle by his side and a broom at his tail. His head was articulated so it could be made to bow up and down before any house where Catholics were known to live, and at this absurdity a great roar of mocking approval and laughter resounded from the crowd. After His Holiness there followed a succession of other hate figures, bishops dressed in sumptuous purple surplices with richly embroidered copes and golden mitres. And finally there came a raggle-taggle of miscellaneous bogey men, including an effigy of Nat Thompson himself, with cross keys at his girdle and a pile of holy catechisms under his arm. All of them were tossed into the flames. Thompson, being the abrasive publicity-seeking character he was, would have been disappointed if he had not been represented. He relished all the personal abuse and gave as good as he got. But when it came to his reporting of Thomas Thynn's murder, just over a couple of months after this event, he overstepped the mark and found himself inside Newgate Gaol for his trouble, alongside the three assassins.

Vosges Mountain Pass

6

THE ROAD FROM STRASBOURG
TO METZ

He takes place of all the thieves as the most heroical, and one
that comes nearest to the old knight errant, though he is really
one of the basest, that never ventures but upon surprizal, and
where he is sure of the advantage.

– Samuel Butler, 'The Character of a Highwayman'[1]

N
ews of Bette's flight to Holland did not remain a secret for more
than a few hours. Henry Sidney knew her plans, and so did King
Charles, and they were both lovers of gossip with no reason not
to broadcast the story. The fact that it would embarrass Thynn intensely
merely added to their pleasure. Vratz probably got wind of it within a day
or so.

In his dealings with Stern, Vratz had always been careful to conceal the
identity of the man he was working for. He had given Stern the impression

that in pursuing a vendetta against Thynn he was acting on his own initiative. The truth was very different. He was actually in the employ of the
young Swedish count, Karl Johann Konigsmark. Karl had been in England
until shortly before Bette's disappearance. His younger brother, Philip,[2]
was still living in London and was an intimate of Court circles. Philip
would have been certain to let Vratz know of Bette's flight at the first opportunity. Immediately Vratz heard the news, he set off across the Channel
for France to join Konigsmark, not even stopping to take a proper farewell
of his new friend, the lugubrious Lieutenant Stern. In order to take full
advantage of the latest dramatic developments he could not afford to delay
for a moment.

In 1681, Count Karl Konigsmark was twenty-two years of age. He was
a young man of an adventurous inclination and restless habits. He had
already spent several years shifting around the Courts of Europe like some
medieval knight errant in search of a chivalrous cause. He came from a
distinguished military family. His grandfather had fought in the Thirty
Years War. His father had died when Karl was thirteen and since then his
upbringing had been left largely to his uncle Otto, a general and a mercenary, who fought in the armies of both Louis XIV and the Holy Roman
Emperor, and managed to remain on good terms with both.

The young Karl was welcomed wherever he went, not least because
he was wealthy, capable of great charm and, according to his admirers of
whom there were many, wonderfully handsome. His most remarkable feature was his long curling fair hair, which reached to below his waist and
was of the finest texture. He disdained to wear a wig, unlike most of the
fashionable young men of his generation, so that he could better display to
the world his extraordinary locks.

In the summer of 1680, Konigsmark presented himself to Charles at
Windsor[3] and offered to serve the royal cause by enlisting as a volunteer
in the English regiment fighting against the infidel in Tangiers. Tangiers
had been acquired by King Charles as part of the dowry of Catherine of
Braganza, and it had proved to be a thorn in his flesh and a drain on his
purse ever since. This wasn't Konigsmark's first visit to England. He had
been in London in the mid-1670s and it is quite possible that it was then
that he first made the acquaintance of Lady Bette, as he knew Bette's
stepfather.[4]

Whether Konigsmark actually went to Tangiers or whether he just
talked about going is unclear. He was certainly in England again during
the following summer, when Bette married Mr Thynn, to her immediate

regret. Konigsmark and Vratz were staying in Richmond together, and it was while they were there that Konigsmark evidently did something to incur Thynn's intense displeasure. According to Vratz, as reported during the course of his later examination, Thynn went about insulting Konigsmark behind his back in a manner that no gentleman could possibly permit or forgive. Thynn apparently called Konigsmark a Hector – that is to say, a bully. Still worse, he was rude about his horse.[5] Exactly what Konigsmark had done to incur such an outburst by Thynn is never spelt out, but it is not difficult to surmise in general terms what must have occurred.

The fact that the Duke of Newcastle, who was very fond of Bette, and was excellently placed to know the gossip about her, links the names of Konigsmark and Bette together as early as November 1681, just after she has run away from Thynn, is a strong indication that there had already been some kind of romantic liaison between them. Why else would Thynn make the remark? The most probable explanation for Thynn's anger is that he had got to hear that Konigsmark had been visiting his newly acquired wife and he did not welcome such attentions.

Konigsmark did not travel with Bette on the *Cleveland* yacht – that much is certain. But it is not surprising that Newcastle thought he might have done. When Bette disappeared, the Count had not been seen for some days in his usual haunts, the Court of Westminster, the glittering salons of London's great houses, the royal theatres, the pleasure gardens, or the private gentlemen's clubs. He had, in fact, already slipped quietly out of town several weeks beforehand, in early October. This is around the same time that Vratz turned up at the Amsterdam Ordinary and first made the acquaintance of Stern. Konigsmark's destination was Strasbourg, in eastern France, where he had some important private business to conduct, and it was in Strasbourg that Vratz caught up with him.

The quickest way from London was to ride post horse to Dover, take the twice-weekly packet to Calais, or possibly hire a fishing boat, and then ride a series of staging horses across northern France. Even if the weather had been favourable it would have taken Vratz well over a week to complete the journey. He had always been intending to meet up with Konigsmark in Strasbourg, but Bette's sudden departure had forced him to bring forward his travel arrangements.

Konigsmark is highly excited by Vratz's news. His own business in Strasbourg has also gone well. The two men now finalise the details of their plans. Vratz writes to Stern telling him that he will be back in London shortly and that the gold dollars will soon start flowing. It is also decided to send off a letter to a servant of Konigsmark's called George Borosky, a Pole living in Hamburg, whose assistance may prove useful. Borosky is told to make his way directly to London. A coach is then hired and Vratz and Konigsmark set off in the direction of Metz, en route for Holland, where Bette is residing.

Konigsmark has two weighty portmanteaux. In addition, they take great care with the stowage of a small wooden box bound with iron hoops and extremely heavy. It is probably placed beneath the coach seat. It contains 1,500 pistoles of gold coin that Konigsmark has just acquired.[6] It is a very large amount of money to be carrying on an open road, in the middle of winter, without an armed guard. The road from Strasbourg to Metz passes through the mountains of the Vosges, an isolated and barren country noted for its bandits.

The coach crosses the Alsace plain with its neat timbered houses and carefully laid out vineyards. The two travellers observe how the tall grey spire of Strasbourg cathedral gradually diminishes in size and the dark mountains with their snow-covered slopes loom ever larger. It is as if they are leaving the protective shadow of the church and slowly entering upon a wild and godless heathland. Konigsmark is tense. He has the disconcerting habit of chewing his lace cuffs when he is feeling anxious. Vratz is coolly laconic as always. He knows a thing or two about bandits. It isn't many years back that he carried out a number of daring robberies himself. He is confident that they can see off any marauders. They are heading for the village of Saverne, where they will spend the first night. The following day they will attempt the pass through the mountains. Outlaws are not their only worry. There is also the risk of being stranded in a heavy snowfall. They examine the sky for that sulphurous yellow light that presages a blizzard. Once winter begins in earnest it is not advisable to attempt the Saverne Pass.

The monotony of their journey grinds on. The village of Stiffen is followed by the village of Wilden.[7] Habitations become sparser, the thatched roofs more mildewed, the trails of wood smoke thinner. There is the occasional branch of a tree hung with black crows or the lone hunter in a leather jerkin trudging along some forlorn trackway. Suddenly the travellers become aware of a changed rhythm of hoofs, a discordant clattering coming at them from a tangent. Vratz pokes his head out of the carriage window and observes five or six ruffians on horseback. He does not bother to engage them in conversation as to their business. He immediately opens fire. There is a skirmish and the attackers are fought off.

According to Vratz's later account of this attack,[8] two of the marauders were shot dead and Konigsmark was wounded in the back, although not seriously. More sensationally Vratz also claimed that their assailants had been hired by Thynn. It is not altogether out of the question, as Konigsmark's visit to Strasbourg had been reported in the English press in mid-November.[9] The mention is very brief, and it is probable that most readers assumed that the Konigsmark being referred to was Karl's uncle Otto, but in fact it was the young Count Karl who was in Strasbourg. It is just possible that Thynn may have picked up on this and so known where to go looking for him. If this is the case, then Thynn's hired thugs must have carried out some very smart detective work to track their quarry down to the Strasbourg–Metz road. It is much more probable that Vratz seized on this incident as providing him with an opportunity for making an easy smear against Thynn's character, in a desperate justification of his own murderous actions.

PART TWO

1667–1680

Bette's mother, Lady Elizabeth Wriothesley

7

PETWORTH MANOR

... when a woman cannot be delivered let her drink a good porringer of her husband's water.

– Anne Glyd, Her Book, 1656[1]

The omens were not good. After the ravages of the plague, there had come the Great Fire, closely followed by the war against the Dutch, and as if these misfortunes were not sufficient, there was the bitter cold of the winter of 1666/7, when the River Thames itself froze over.

At Petworth Manor in Sussex there was a particular cause for anxiety. Lady Elizabeth Wriothesley was about to give birth. Her husband, Joscelyn Percy, was the son and heir to Algernon, 10th Earl of Northumberland. On the death of his father, who was already gravely ill, he would inherit vast estates, not just at Petworth but at Syon in the county of Middlesex, and at Alnwick Castle in the North of England, as well as their palatial London establishment, Northumberland House, with its magnificent façade created by Inigo Jones and its walled gardens stretching from the Strand to the river. The Percy line of succession, and the securing of this enormous property empire, depended upon Lady Elizabeth giving birth to a healthy child, and, as the wife to a great nobleman, the production of a male heir was her primary duty. She had married Joscelyn at sixteen and was now twenty years old. Her first baby had died at birth two years previously.

Visiting Petworth today, it is difficult to see it except through the lens of Turner's glorious paintings, with their visionary sunsets and softly un-dulating hills. In the 1660s it was a much wilder and more barren landscape. The picturesque deer park of Capability Brown had not yet been created. There were no views of the lake with its sail boats and its entrancing re-flections. The graceful Palladian mansion had not yet emerged from the chrysalis of a large rambling Tudor manor house with its tall gabled roof and echoing stone hallways. The rooms were dark, the corridors draughty, the stairs winding. It was a house more suited to the clanking of armour than the playing of a string quartet. The formal gardens, surrounded by ramparts, ditches and high walls, provided a retreat from the outside world, not a perspective upon it. It was to this windy hilltop fortress that Lady Elizabeth had come to give birth.[2]

As the leaves fell from the ancient trees and the days grew steadily shorter and colder, Elizabeth must have longed for this pregnancy to reach its full term. She was, no doubt, tired with all the advice and the endless constraints placed upon her. A pregnant woman must not dance, for the turning in circles could lead to the cord becoming twisted and the baby strangled in the womb. She must not ride a horse, for the jolting could dislodge the foetus and result in a miscarriage. She must not sit with her legs crossed or she might suffocate the baby and so bring forth a stillborn child. Like many women in her condition, she must have felt that her body was no longer her own.[3]

When the mornings were sufficiently warm, Elizabeth took the air along the gravelled pathways of the pretty parterre to the south and west of the house, sheltered from the prevailing winds behind tall brick walls. Walking along the diagonal alleys, with their closely clipped box hedges wrought into fantastical geometric shapes by the ingenious gardeners, was one of the few pleasures she was still allowed. The family physician, Dr Mapletoft, told her that it was good for her to take exercise. She liked and trusted Dr Mapletoft, who, as well as being an esteemed doctor and uni-versity scholar, was the friend and former tutor of her husband, Joscelyn.

Dr Mapletoft was a knowledgeable, well-travelled, witty and sensible man with modern rational views on women, politics and the workings of the universe. His opinions provided her with a useful counterweight to the old-fashioned attitudes of her mother-in-law, the formidable and energetic Countess Howard.[4]

But even within the tranquillity and protection of this enclosed garden it was possible to be overwhelmed by a sudden sense of dread. However much Elizabeth might long for the birth to take place, she must also have been acutely aware of the danger it would place her in. Small things could unsettle. The innocent noise of pigeons, for instance, huskily clearing their throats in the tall sycamores. Women whose afterbirth had not come clean away often developed puerperal fever, which led to an agonising death. In these desperate circumstances caged and half-starved pigeons were brought to the bedside of the sick woman and encouraged to peck at the bare soles of her feet in the vain hope that their cruel lacerations would bring about a cure. Countess Howard was of a generation that believed in the efficacy of pigeons. Dr Mapletoft laughed at such backward beliefs. But then it was easy for Dr Mapletoft, or Elizabeth's husband, to poke fun. They were men. The closest they ever got to a pigeon was to eat it.

As well as having to suffer the accumulated ignorance of previous generations, there was also the constant speculation on the sex of the unborn child to endure. Privately, Elizabeth may have been certain that conception had taken place when the moon had been waxing, which according to the astrologers was guaranteed to bring forth a male baby. But when examining her abdomen before she retired for the night, doubt might creep in. If the left side was the more swollen, it was a certain sign of a girl. An association of maleness with the right-hand side went all the way back to Hippocrates and his theory that it was the right-hand testicle that produced a boy, while the left-hand, the sinister side, contained the seeds for a girl. Two thousand years of learning could hardly be wrong.

On 24 January there was a slight thaw and the wind rose. At about this time Elizabeth's contractions became intense. The gossips, Lady Elizabeth's closest friends in the locality, were summoned, as well as her personal midwife, and the under midwife. Suddenly all was activity and bustle. The arching trees along the drive to the gates of Petworth Manor dripped with increasing rapidity upon those who hurried beneath.

The process of giving birth was surrounded with ritual. The lying-in chamber was carefully prepared with an abundance of fresh white linen, bleached in a solution of urine and beech ash. The room was lit with the subdued light of a white wax candle. It was dark and quiet, warm and free of draughts. A wood fire was burning. Heavy curtains made from sky-coloured sarsnett and lined with serge were drawn across the casements. The walls were muffled with five separate nine-foot-long tapestries with a modish flower-pot pattern.[5] The large bed, a room within a room, was also hung with floral-patterned perpetuana wool drapes. Even the keyhole in the door was covered to keep out chill air and evil spirits. Nothing was left to chance.

Once the contractions began to come regularly Elizabeth withdrew to this upper chamber. Various potions were at hand to ease delivery. Ten grains of dittany of Crete, pennyroyal and round birthwort, together with twelve grains of cinnamon and saffron, beaten to a fine powder and dissolved in white wine, was thought to quicken dilation. The clutching of eagle stones, a stone within a stone, itself a symbol of the infant enclosed within the womb, was also believed to speed the baby's arrival.

On 26 January, Lady Elizabeth at last gave birth. It was a baby girl, red-skinned and with a lusty cry, both of which were good signs. She was immediately swaddled. A few drops of blood from the severed cord were touched upon the baby's lips to protect it from disease and the evils of the world. Two days later she was carried into the Petworth family chapel with its stained-glass windows and its dark oak pews and solemnly christened Elizabeth Percy, but she was always to be called Lady Bette.

Bette's father, Joscelyn, 11th Earl of Northumberland

8

HÔTEL DE LA BAZINIÈRE

It is not enough that persons of my Lord Percy's quality be taught to dance and to ride, to speak languages and weare his clothes with a good grace (which are the very shells of travel); but besides all these that he know men, customs, courts, and disciplines, and whatsoever superior excellencies the places afford, befitting a person of birth and noble impressions. This is, Sir, the fruit of travel.

– John Evelyn to Edward Thurland, 8 November 1658,
referring to Joscelyn Percy's imminent Grand Tour[1]

L ady Bette's father, Joscelyn, was to be the role model for his generation. His father, Algernon, 10th Earl of Northumberland, had been a distinguished statesman, one of the few to emerge from the upheavals of the Civil War with his reputation still intact. He stood for the Church of England, family honour and social responsibility.[2] It was hoped that Joscelyn would follow in his footsteps. The problem was that the new generation of young gallants were notorious for their cynicism, hedonism and casual violence. They were typified by the dissolute poet and wit John Wilmot, Earl of Rochester, and the coterie that crowded around him, which included Thomas Thynn. These men no longer defined themselves through some ideal of service to the nation but through feats of duelling, drinking, and fucking, or 'swiving', to use one of their preferred terms. Their selfish and extravagant depravity was given intellectual respectability by the bleak pessimism of philosophers like Hobbes. The typical 'town gallant' was described as a man who had never read *Leviathan* but someone who had 'caught the rattle of it at the coffee houses' and the chatter 'had taught him to laugh at spirits and maintain that there are no angels but those in petticoats'.[3] John Evelyn was scathing about this younger generation of courtiers, referring to them as 'insolent, ignorant, debauched, and without the least tincture of those advantages to be hoped for'. He goes on to add: 'unless we thus cultivate our youth, and noblemen make wiser provision for their education abroad, ... I despaire of ever seeing a man truly noble indeed.'[4] Evelyn, an avid tourist himself, may have overestimated the civilising effect of foreign travel.

In 1662, at the age of eighteen, Joscelyn had married the noted beauty Elizabeth Wriothesley, daughter of Thomas, Earl of Southampton. He had originally been betrothed to Elizabeth's elder sister Audrey, but on Audrey's death in 1660 the mantle of prospective bride was passed seamlessly on to the next daughter in line. An alliance between these two great landowning families, the Northumberlands and the Southamptons, had long been planned, and a mishap like the demise of the intended bride was not sufficient reason for altering the general strategy. If Joscelyn's letters to his old friend and tutor Dr Mapletoft are to be believed, it was not just a marriage of dynastic convenience. It seems there was also genuine affection and respect on both sides. Joscelyn talks enthusiastically about Elizabeth's kindliness.[5]

It isn't long though before Joscelyn is behaving badly. Mapletoft feels obliged to send him a note, written in Greek in case it fell into the wrong hands. Women were not generally taught Greek. Joscelyn's exact misdemeanour is not known because Mapletoft's letter has not survived, but what is interesting is Joscelyn's reaction to the reprimand. He thanks Mapletoft:

for the little Greek note you sent me and desire you would both by letters now and by word of mouth when I see you continue to use that freedom that have been between us for I have so little truth from anybody, that I am the last that hears anything amiss concerning myself, and therefore desire you not to stay from writing anything of admonition to me, which will as your discourses have been much to my advantage.[6]

There is something touchingly earnest about this request to be told off when he is deserving of it. It is as if he is conscientiously trying to live up to an ideal, but also troublingly aware that he is constantly falling short. Perhaps the weight of expectation on him was too heavy a burden. Sir Peter Lely's portrait of him shows a callow, diffident-looking youth, not unhandsome but rather uncertain of himself.

He did not appear much at Court. He was not part of the wild and depraved set of young men that surrounded the royal brothers. He was also noticeably absent from the great naval battles of 1666 against the Dutch, unlike so many of his peer group, who enlisted as gentlemen volunteers, and clustered noisily around James, Duke of York, aboard his ship the *Royal Prince*. Joscelyn's absence from the scene of action may have had something to do with his father's disapproval of the Court Party, but an equally probable explanation is that he was so often ill. He writes to Mapletoft at one point: 'I believe that few persons have suffered more in diseases without dying than I have.'[7] The remark is both humorous and, in view of what was shortly to follow, extremely poignant.

So Joscelyn spends most of the early years of his married life and manhood languishing in the country, cosseted by his domineering mother and waited on by his young wife. He learns to play the guitar and practises his tennis. He writes to Mapletoft, who is in Paris, and asks him to buy 'some things that belong to my guns', explaining that the shooting of wild game is his 'principal recreation ... at Petworth'.[8] He shoots wild duck, pheasants, partridges, hares, leverets and lapwings, paying his gamekeeper to have them hatched, bred and tracked. Mindful of the need to charm the ladies with appropriate gifts, he requests Mapletoft to purchase 'half a dozen pairs of the finest and newest fashioned estuys [ornamental needle cases] and some handsome pocket knives as well as a few little bottles of the best essence, or any other little things of no great price, such that I may present to our ladies here'.[9]

Joscelyn's meticulously preserved accounts, which still survive in the Petworth archive, provide a fascinating insight into his priorities for expenditure. Like most of the men of his generation he is fastidious about his appearance. During 1667, for instance, the year before Bette's birth, he has his teeth cleaned by a Mr Goslin at the not inconsiderable price of twenty-four shillings and eight pence a time. He asks the patrician diplomat and old friend of the family William Temple to make a special purchase on his behalf of a particular kind of cloth, only available in Brussels, and tips the footman five shillings for delivering it. But his real weakness is for shoes. In the space of just twelve months he purchases eighteen pairs of shoes from Mr Trinder, as well as two pairs of galoshes, a pair of black velvet slippers and two pairs of tennis shoes. In addition, he buys two pairs of winter boots from Mr Kendall and has three further pairs waxed, and two new pairs of winter shoes from Robert Shorter. His older boots he gets John Quinnell to 'liquor' (presumably a kind of protective lacquering). His most ominous purchase, however, was a fashionable black rapier and a new scabbard to match, which he acquired from a Mr King. He may not have fought against the Dutch but he clearly felt the need to present himself as a man of action. He was very much the grand courtier in waiting, polishing up his accomplishments ready for display.[10]

The year after Bette's birth, 1668, Joscelyn's father Algernon died and Joscelyn succeeded to the title of 11th Earl of Northumberland. In his immediate circle there was renewed anxiety as to how he would react to his new position of immense wealth and prestige, and once again there was no shortage of advice proffered. William Temple, for instance, immediately took it upon himself to write to Joscelyn in paternalistic and somewhat admonishing tones. Like Evelyn, he remarks that he has never seen a younger generation 'so generally corrupted as ours by a common pride and affectation of despising and laughing at all face of order and virtue, and conformity to laws'.[11] The inference is clear. Joscelyn must take care not to succumb to similar temptations. So the world waited with bated breath to see what role Joscelyn would choose to play. In the event, like many young men faced with making a life-determining decision, he opted to go travelling.

The decision to tour Europe must have come as music to Elizabeth's ears. Soon after Algernon's death she had lost another child, a boy this time. A complete change of scene would help revive her spirits. It would also have the added advantage that she could escape her mother-in-law. The Countess Howard might have become the Dowager Countess, but she did not withdraw quietly to a dower house on the hill. She may have adopted the black weeds of the widow, the peaked cap and close-fitting hood, the nun-like robes, but she was not yet ready for the convent, far from it. The garments must have had the effect of making her demeanour even more terrifying than before. She was described by a contemporary as 'a divell of a woman'.[12] It was not in her nature to relinquish the reins of power easily, and she was more than ready for the fight that lay ahead.

For Elizabeth and Joscelyn the lure of warm weather, the seductiveness of foreign architecture, the absence of nagging relations and the avoidance of having to make any decisions about a political career must all have seemed an idyllic prospect. They chose to travel with their close friends Thomas Blomer, who went as chaplain, and his wife Dorothy, Elizabeth's long-standing companion. The mood was light-hearted and carefree. They were all great admirers of France and French manners. The toddler Bette travelled with them, with her own special travel cot, 'a travelling bedstead . . . with a furniture of dove coloured hair camlet lined with sersnett and a quilt suitable to it'.[13] To take such a young child abroad was unusual, but Elizabeth did not choose to trust her mother-in-law with her daughter's care at this tender stage of her young life.

It was Ralph Montagu, English ambassador to the court of Louis XIV at the time, a position that suited his predilection for intrigue and mischief-making, who made the arrangements for the Northumberlands' visit. He rented the magnificent Hôtel de la Bazinière on their behalf at a cost of eight thousand livres a year. It had previously been the residence of Charles I's widow, Henrietta Maria, after she fled England. Montagu probably took a secret commission for being so obliging. It would have been very out of character if he had not. This was, after all, the man who accepted a bribe of 100,000 crowns from the French to pursue a policy that was designed to weaken English interests.[14]

Hôtel de la Bazinière was a grandiose chateau, situated in the heart of Paris, on the Quai du Pont Rouge, in the sixth arrondissement. Today it is called the Hôtel de Chimay, and has undergone several transformations in the interim, but it still has something of the same self-regarding pomp about it. When Elizabeth arrived, the rooms had been recently decorated by that master of baroque bombast, Charles le Brun. He was fond of allegorical paeans of praise to the virtues of the Sun King, Louis XIV, which generally involved a great deal of cresting of clouds by gilded chariots.[15]

There was much to see and do in Paris. A visit to Versailles was an absolute requirement. If you were lucky enough to arrive at the right time you might have the honour to observe Louis himself eating his dinner. The traveller Richard Ferrier was, however, a little disappointed at the modesty of the feast that he witnessed going down the royal gullet. 'The dinner the King had was but ordinary, there being a dish of soup, some chicken and a quarter of lamb.'[16] Ferrier also takes the opportunity to caution against the danger of pickpockets operating within the palace precincts. Christopher Wren, when he visited Paris just a few years before the Percys, was more interested in the massive new building works going on at the Louvre, rather than what Louis ate:

> The Louvre for a while was my daily object, where no less than a thousand Hands are constantly employ'd in the Works, some in laying mighty Foundations, some in raising the Stories, Columns, Entablements, etc. with vast Stones, by great and useful Engines; others in Carving, Inlaying of marbles, Plaistering, Painting, Gilding etc. Which altogether make a school of architecture, the best probably at this day in Europe.[17]

Perhaps more to Elizabeth's taste were visits to the opera at the Palais Royale or sauntering along the rue des Chargeurs at night, with its luxury shops splendidly lit by lanterns, so that in the dark it shone like a cavern of jewels. Permanent street lighting like this was unheard of in London. If she was feeling adventurous she might have taken a *rouillons*[18] to the pottery at St Cloud, or visited the manufactory of Les Gobelins, famous for its furnishings and tapestries, or even gone as far as the house of mirrors beyond the gate of St Antoine, where every conceivable shape of looking glass could be purchased. On sunny mornings there were walks through the Tuileries or the Royal Physick Garden, and for more melancholy moments the churchyard of St Innocent, filled with skulls.[19]

The arrangements for Joscelyn and Elizabeth's visit to the Continent were lavish. Their entourage included no fewer than thirty horses. There was, predictably enough, a bureaucratic hiccup with importing this number of horses into France. The French customs impounded them. The ubiquitous and energetic Ralph Montagu immediately weighed in. He wrote indignantly on 11 January 1670: 'My Lord Northumberland has been extremely ill used here by the offices of the customs house, about some Spanish horses that they have seized, and if they do not give him all satisfaction, I shall be obliged to make a public complaint.'[20] The customs men quickly backed down. None of this detracted from the grandeur of the visit. If anything it added to its glory. As William Perwich, Charles II's special envoy, observed in his dispatch of 18 January 1670, it seemed to be Joscelyn's intention 'to spend some time and money in Paris'.[21] At long last the young Earl was about to cut a figure on the grand stage.

Carnival in the Piazza in front of the Palazzo Colonna 1675

PALAZZO COLONNA

A place where people live without ever taking their masks off.
– The *Avvisi di Roma*, 15 February 1670[1]

J oscelyn did not stop in Paris. Within a few weeks he was heading south, for Italy. It is possible that he was ill again and that his physician considered that the warmer air of the South would be beneficial. Elizabeth did not travel with him. She was pregnant for the fourth time, and had most probably been advised to avoid such a long, tiring and jolting journey.

Joscelyn hadn't been in Rome for long before there came a whiff of scandal. It is alluded to in a memo, dated 23 April 1670, buried among the papers of Sir Joseph Williamson, the King's secretary of state. Williamson employed a network of spies to provide him with intelligence of what was going on throughout the Courts of Europe. The memo reads: 'I have taken a copy of the account of Lord Northumberland's business in Rome, and intend showing it to my Lord tomorrow, I believe Lord Northumberland's

relations would rather that it went no further.'² The clear implication of
this is that Joscelyn's conduct had in some way been deeply compromising
to his reputation. His 'business', it turns out, was the seductive Hortense
Mancini, Duchess of Mazarin, 'An extraordinary beauty and wit, but dissolute and impatient of matrimonial restraint' according to Evelyn's rather
prim verdict on her character.³

Hortense was staying at the magnificent Palazzo Colonna, built around
an enchanting central garden with cooling fountains and scented flowers.
This was the home of her sister Marie and her brother-in-law, Lorenzo
Onofrio Colonna. She had just recently fled from her oppressive and
wealthy husband, the Duc de La Meilleraye. The latter may have been one
of the richest men in France, but he was also a crazed psychopath. He used
to have the front teeth of his female servants removed to prevent them
from being attractive to men, and on inheriting Cardinal Mazarin's great
art collection, through his marriage to Hortense, he had all the erotic areas
of female flesh scraped off the oil paintings and chipped from the sculp-
tures. He was singularly ill suited as a husband for Hortense, who liked to
surround herself with artists, philosophers and poets. She was a woman of
the salon and was very much part of that sophisticated modern world to
which Joscelyn and his wife aspired. She was also well known for her les-
bian and heterosexual affairs, and indulged a fondness for cross-dressing.

In 1670, the Palazzo Colonna was the centre of the fast life in the Eternal City, the place where all the smart people went. Its dazzling Long
Gallery remains largely unchanged today, with tall mirrors and a frescoed
ceiling depicting the famous sea battle of Lepanto, when the infidel Turks
had been defeated, and in which one of Lorenzo's ancestors had played a
key role. It was in this room that Marie Mancini loved to put on balls and
plays, spectacles and concerts. That February, during carnival time, when
Joscelyn first became a regular visitor, she stage-managed a performance of
the *Ballet of the Nymphs of the Winds*, a suitably dreamy and ethereal title.
Marie and Hortense adored the Carnival floats that were pulled through
the noisy streets and they both dressed up in elaborate costumes of pearls
and feathers and paraded themselves as living works of art, much to the
scandal of more staid Roman society. Women were not supposed to appear
on the floats, but merely to watch from the upper windows.

Marie Mancini was not reticent when it came to describing the pleasures of the Palazzo Colonna. In her memoirs she recalls breathlessly 'the
throng of excellent society who frequented our house, which teemed with
delights as if it were the very centre of pleasure. For indeed, I can say

without exceeding the truth in the least, that the plays, the conversation, the brilliant gaming, the music, the magnificent meals – in short all the entertainment that one can imagine – followed one after another.'⁴ There were, of course, dissenting voices, writing in the *Avvisi di Roma*, who considered the Palazzo Colonna to be little better than a brothel. But whatever one's view it was certainly a far cry from the world of hunting and shooting at Petworth, presided over by the Dowager Countess Howard. It is hardly surprising that it turned Joscelyn's head. He fell in love with Hortense and his attentions were evidently welcomed. She sat for a painting that was to be delivered into his hands and his hands only.

It was all very romantic. The problems started when Joscelyn went to the artist's studio to collect the finished work, most probably a miniature that he could easily conceal in his luggage, only to discover that it had already been disposed of elsewhere. Close cross-questioning of the artist concerned revealed that it had been collected by Don Domingo Guzman, brother to the Duke of Medina de la Torres. Don Domingo was another of Hortense's admirers who clearly felt he had a prior claim on any images that were produced of her.

Joscelyn was furious. He promptly challenged the duplicitous Don to a duel. He sent the challenge in the proper manner and with all due formality via his good friend the Duc de Rohan. A place and time was agreed for the two rival lovers to settle their differences. This was Joscelyn's big moment. He had not taken part in the wars against the Dutch. He had never proved his manhood on the battlefield. Now was his chance to show his mettle.

It is easy to imagine the scene. Early morning, not many people about, a quiet grove just outside the main precincts of the town, the leaves of the olive trees a tender grey-green, a wreath of mist upon the surface of the Tiber, a fierce sun rising above the red tiles of the city rooftops. Joscelyn arrives with a full retinue of followers, valets, footmen, and the elegant Duc de Rohan as his second. He unsheathes the black-hilted rapier that he has recently purchased and practises his thrusts, his passeres and his contratempos, slicing the trembling air with a thin blade of steel. He strikes a pose with his right foot flexed forward, the torso angled, his shoulders in line with his bent knee, so presenting the narrowest of targets to his opponent. He looks eminently glamorous in his tight-fitting breeches and white silk and lace shirt. There is only one problem. There is no sign of Don Guzman. The slothful Spaniard has yet to show his face. This lack of punctuality is an expression of the most intolerable contempt.

The Don eventually turns up, but it is immediately evident that something is amiss. For a start he has only one servant in attendance. One servant suggests a deliberate lack of seriousness. It is insulting. Worse still, the Don alights from his horse smiling broadly, fails to draw his sword and instead walks straight up to Joscelyn, and throws his arms about his neck in an attempt to 'droll' it all off. According to the Don, the whole Hortense picture business is nothing more than the result of a silly misunderstanding.

Joscelyn is not to be quite so easily appeased. He still wants the portrait and demands that it is handed over. The Don does not have it on him. The argument goes back and forth. But the moment of extreme tension is past. As the morning heats up, tempers gradually cool. Don Guzman suggests that the Duc de Rohan and Joscelyn should both get into his coach and together they will drive to the Spanish ambassador's house, where the disputed picture is in safe-keeping. Joscelyn is most welcome to it. The short journey is made and the picture restored to its rightful owner. This transfer of possession having been successfully accomplished to everyone's satisfaction, all three men pledge eternal friendship and proceed to drink each other's health in the time-honoured manner. They then decide it will be even more fun if they visit Hortense, who presumably has some explaining to do.

This entire episode was detailed in a newsletter dated 3 May. It seems probable that it is essentially the same as the report that Whitehall was so concerned should be hushed up. Neither Joscelyn's mother, nor his pregnant wife, would have been overjoyed to hear of his affair with the notorious Duchess. The writer of the newsletter, on the other hand, a hack appropriately called Muddiman, felt no such inhibiting sensitivities. He regarded the entire escapade as redounding to Joscelyn's credit: 'The Earl of Northumberland, who is esteemed for his general deportment in all places, has gained much at Rome, especially with the French, who challenge to themselves a kind of mastership in the punctilios of honour.'[5]

Not long after the Hortense portrait episode, Joscelyn left Rome to return to Paris. He was in a hurry to get back. He is described as having 'heated himself with travelling post for many days' – that is riding a series of horses along sun-soaked roads rather than sitting in the relative cool and shade of the slower carriage.[6] Perhaps he was suffering from a guilty conscience. Whatever the explanation for his great haste, his exertions were evidently too much for him. He died in Turin on 21 May. He was twenty-six years old. When Elizabeth was informed, she miscarried and lost yet another boy child. It was observed in dispatches that 'the losse of this nobleman is the greater because the family is extinct for want of issue male'.[7]

Joscelyn's death was quick. The return of his corpse was a much more protracted business. Firstly, it needed to be embalmed to prevent it from becoming putrid and stinking long before it reached its grave. The soft organs, the stomach, bowels, kidneys, heart and lungs were all carefully removed. The heart was placed in a separate lead-lined casket, for the bereaved to keep close by them should they so desire it. The remaining flesh was washed in a solution of vinegar and anointed with aromatics and spices. The beard and other body hair were shaved. The freshly cleansed flesh was then wrapped in waxed cloths and dressed in a shirt of flannel that extended at least six inches beyond the feet. A cap was placed upon the head and fastened with a chin cloth, gloves pulled on to the hands, a cravat wound around the neck. The exact art of embalming was a closely guarded secret.[8]

Once secured against the indignity of immediate putrefaction, Joscelyn's body would have been placed in a coffin on a bed of loose bran to absorb leaking fluids. It was then trundled from Turin by coach across southern France in the broiling heat. The young Thomas Clifford, another English courtier of noble family, who was to die in Florence the following year while on his Grand Tour, supposedly from drinking too much iced Italian beer, had his hearse draped with a pall of black velvet, emblazoned with the family escutcheons, and pulled by two donkeys. Eight trumpeters walked half a mile ahead of the cortege, 'sounding the doleful notes fitted for this sad solemnity'.[9] It is unlikely that the corpse of Joscelyn, the eleventh and last Earl of Northumberland, would have been treated with any less dignity and splendour.

The roads were long, straight and wearisome, relieved only by the shadows of the occasional row of poplars. The corpse reached Blois in the Loire Valley early in June. Louis XIV did not help matters by seizing the Earl's horses, 'and most of what he has left in France'. He could do this through the exercise of an ancient law, *droit d'aubaine*.[10] Once again it was left to the ever-obliging Montagu to intervene. Elizabeth was described as 'disconsolate'.[11] By mid-June she was in Calais but was delayed from crossing the Channel 'through the illness of her child'. Bette was feverish. It seemed there was to be no end to her tribulations.[12]

Montagu bustled about the newly bereaved widow and made all the necessary arrangements. He is described by Macky, a contemporary of his, as 'not very tall, inclining to fat, and the owner of a coarse and rather swarthy countenance'.[13] But he had the reputation for being a great charmer of women. Comte Gramont goes some way to explaining the nature of his special attraction to the opposite sex: 'It was Montagu, a person not at all formidable as far as his face was concerned, but very much to be feared on account of his assiduity, the agility of his wit, and certain other talents by no means despicable when once a suitor has received permission to bring them into play.'[14]

Elizabeth finally landed at Dover on 25 June, went first to London and then immediately on to Petworth to make arrangements for her husband's funeral. The body came back via Le Havre. The royal yacht *Henrietta* brought it from there to Portsmouth, arriving around 12 July.[15] Salutes were fired from all the guns of the assembled ships at anchor. The noise was sombre and deafening, as if the earth itself was being riven apart. From Portsmouth it was a relatively short staging post to Petworth Manor. The corpse was laid out in Joscelyn's former chamber upon the great French bedstead with its hangings of crimson velvet laced with gold and silver.[16] He was interred in the family tomb.

The magnificent parties at the Palazzo Colonna did not continue for very long after Joscelyn's abrupt departure. The two flamboyant sisters, Hortense and Marie, were fiercely competitive, each trying to outdo the other with the brilliance of their accomplishments. It was inevitable that they would soon quarrel. The immediate trigger was a pointedly cruel remark by their brother Philippe on the artistic merits of Marie's latest concert. He told Marie to her face that 'the music and the lyrics were the most pitiful thing in the world and that the symphony was worse than the rest'. Marie might have been able to ignore such spite from an unfeeling man, dismissing it as nothing more than the grossness typical of the sex, but when she saw her sister 'giving looks and gestures of approval', it was all too much for her. Her anger was understandable. She had after all provided Hortense with a home in her hour of need. The least she could do in return was show some support for her artistic endeavours.[17] There followed many tears and much mutual recrimination. A few days later Hortense and Philippe headed back to France together, he to get married, and Hortense to pursue her independence from her husband through the French courts, and try and win back possession of her private fortune. In the latter she was unsuccessful. Before long she was seeking the protection of and offering favours to the Duke of Savoy, and when he died unexpectedly, she fell into the hands of the ever-conniving Ralph Montagu.

In the summer of 1670, back at Petworth, all was gloom. Dorothy

Blomer, who had been one of the French party, wrote to John Locke, in London, informing him that Lady Elizabeth 'had not been well since she came into the country' and explaining that 'if she does not mend a few weeks may bring us into your neighbourhood'.[18] If London did not prove effectual she thought they might have to return to France again, 'which I can not think of with any pleasure', she hastily adds. She had described Petworth in a previous letter as 'an honest ignorant place',[19] presumably referring to its lack of sophisticated culture as well as its unaffected rural integrity, in contrast to the dazzling mirrored decadence of somewhere like Paris, which they had just left in such miserable circumstances.

There exists a curious coda to the history of Joscelyn's affair with Hortense. An inventory of the possessions to be found at Petworth a few months after his death contains a reference to 'a large wainscot cabinet' in the closet, situated within the withdrawing room, used exclusively by Lady Elizabeth. The contents of this cabinet are enumerated: 'eight old purses, some scissors, knives and pen knives, a drawer with heads for sticks and other tops, a china cup and cover with silver hooks and other small silver instruments, a box full of little toys, writing papers, two little pictures, the one a landskip, the other a naked piece ...'[20] Some of these items were almost certainly among the small presents given to Elizabeth by Joscelyn, which he had John Mapletoft purchase for him from Paris. Others may have been toys kept from her childhood. The oddest item listed is the little picture described as 'a naked piece'. Small nude pictures of women were common in this period. Pepys famously kept one of Nell Gwyn wearing only angel wings tucked away in one of his drawers.[21] It seems a little strange though for Lady Elizabeth to have been in possession of such a picture, unless, of course, it was the miniature of Hortense. She may have come across it among her husband's baggage when the body had finally been returned to her, and not knowing quite what to do with it stuffed it in the cabinet along with other discarded and unwanted objects. Whatever the explanation, it was a sad end to what had been planned as a magnificent process through the pre-eminent Courts of Europe.

Joscelyn's death also had the consequence that the three-year-old Bette Percy was now sole heir to the vast Northumberland inheritance. Overnight, she had become the most desirable marriage prospect in the kingdom. It was an enormous legacy which was also to prove the most unenviable of burdens. She was no longer just a child. She was an eminently tradable commodity the rights to which would be fiercely fought over.

There is a painting by Peter Lely of the little three-year-old girl. She is shown seated, cherubic mouth, plump limbs, full face, pointing towards the inevitable spaniel and staring boldly at the viewer. You can almost touch the soft silky texture of the exquisite pinky mauve dress she wears. What strikes one most, however, is the isolation of this small figure poised against the conventional classical backdrop of rich drapes and Arcadian landscape. She is entirely alone. She is not part of any family grouping. Even the dog keeps its distance. It was no doubt the protocol that a great heiress, even if aged only three, should receive the dignity of a portrait seated alone, without the distraction of other figures. There remains, however, something rather forlorn about it.[22]

Thomas Thynn

10

WHETSTONE PARK

A wild unthinking dissolute age, an age whose business is sense-less riot, Neronian gambols, and ridiculous debauchery.

– Nathaniel Lee, *The Rival Queens*, 1677

In the year 1670, the same year in which Joscelyn Percy died, Thomas Thynn, at the age of twenty-two, inherited the house and estate of Longleat in Wiltshire from his uncle Sir James Thynn. It was his great good fortune that his uncle had died childless. Longleat came with one of the handsomest rent rolls in the country. Thynn was promptly dubbed 'Tom of Ten Thousand', a none too subtle reference to his enormous annual income. The windfall had come to him not a moment too soon. Only a few months before his uncle's death he had been writing self-pitying letters begging for funds, 'for I am left here without Company and without support, not owned by my father, nor encouraged by anybody, and now I must give my creditors a verbal satisfaction, for I despair of giving them a real one'.[1] His indebted state was hardly surprising, since he was already in the habit of purchasing eighty dozen bottles of wine a month.

As soon as Longleat came into his possession he headed for London. Like many of his generation, he had absolutely no interest in languishing in the country and overseeing the lot of his tenants. He left that to his steward. He clearly subscribed to the prevailing view expressed by Horner in Wycherley's play *The Country Wife*, that 'People really do live nowhere else'. Country dwellers might 'breathe, and move, and have a kind of insipid dull being, but there is no life' except in London. So Tom Thynn spent most of his time in his town house in Canon Row, where he indulged his fondness for fine wines, loose women and foppish garments. It was his gaudy taste in clothes that he was most noted for. Around this time, for instance, one outfit he purchased comprised a coat of violet, striped and richly laced with gold and silver, a pair of pink morello breeches trimmed with silver lace, a pair of pearl-coloured silk stockings, a white tabby waistcoat laced with silver black lace, and silk drawers. If he was going to fritter away his time, money and energies in the brothels and taverns of the capital he intended to do it in style.[2]

He quickly began to move in the smartest and most debauched of circles. The Duke of Monmouth was soon a bosom friend, but his coterie also included the likes of Rochester, Pembroke, Harry Savile and the Duke of Albemarle. They called themselves 'The Merry Gang'.

Rochester appears not to have been particularly impressed by Thynn's intellectual abilities, judging by the acerbic couplet that he penned on the subject:

> Who'd be a wit in Dryden's cudgel'd skin,
> Or who'd be rich and senseless like Tom ... ?[3]

Monmouth, one year younger than Thynn, was, by all accounts, none too bright either. Pepys describes him in adolescence as being 'the most skittish, leaping gallant that ever I saw, always in action, vaulting or leaping or clambering'.[4] The traveller Lorenzo Magalotti was rather more scathing in his verdict on the grown man:

> He is rather weak and ignorant, and as cold as can be. He is most unhappy in conversation and in paying compliments ... His inclination leads him to the pleasures of the senses and of wine; he has lately recovered somewhat from the latter, but in the former he is easily pleased, and very often has paid,

in the hands of the doctors, the penalty of his too ignoble and imprudent sensuality.[5]

In short, Monmouth had the pox.

The burgeoning friendship between Thynn and Monmouth was based on a conjunction of needs. Monmouth was short of money. Thynn had plenty of it. Thynn was politically ambitious and Monmouth appeared to offer a useful conduit to power. Add to this the fact they shared a taste for vicious amusements and it was inevitable that they would soon run into trouble.

Early on the Sunday morning of 26 February 1671, still continuing their revels of the previous evening, Monmouth, Thynn, Rochester and a whole crowd of other young 'Hectors', as they were popularly termed, decided to pay a visit to Whetstone Park. Today Whetstone Park is an elegant street just to the north of Lincoln's Inn Fields in the heart of the genteel Bloomsbury area of London. In the 1670s it was one of the most depraved and deprived parts of the city, notorious for its cheap brothels and its downmarket street whores. This is where Sue Willis, a notorious bawd, had her establishment, distinguished by two large white stone balls on top of the pillars that led to her front door. In the spring of 1671 trade in the area was poor. The new rival hot spot of Middle Park near Charing Cross was drawing away custom. Prostitutes had to work hard for their living, none harder perhaps than Priss Fotheringham, who used to stand naked on her head at the Six Windmills and spread her legs, while 'four cully-rompers chuck'd in sixteen half crowns into her Commoditie'. Sometimes over-enthusiastic bystanders poured in Rhenish wine in addition, which had a 'smarting and searing quality'. Other whores had different specialities, including dancing naked before a lighted candle placed on a large pewter plate and when the dance ended snuffing the flame by inserting the candle into the vagina.[6]

The weeks of late February running up to Lent were by tradition an exceptionally difficult time for women working in the sex trade. Shrovetide was widely regarded as a free-for-all, a festive season during which young men had a licence to attack and abuse prostitutes as they wished. The motives for this in the past had been in part political. Fear of sexual disease often became confused in the popular imagination with a fear of Catholics. Syphilis was the taint of whores, and there were no greater whores than the King's mistresses, Barbara Palmer and Louise de Kérouaille, who were both Catholics.[7]

But when the Merry Gang decided it would be fun to target Whetstone

Park, political protest was not on their agenda. This was purely and simply a misogynistic grudge visit. It is Rochester again who best sums up the prevailing mood of post-coital disillusion that fired them up, in his poem 'Regime de Vivre':

> I rise at eleven, I dine about two,
> I get drunk before seven, and the next thing I do,
> I send for my whore, when for fear of a clap,
> I spend in her hand, and I spew in her lap:
> Then we quarrel and scold, till I fall fast asleep,
> When the bitch growing bold, to my pocket does creep.
> Then slyly she leaves me, and to revenge the affront,
> At once she bereaves me of money and cunt.[8]

There is very little official reporting of the Whetstone Park incident, for obvious reasons, but an anonymous contemporary poem describes the precise events that led up to it:

> . . . twas an injury beyond repair
> To clap a king's son and a great duke's heir.
> And therefore in their fury 'tis decreed
> This Jezebel must fall . . .[9]

It seems that Monmouth and several of his friends believed they had contracted the pox from one of Sue Willis's girls, and they were now determined to have their revenge.

Another contemporary ballad, entitled 'On The Three Dukes Killing the Beadle on Sunday Morning',[10] records what happened next. The chosen victim is described as 'a sickly damsel'. Her aggrieved and wealthy clients had decided it would be amusing to seize her few possessions, and so 'against law her castle did invade/ to take from her her instruments of trade'. The invaders were, of course, drunk. They were also in masquerade. Masquerading was all the rage. Only the previous month there had been 'a great ball at the French Ambassador's where most of the court were in masquerade, on Friday . . . one at the Temple, on Saturday at Lincoln's Inn, and on Candlemas night a great one at Court'.[11] Dryden wrote: 'to wear a mask 'tis extremely pleasant, for to go unknown, is the next degree to going invisible.'[12] In this state of irresponsible anonymity, the Merry Gang burst in to their chosen brothel, stole the poor prostitute's loose shifts and revealing petticoats, as well as her cosmetics, creams, patches, mirrors, dildos, whips and other accoutrements, and created a great uproar. In the chaos and screaming that ensued someone must have gone and fetched the local constables.

> In came the Watch, disturbed with sleep and ale,
> By shrill noises, but they could not prevail,
> T'appease their Graces.[13]

In the fracas that ensued, a beadle called Peter Virnill was attacked. He pleaded for mercy, but the entire posse of drunken and overprivileged young men was too fired up to listen. They fell on him in a vindictive orgy of violence and hacked him to death. An unrepentant Rochester later reminisced in mock heroic couplets on the role he himself had played in this gang killing:

> I'll tell of whores attacked, their lords at home,
> Bawds' quarters beaten up and fortress won,
> Windows demolished, watches overcome,
> And handsome ills by my contrivance done.[14]

The immediate upshot of this particular outrage was that a grand ball that had been planned to take place in Whitehall had to be cancelled. Presumably it was thought it would be unseemly if the perpetrators of such scandalous violence were to be seen dancing in the company of the King and his mistresses, 'all daubed with lace and blood'.[15] This minor setback to the social calendar was the only tangible discomfiture suffered by the world of the Court as a result of the murder of a constable going about his duty. The King hurriedly issued warrants of pardon for all those involved, including Monmouth, Thynn and Rochester. The cynicism with which such royal pardons were issued by Charles to protect those who were close to him was not lost on his critics. The author of the anonymous ballad concluded bitterly:

> What storms may rise out of so black a Cause,
> If such Turd-Flies shall break through Cobweb Laws.[16]

Althorp in 1677

11

ALTHORP

Oh that second bottle, Harry, is the wisest and most impartial
downright friend we have, tells us truth of ourselves, and forces
us to speak truths of others, banishes flattery from our tongues
and distrust from our hearts, sets us above the mean policy of
Court prudence, which makes us lie to one another all day for
fear of being betrayed by each other at night! And, before God,
I believe the errantest villain breathing is honest, as long as that
bottle lives.

— Letter from Rochester, while at Bath, June 1671, to Harry Savile[1]

I t was the late summer of 1671. The year of formal mourning for
the death of Joscelyn was over. During that time Elizabeth had
lived a secluded existence at Petworth, with only her closest companions such as Dorothy Blomer in attendance. She had been suffering
from numerous agues and rheums whose origins her physicians could not
explain. Then came an invitation to travel to Althorp, country home of

the rising politician Robert Spencer, 2nd Earl of Sunderland, for a season of parties and entertainments. It promised a most welcome distraction. A change of air would do her good.

Elizabeth accepted the invitation, even though it involved a long and exhausting journey. At the very least it had the merit that she would escape for a few weeks from the interferences and condescensions of her mother-in-law. Her half-sister Rachel, with whom she had a close friendship, and Rachel's husband William Russell were going, as also were Lord and Lady Clanbrazil and Lord and Lady Shaftesbury.

Anne Digby, Sunderland's young socialite wife, was a cousin of Rachel and Elizabeth's. She had already acquired a reputation as a hostess of wild and extravagant festivities. At one such recent gathering attended by Barbara Palmer and the King, Barbara had undergone a mock wedding with Charles, much to everyone's amusement, although it was perhaps just as well that Charles's long-suffering wife Catherine of Braganza was not present to witness the hilarity of it all. No doubt Elizabeth and Rachel discussed what amusements might await them as they travelled north together. There would be musicians, of course, and most probably opera singers. But would there also be fire eaters and stone eaters, acrobats and contortionists, freaks and clowns?

Included among the numerous other house guests was Harry Savile, younger brother of the Earl of Halifax. Savile was of that not uncommon species, a younger son in urgent need of a rich wife. He had few resources of his own, and while he had dabbled at a career in the navy and a career in politics, he had so far failed to make much headway in either sphere. He attributed his lack of worldly success to his outspokenness and his impatience with the rituals of court sycophancy, complaining in a letter to his elder brother how advancement required 'fawning, creeping, and serving in offices troublesome and servile enough in themselves, although gilded by the fancies of men'.[2] Less charitable observers may have considered that his career setbacks had more to do with his habit of whoring and drinking to excess. According to Lord Clarendon he was 'a young man of no wit and incredible confidence and presumption'.[3]

Savile and Sunderland had gone on their Grand Tour together back in 1661, which on that occasion took in Spain as well as France and Italy. The two men had remained firm friends ever since. Sunderland appealed to the more politically ambitious side of Harry Savile's character. But Savile was also a close friend and hardened drinking companion of the notorious

Rochester, and in the early 1670s it was Rochester who held the stronger sway with him.

To get from London to Althorp in one day, the two sisters needed to make an early start, ride in a well sprung coach and change horses at Dunstable, which also made a convenient stopping point for lunch. This is what Evelyn, who was a frequent visitor, recommended. Even keeping to this tight schedule it would still have been dusk before they obtained their first anxious glimpses of Althorp through the coach windows. The house was situated in the hollow of a small valley and surrounded by wooded hills. When Magalotti had visited in the company of Grand Duke Cosimo III of Tuscany just two years beforehand he had been impressed by the whiteness of the stone, dug from the nearby quarry at Weldon, but regretted that it had not been polished by the masons until it shone, for then it would have looked almost as brilliant as white Italian marble. Elizabeth was probably less exacting in her appreciation. Compared with Petworth, Althorp was excitingly modern. It was perfectly symmetrical in the classical manner, with much rich ornamentation.

Anne, Countess of Sunderland, was not one to penny-pinch when she desired to impress. A thousand candles glittered in the tall windows. The drive was lit by servants carrying flambeaux. The surrounding park was full of deer and herons. There were always those who sniped, of course. The Princess of Denmark claimed that the Sunderlands didn't pay their bills – 'she cares not at what rate she lives but never pays anybody. She will cheat, though it be for a little.'[4] There was very probably something in this accusation. Evelyn, for instance, who was always rather susceptible to the flattery of young and attractive women, and whose income was far more modest than that of the Sunderlands, lent Anne £500, which she not only failed to pay back, but repeatedly forgot to pay the interest on.

Money was never a problem for Elizabeth. As her coach rolled over the old stone-flagged bridge she was much more likely to be thinking about who else was on the guest list than how she could pay her bills. For her this was the beginning of her new life. She was just twenty-four years old. She was generally acknowledged to be beautiful. More importantly she was in possession of a private fortune worth more than £5,000 a year, independent of her husband's jointure. She could begin to look around her again at what life had to offer. In her excitement she probably did not notice that the canal beneath the bridge was empty of water, a defect in the irrigation system that Evelyn, as the foremost gardener of his generation, was quick to comment on.[5]

The new guests were announced and gathered in the grand saloon with its echoing, black and white marble tiled flooring, and sculptured busts of ancient heroes. A superb sweep of walnut staircase enabled the Countess of Sunderland to make an impressive descent, in order to greet them. She was a powerful-looking woman with broad shoulders, bosoms thrusting like the proud prow of a ship, and a tumble of ringlets of blonde hair. Her manner was warm and effusive. She knew how to ingratiate herself. According to the Princess of Denmark, 'she had so fawning and endearing a way she will deceive anybody at first.'[6]

Initial conversation probably centred on what a wondrous charming place Althorp was and how very convenient and clever it was to have repositioned the kitchens in the plumb centre of the house and on the ground floor, an innovation that Evelyn privately deplored. Perhaps even the tactful Elizabeth raised a surprised eyebrow towards her sister when she noticed this unusual arrangement. Anne would have lapped up the praise of all her new improvements and told everyone how anxious she was to demolish the mean old outhouses that detracted so from the overall effect she was trying to achieve.

Meals were eaten in the dining room, situated at the front of the west wing, with windows on three sides. It was hung with paintings by Caravaggio, Rubens, Rembrandt and Veronese. Robert had been a keen collector on his travels and liked to show off his spoils. Stuffed quails were swallowed and claret quaffed in increasing quantities. Conversations swirled beneath the frescoed ceilings. Among the women the hot topic of the day was how young children were disappearing, spirited away to be killed for their blood, which was supposedly being transported to France to be used to cure the French King of a leprosy. There were mothers who were so terrified at the rumours that they had taken to keeping their children at home from school.[7] It was typical of the insidious manner in which fears about secret Catholic conspiracies and diabolical witchcraft had become commingled.

After dinner the men paced the long library smoking sweet cigars of best Virginia tobacco and talking of the last Dutch war and the likelihood of another starting. Those who liked to think of themselves as being 'in the know' stood in conspiratorial huddles and questioned Sunderland as to whether he had yet received orders from the King to go to Madrid as his special envoy. Rumours of such an appointment had been circulating for some time, but there had been inexplicable delays. The purpose of the mission was to persuade the Spanish not to join the Dutch in a new war against the French, but that was not widely broadcast, for it looked far too much like siding with the Catholics against the Protestants, which was not a popular policy in the country. Sunderland himself did not give a jot for Catholicism or Protestantism. He was interested only in power and money. 'The most mercenary man in the world' was the verdict of James, Duke of York, who was not exactly renowned for his own lack of interest in material wealth.[8]

Savile was bored with all the dry talk of politics. The recent seizure of a consignment of French-manufactured dildos by customs officers was more up his street. Rochester and Savile were both members of a club called the Ballers. Killigrew was another member, and it was he who coined their ringing slogan, 'Grant us our wine and our dildos custom free.'[9]

At some point during the evening Savile singled out Elizabeth for his diversion. For a man in Savile's situation, who had a high opinion of his own personal charms and a low bank balance, Elizabeth was a particularly attractive proposition. She was possessed of a fortune and was in a position to make an independent decision about exactly on whom she wished to bestow it. She was no longer a pawn in the dynastic ambitions of some elder male relative. Savile, no doubt, offered her comfort in the grief of her widowhood and complimented her on her unblemished complexion and perfect figure. He was well known for his gallantries. Elizabeth, no doubt, was civil in her responses. Perhaps Harry misinterpreted her natural politeness as something more flirtatious. Perhaps he was already too drunk to make such a fine distinction.

As the evening wore on, the guests gradually departed to their allotted bedchambers. At the top of the grand staircase the gallery bifurcated and the rooms were neatly arranged in two long rows in the Italian manner. Elizabeth made her excuses and retired. Other house guests drifted away in ones and twos. Savile lingered and continued to drink. He wanted to play billiards. The billiard room was on the north side of the house, just beyond the staircase. There was a door from there into the garden. According to the Attorney General, Sir Heneage Finch,[10] Savile borrowed a master key off Sunderland so that he could secure the building after everyone else had gone to bed, or that at any rate was what he said. He was restless and had no desire to sleep. He wished to walk a while in the park and cool his thoughts. There was a fine view to be had

from there of Holmby House, which had been ransacked during the
Great Civil War and now stood as an awesome monument to the folly
of fanaticism.

It was well gone midnight, and the rest of Althorp had long fallen
quiet, when Savile returned to his room. He struggled out of his breeches
and put on his nightshirt. He had been careful to note beforehand which
chamber Elizabeth had been given. He was extremely drunk, but not so
drunk that he could not remember in which direction to go. He groped
his way along the dark galleried landing, his nightshirt flapping like a
slack sail about his portly buttocks. The merciless Rochester had memorialised the sight of his friend naked, when he described how a whole
gang of them had been roistering together in the open at Woodstock Park,
Rochester's country place: 'Prick, 'tis confessed, you showed but little of;
but for arse and buttock (a filthier ostentation, God wot!) you exposed
more of that nastiness in your two folio volumes than we altogether in our
six quartos.'[11]

He made it to Elizabeth's door undiscovered. He then used the recently acquired master key to gain entry to her bedroom. The Attorney
General, Sir Heneage Finch, was clearly of the opinion that Savile's previously expressed desire to play billiards was nothing more than a ruse
and that he had all along been planning this assault. John Muddiman,
who was quick to send news of the great scandal to Rochester, did not
mention the key or billiards, but had it that Savile had earlier in the day
removed the bolt from Elizabeth's door, so that all he had to do to breach
it was lift the latch.[12] Either way his entry was clearly premeditated and
clandestine.

It was one in the morning when Savile burst in. He immediately tried
to force himself on Elizabeth, while simultaneously declaring his passion.
Elizabeth woke in a state of terror. It was pitch-black. At first, in her confusion, she was not even aware of the identity of her assailant. He was just
a big heavy lumbering man, stinking of wine and sweat. She screamed and
he attempted to stifle her screams with his large hands. She managed to
free herself from his grasp sufficiently to grab hold of a handbell beside her
bed. She rang it repeatedly and desperately, while continuing to scream.
Its urgent clanging drowned out Savile's self-pitying drunken whine as
he fumbled at her night linen and ranted about how long he had been
suffering from the pangs of love. Fortunately for Elizabeth there was a
second exit onto an inner gallery, and she managed to escape. It seems that
for all Harry's careful reconnaissance and military-style planning he had

not been aware of this second door. Distraught and incoherent, Elizabeth ran barefoot over the cold tiles and sought refuge in the bedroom of Lady Ashley, wife of Lord Shaftesbury, who had already been wakened by the furious bell ringing and was quick to respond to the desperate knocks on her door.

In moments the entire household was awake. Small groups gathered on the stone landings, slightly dazed gentlemen in flannel nightshirts and nightcaps holding candles, gawping ladies wrapped in silk shawls whispering furiously. Harry Savile, who was noticably absent, had already slunk off back to his own quarters.

Savile's initial strategy the following morning was to try and laugh off the entire episode. He claimed that Lady Northumberland must have seen a ghost of himself rather than his true person in flesh and blood. Elizabeth was still too shocked to speak coherently about what had happened. She had 'scarce recovered so much breath and spirit by morning as to be able to tell her story', wrote Sir Heneage Finch. But no one believed Savile. Lady Ashley knew very well that it hadn't been a nightmare. Perhaps she had seen bruises on Elizabeth's arms or glimpsed Savile's retreating posterior. Quickly realising that his version of events was not going to carry the day, Savile changed tack. He slipped out of the house, seized a horse from the stables and set out for London.

Among 'The Ballers' the whole affair was dismissed as a light-hearted escapade, the kind of scrape that Harry was always getting himself into. Rochester, in particular, greatly enjoyed the story of his friend's disgrace. He was lying ill in bed at Woodstock, suffering from a renewed bout of syphilitic pains, when he received the news. Those closer to Elizabeth were outraged. 'The famyly breath nothing but battell murther and suddain death,' wrote Muddiman.

What Savile himself imagined he was going to achieve by his night-time perambulations and assaults is none too clear. He may have thought that if he succeeded in forcing himself on Elizabeth she would then have no choice but to accept his hand in marriage in order to preserve her reputation, particularly if he was lucky enough to get her pregnant. 'The Ballers' made little distinction between wooing, abduction and rape.

Once it was realised that Savile had fled, William Russell went in hot pursuit to avenge the honour of his affronted sister-in-law. It does not appear that he ever caught up with his quarry. It was probably more of a gesture, a nod in the direction of chivalrous outrage, rather than a chase motivated by any real desire for a confrontation. Sunderland also was furious. His friend had gone too far this time. This was not the kind of scandal that he wished to occur beneath his roof. It would do nothing to further his ambitions.

Ralph Montagu, English Ambassador in Paris

12 ≋

NUMÉRO 50, RUE DE VAUGIRARD

> I sleep at a neigbour's at present, because they are building
> just opposite my chamber window . . . in the afternoon I have
> the headache . . . in the morning I am still worse, and take herb
> tea.
>
> – Madame de la Fayette, Paris, 30 June 1673[1]

In the autumn of 1672, Elizabeth Wriothesley returned to France. It was her intention to spend the winter in the south, in Aix-en-Provence, for her health was still a cause for concern. She travelled, as before, in the company of her close friends Dr Mapletoft and the Blomers, together with Bette, who was now five years old. Included in the party on this occasion was John Locke. They left London on 11 September, arriving in Paris thirteen days later. Locke's correspondence gives a good feel for the mood of the party. It is light-hearted and mocking. He writes to his friend John Strachey in the middle of October 1672, explaining the meaning and use of an '*audace*':[2]

O the advantage of travel! You see what a blessing it is to visit foreign coun-tries and improve in the knowledge of men and manners. When could you have found out this by living at Sutton Court and eating crammed capons and apple pies? But now I have communicated this to you and enriched your understanding with the notice of a new fashionable French word, let it not make you proud, that belongs to us only that have taken pains and gone a great way for it.[3]

Elizabeth Wriothesley was not without her admirers on the other side of the Channel. The conniving Ralph Montagu was still the English am-bassador in Paris and he was very quick to renew his acquaintance with her, much to the annoyance of his mistress, the Duchesse de Brissac. Elizabeth did not seem flattered by his attentions and hastened to continue her jour-ney southwards. Undeterred, Montagu followed her to Aix, but it seems his usual charm failed to work its magic. Madame de la Fayette, a French lady novelist much admired by Voltaire, wrote with waspish satisfaction to her friend Madame de Sévigné regarding his disappointment: 'It is said Lord Montagu's journey has not succeeded as he would have wished, so that he will proceed to Italy, to show the world that Lady Northumber-land's fine eyes were not the only motives that induced him to travel. Pray let us know what you perceive of this affair, and how you think it will end.'[4]

By the following April, Elizabeth was back in Paris. A curious Madame de la Fayette paid her a visit and Elizabeth courteously returned it. The French lady was not impressed. She writes again to her friend Madame de Sévigné: 'She seems to me to have been a very handsome woman but there is not a feature of beauty remaining in her face, nor the slightest appear-ance of youth, at which I am greatly surprised: add to this that she dresses badly and without the least taste. In short I was not at all captivated with her.'[5]

Madame de la Fayette was thirty-nine years old, fourteen years older than Elizabeth, and living separated from her husband, with none of Elizabeth's financial advantages. She had enjoyed a close and intimate friendship with Montagu and was more than a little put out that he now appeared to be so infatuated with the English woman. 'I have talked a great deal to him about her: he has declared himself her humble servant without the least reserve,' she writes with evident annoyance. She ends her letter with a flounce of irritation: 'My blood is so heated, and I am so much out of sorts with the bustle and noise I have had to encounter, for the last two or three days, that I am perfectly exhausted.'

However, all was not lost. Montagu's attempts to woo Elizabeth were not making much headway. Elizabeth returned to England. Montagu doggedly followed her but Madame de la Fayette was now reasonably confident that all his efforts would come to nothing. 'It is said that he will find all his hopes baffled. I have a notion there is something a little wrong in the mind of the nymph,'[6] she wrote with malicious glee.

St James's Park during the reign of Charles II

13 〜

ST JAMES'S PARK

[Elizabeth Wriothesley] is grown so flippant since her adventure at Court of which she has already informed your Ladyship, that now she trys it every day in St James' Park, meets the person you wot of [the Duke of York] and ogles and curtsies do pass at that rate that her friends, knowing not what to make of it, only pray that her honour may be safe.

– Sir Henry Sidney to Lady Rachel Vaughan,
Elizabeth Wriothesley's half-sister[1]

The pleasure gardens of St James's Park had been laid out by the Queen Mother's favourite French garden designer, André Mollet, in the early 1660s. Previously swampy land was turned into a Pleasure Garden. The King liked to stride out there early in the mornings, outpacing his gouty and obese courtiers, desperately hanging on his every foam-flecked syllable. Central to the design was a rectangular sheet of water or canal, half a mile long and over thirty yards wide. It formed a perfect skating rink in the winter, and in the summer dragonflies hovered. Avenues of lime trees radiated from the central concourse, pale green sunlight filtering through their leaves. Parrots and cassowaries in gilded cages squawked in the shade. Wild waterfowl populated the ponds. There was an island designated for breeding, and a newly created Royal Office to go with it, called Groom of Duck Island. It was one of Charles's little teasingly sadistic jokes. If you were made Groom of Duck Island you knew your star was no longer in the ascendant.

Charles was a great collector of exotic species. He loved the bizarre and the freakish. The park swiftly turned into a menagerie, full of Solan geese, Guinea goats and Arabian sheep. There was a famous albino raven and a Balearican Crane with a wooden splint for a broken leg, perfectly tooled by an ingenious ex-soldier. A new strip of road was laid down called Pell Mell, that bisected the Park and was intended for the playing of the game pell mell, a more muscular version of croquet. It was surfaced with crushed and powdered cockle shells, the glitter almost as dazzling as the satin of the dresses of the women who sauntered there. When the wind blew, swirls and eddies of dust rose and besmirched the beautiful fabrics, but grime was an accepted part of London living. It did not stop the daily hordes of gallants and belles dames coming to parade themselves and spread their own gaudy but quickly soiled plumage.[2]

In the early summer of 1673 there was a new and somewhat unexpected participant in this elaborate daily ritual of public flaunting. Lady Elizabeth Wriothesley was joining in the fun. She had returned to London in rare good health. Even more noteworthy, she was observed exchanging meaningful glances not with her Parisian admirer, the squat Ralph Montagu, but the tall and glamorous Duke of York, heir to the throne. The sensational news, that quickly went the rounds, was that she had come back from France to marry James. 'The Countess of Northumberland is extraordinary gallant, so that the people say His Royal Highness is to marry her, and that shee . . . came home on purpose to receive the motion, and it's much liked by all the people and his Royal Highness's servants,' writes Henry Ball, one of Sir Joseph Williamson's intelligencers, from Whitehall on 13 June.[3]

The linking of Elizabeth's name with the Duke of York was not entirely new. For some two years there had been suggestions and rumours of an intended marriage. The Earl of Anglesey, for instance, made the following entry in his diary for 3 September 1671: 'Went to London in the morning and saw the Duke of York early, taking the liberty to discourse with him of what people talked of him ... commending the Countess of Northumberland to him for a wife, giving her her due praises ...'[4]

Nothing was to come of it, however. Henry Ball, in his next letter, dated 15 August 1673, was soon busy peddling new rumours: 'The towne is now full of the marriage, which they say is concluded on between Mr Montagu and the Countess of Northumberland, which is to be as reported on Monday, and that his Majesty has given his consent ... people say shee, having missed her ayme of Duchesse of York, will not long continue a widow.'[5] It seemed that Montagu's persistence had triumphed after all.

The marriage between Elizabeth and Montagu was arranged for 26 August, to be solemnised at Titchfield, the Wriothesley family home. The following month, the Duke of York married the fifteen-year-old Mary of Modena. There were political pressures on him to do so. It was a marriage in the French interest and it helped cement Charles's secret alliance with Louis XIV.

There was still one important stumbling block to Elizabeth's marriage to Montagu, however, that needed to be overcome. It concerned the custody of little Bette. James Vernon, a Whitehall civil servant, described the problem:

> If there be any thing that may make my Lady less satisfied with a second marriage, and which perhaps have kept her from it all this while, it is a clause in her late husband's will, which takes away from her the care of bringing up her daughter, and puts the child in the hands of the Dowager; this is of extreme hard digestion and no stone will be left unturned, if either King or Parliament can be prevailed with to keep up the mother's right.[6]

The motive for this clause in Joscelyn's will was not altogether unreasonable. Bette was invested with great wealth and Joscelyn did not want an unscrupulous second husband milking that vast estate for his own purposes. Perhaps even more importantly, he did not want some new man deciding who it was that Bette was to marry. Far safer, he thought, to place Bette's future welfare in the hands of his own dearly beloved mother, a woman old and wise enough to make it unlikely she would fall under the influence of some unprincipled rogue. That, at any rate, was the theory.

Elizabeth went ahead with the marriage to Ralph, but if she thought her mother-in-law would not try to assert her legal rights over Bette, she seriously miscalculated. 'The day after they were married the Countess Dowager sent a gentleman with a letter to Titchfield to claim the little Lady Bette.'[7] Elizabeth refused to comply. She had almost certainly been assured by Montagu that the Dowager Countess would find it impossible to claim the child in the face of opposition from the King, and Montagu had a characteristically ingenious plan for enlisting the King's support. Montagu was the kind of man who had an ingenious plan for every situation. Few of them worked out, but this never appeared to diminish his extraordinary self-confidence.

In this instance he was relying on his previous close relationship with and intimate knowledge of Barbara Palmer, Duchess of Cleveland, one of the King's most influential mistresses. The venal and upwardly socially mobile Barbara was anxious to make a brilliant marriage for her bastard son by Charles, Lord George Fitzroy. There was no more brilliant marriage to be had than the hand of Bette, and Charles, with his usual lassitude, tended to adopt the line of least resistance where the wishes of Barbara were concerned. The rumour quickly went round Whitehall that it was a done deal. Bette was destined for Fitzroy and the King would overrule the Dowager Countess, leaving Bette in the hands of her mother. 'Since Mr Montagu was in possession of his bright purchase the old lady has sent for the child, but was answered in the negative, and preparations are making to assert this refusal, and the Towne has already disposed her to my Lord George and made the mother a Dutchesse,' was the gossip.[8] Whether or not Elizabeth Wriothesley seriously anticipated being made a Duchess in return for marrying her daughter off to one of the King's impecunious and illegitimate children is questionable, but Montagu was seriously overplaying his hand in thinking he could manage to pull this off. The Dowager Countess Howard had no intention of allowing Bette to remain in the possession of her mother.

On 22 September 1673 a meeting was arranged between the two disputing parties. Elizabeth and Montagu were residing temporarily at Northumberland House. Countess Howard agreed to visit them there. The Lord Chancellor was present, presumably in his capacity of legal adviser to the Crown. Lord Suffolk was also present offering support to his sister, the Countess Howard. Not that she needed it. Rachel Russell, who reported on the meeting to her husband in a letter written the next day, remarked that the old lady was 'stout yesterday, and would not hear patiently'.[9] As usual the Countess Howard was short-tempered, outspoken, impatient of any restraint or opposition. Even the infinitely subtle and resourceful Montagu must have wondered quite how he was going to handle her.

The law was not on Lady Wriothesley's side. She eventually offered to surrender Bette on condition that she could have her to visit for ten days to a month at a time. She also wanted the Countess to enter into a formal bond not to marry the child off without her own permission, nor to betroth her until she was of an age of consent, which was twelve. Rachel Russell was still hopeful that an agreement between both the parties could be reached. But her sympathies, as might be expected, were all with her sister. 'My sister urges, it is hard her child (that if she has no other children must be her heir) should be disposed of without her consent; and in my judgement it is hard.'[10]

It does not appear that Elizabeth's proposal was ever formally accepted by the Dowager. What is clear is that shortly afterwards Bette was handed over into the grandmother's custody. The person entrusted with this task was the faithful Dr Mapletoft. It is the occasion of one of the few letters from Lady Wriothesley that have survived:

> I am very glad the dear child is soe well ... I leave her wholly to your care to remove her when you think fitt, and I desire that you would stay to come with her; for I shall not be at ease if you are not with her. And pray take care to defend her from her grandmother, who has not so much civilite left as to come and speak to me herself; but by a letter has let me know that she does expect to have her delivered up; if not, she must use force.[11]

The Montagu marriage was soon in disarray, much to the amusement of the Whitehall gossips. On 5 November Thomas Derham, another of Secretary of State Sir Joseph Williamson's informers, writes: 'Mr Montagu and his Lady begin already to live like man and wife, neither caring a rush for the other, which makes her marrying of him more and more to be wondered at.'[12] A week later Sir Gilbert Talbot adds further to the running farce: 'Your friend R.M. hath managed his matters soe that he and his Countesse lye in two beds.'[13] If you were part of Charles's Court there was precious little privacy to be had.

Elizabeth's despair at the loss of her child cannot have helped. Perhaps Montagu had talked her into the marriage with him on the promise that he could fix the custody issue. If that was the case Elizabeth had been naïve, and now she was regretting it. 'Poor childe I pray God send her health and protect her from all the designs that are upon her at this time,'[14] she writes, with ominous prescience.

Entrance to Northumberland House from the Strand

14

NORTHUMBERLAND HOUSE

refraining much speech before them, in patient hearkening to
them, in giving reverend titles to them, and humble and ready
answers, without pride or stoutnesse . . . Avoiding all unmannerly
rudenesse, disdainful statelinesse, toyish wantonnesse, over-
much boldnesse, and high-mindednesse.

– Prayer for a child to use, 1634, William Gouge[1]

It is 26 January 1676, and Bette is seated on a stool in her closet
before her dressing-table mirror. There is a yellow-patterned carpet
on the floor. Bette is fond of yellow, the colour of sunlight and
happiness, but outside it is wintry and grey. It is her ninth birthday and she
is preparing herself for the party that her mother is holding in her honour.
She knows that it is vitally important that she should make a favourable
impression on the assembled guests, as several prospective suitors have
been invited to the festivities.

It is possible to reconstruct the scene. Bette's table is covered in little lacquered or silvered trinkets and small boxes made from ivory or tortoise-shell, cedar or olive wood. They contain brushes, tweezers, scissors, combs, powders, ointments, perfumes and jewels. Two japanned candlesticks stand either side of the mirror, emphasising its resemblance to an altarpiece. The candles are lit, for the light is rapidly fading. She has already bathed her face in a lotion of puppy water, produced from wine mixed with the juices of roast puppy, a combination excellent for the complexion. She now settles herself before the mirror and applies ceruse to her cheeks to erase the worst of her freckles, which were considered a great disfigurement. Ceruse contains white lead, but the debilitating effects of lead poisoning have yet to be discovered. A maid assists her to pluck her eyebrows and stick on false replacements made from mouse skin, using an aromatic gum. These new eyebrows are placed a little higher up than is quite natural to give her a desirable startled look.

Even girls as young as nine must dress themselves as miniature adults for important and formal occasions such as this. So Bette's hair is elaborately coiffeured and undergoes the painful application of heated curlers and tongs. Her particular style for that evening was probably similar to that of another great heiress, Bridget Hyde, who was exquisitely painted by John Wright at around this time. The hair is parted in the middle and cleverly festooned at the sides, so that it projects from the head like a perfectly wrought wasp nest, a tracery of silver and diamonds sparkling from amid its whorls. An arrangement of curls is permitted to dangle loose. The curls are not a random selection. Each one is exactly placed and has its own name. There are the *'crèves coeurs'* or heartbreakers at the nape, and the *'confidantes'*, tickling the lobes of the ears. Her white neck is adorned with three ropes of pearls. The dress is gorgeous, a misty grey-blue silk, low-necked and off the shoulder, even though the young wearer has yet to develop a bosom. It is designed in the French fashion with full sleeves, a long pointed bodice and a full skirt split at the sides so that it can be easily lifted to reveal a pleated petticoat in a subtly contrasting colour.[2]

Mrs Stanhope,[3] Bette's faithful companion, stands behind her and makes any necessary last-minute adjustments. When preparations are finally complete Bette descends the stairs. The Dowager Countess's coach is already waiting in the forecourt, emblazoned with the Percy arms: six silver fish and two rampant lions.

Bette's grandmother would also be attending this birthday party. Two years had passed since the great shouting match had taken place between her and Elizabeth, and relations were still very frosty between the two women. The issue of who would make a fit and proper husband for Bette was the great bone of contention.

As usual the night air is foul with the fumes of fermenting hops blowing from the nearby brewhouses in St Martin's Lane. John Evelyn noted how, whenever the wind blew from that direction, Northumberland House was frequently 'wrapped in a horrid cloud of this smoake'.[4] The Dowager disapproves, but there is little even she can do about it other than command that the carriage door is closed as quickly as possible, before she chokes. The coach swings out through the great wrought-iron gates and onto the Strand. It is drawn by four of those fine Spanish black horses that had been twice impounded during their brief excursion across the Channel when Joscelyn had been en route for Italy. The pace of progress through the crowded streets is slow. The partygoers are preceded by two footmen in full livery to clear the road of riff-raff, as well as trumpeters to announce her Ladyship's noble presence to the world at large, and link boys with flambeaux to light the way.[5]

Elizabeth and Montagu were renting the Earl of Leicester's town house on Cranbourn Street, opposite Leicester Fields, in the heart of what is today called Soho. It was an interim measure while their new house was being built. Soon after his marriage Ralph Montagu had set about constructing a great monument to his own glory with his wife's money. It was to be a grand design in the French style, built where the British Museum now stands. Elizabeth was anxious to move in as soon as possible, but Montagu's plans grew ever more elaborate. The chimneys needed to be taller, the cupolas more bulging, the porticos grander. He hired the ingenious scientist Robert Hooke as his architect. To emphasise the building's semi-royal status, the domed sloping roof of the central portion was to be crowned by a gilt balustrade like a glinting coronet catching the sunlight, and the chimneys of the pavilion section were to be adorned with copper gilt balls.[6]

There was hardly a word written by any of the Court gossips or Bette's numerous relations, as to what kind of girl she was, her tastes, accomplishments, interests, thoughts. But there was much general speculation on the subject of her future husband. It is as if all who looked at her could see only the glittering potential for plunder. From the moment that Joscelyn died, Bette had little identity of her own other than that of being the greatest marriage prospect in the kingdom.

So the nine-year-old Bette can be pictured in her party finery standing dutifully in the entrance hall to Leicester Place, flanked by her mother and her grandmother, towering over her like warring gorgons. She politely welcomes her guests, the Marquess and Marchioness of Winchester with their son Lord St John, the Earl and Countess of Salisbury with their son Lord Cranborne, the Earl and Countess of Clare with their son Lord Haughton, the Duke and Duchess of Newcastle with their son Lord Ogle, and last but not least the mischievous George Fitzroy, the illegitimate son of the King.

Montagu is bound to have been late. He had probably just come from a meeting with Fitch the bricklayer, who was complaining that his bills had yet to be paid. It would be interesting to know whether Count Konigsmark was also at the party. It is quite possible that he was. He would have been about sixteen years old. He had certainly been in London at about this time, because a few months earlier Robert Hooke had noted in his diary: 'Count Konigsmark well satisfied with quadrant'.[7] Hooke was an innovative maker of instruments and Konigsmark had commissioned from him one of his new reflecting quadrants used for measuring distances at sea by means of triangulation. It is probable that it was Montagu who had introduced Konigsmark to Hooke, for Konigsmark and Montagu had both spent time in Paris together. It could well have been on such an occasion as her birthday that the little red-haired heiress first caught Konigsmark's eye.

Montagu was acutely aware of Bette's marriage potential and how it could be best exploited for his own political advancement. His wife Elizabeth might have lost the custody battle, but with his characteristic tenacity and self-confidence he was still giving everyone the impression that Bette's hand in marriage was within his personal gift. He told Danby, Charles's first minister, that he could deliver Bette to Fitzroy. If Montagu could bring off this great coup it would much improve his standing in Charles's eyes.

Montagu was frank with Danby as to where the main opposition threat was coming from. The grandmother was pushing for Lord Henry Ogle. 'I find by her letters to my wife she is extremely set upon marrying her to my Lord Ogle,' he wrote to Danby.[8] But Montagu was confident that he held the trump card. He told Danby that Bette would never go against her mother's wishes no matter how hard the grandmother pushed. And Elizabeth would do as Montagu told her to do.

During the party George Fitzroy took every opportunity of mocking his great rival Henry Ogle behind his back, by pulling faces. Whether Bette found him amusing is not recorded. Montagu obviously did, for he writes to Danby: '[Fitzroy] is already cunning enough to be enquiring of me after my lady Betty Percy and has taken such an aversion to my Lord Ogle ... that when they meet at my house he is always ready to laugh or make mouths at him.'[9]

Henry Ogle was the favourite grandchild of Margaret Cavendish, the author and pioneer for female education, and he seems to have been a serious-minded and sensitive child, if not particularly prepossessing in appearance. The Countess of Sunderland famously described him as being 'as ugly as anything young can be'.[10] George Fitzroy on the other hand may have been proficient at vaulting, shooting and horse riding, as well as handsome, but he was not much of a reader.[11]

Bette's mother, Elizabeth, meanwhile, was not on the best of form. She was just recovering from yet another of those bad colds that continually afflicted her. 'I was so very ill that I was forced to keep to my bed on Sunday,' she wrote to her sister Rachel a few days later.[12] She often took to her bed. Of course, she did not have the benefit of antibiotics and all the other remedies and palliatives so readily available today. And like most married women of her age she was repeatedly pregnant, which was a constant drain on her energy levels. She was frequently languid and fretful, always thinking about that next spa resort she was off to, and visiting fortune tellers for reassurance.

The birthday party was not a success. Not only were Henry and George constantly squabbling with each other, but suddenly the Dowager Countess announced in a resounding voice that she was leaving and taking Bette with her. The party was not halfway through. The music and the dancing had yet to start. Bette loved dancing. It was what she had most been looking forward to.

'It did not pass so well as the last she kept with me,' admitted a weary Elizabeth.[13] The problem was that the Dowager Countess's gambling friends had failed to turn up. Lacking any other form of distraction, 'play being the only thing can engage her grandmother to stay abroad past her hour', the disgruntled Countess took Bette home at seven o'clock. Elizabeth does not describe Bette's response beyond saying: 'a great disappointment having some of her young company and fiddles'. Were there tears, tantrums, footstampings and harsh words? It seems more likely that Bette was so well schooled in the doctrine of obedience, as advised by William Gouge in his 'Prayer for a Child', that she said nothing. She no doubt dutifully removed her satin dancing slippers and put on her outdoor boots, to be once more shuttled through the night in the stately Percy coach, back to the interminable and gloomy corridors of Northumberland House, with their ancestral suits of armour upon the landings, and their ancient carbines and musquetoons in racks upon the walls.

It was common enough for children of the great aristocratic families to have only limited contact with their parents, but Bette's isolation must have been intense. Her father was dead, her mother she saw only rarely, and her ill-tempered grandmother was more and more obsessed with her own self-importance and the playing of backgammon, bizet or ombre for ever larger stakes of money. Bette had no siblings living with her in the various grand houses where she dwelled. She moved ceremoniously between these gilded palaces, much as the seasons themselves moved. But the vast echoing hallways with their marble busts, and the long silent picture galleries with their watching eyes, were all equally empty. The few children of her own age that she had contact with were generally of too low a class for her to be allowed to associate freely with them. She would have been acutely aware of her difference from others. The magnificence of her pedigree had been dinned into her by the old Countess from an early age. But all this only underlined her separateness from the rest of humanity. She was to grow up very clever, intensely private, serious, wilful and lonely.

John Wilmot, 2nd Earl of Rochester

15 ⤜

ST JAMES'S PARK AT NIGHT

Nightly now beneath their shade
Are buggeries, rapes and incests made,
Unto this all sin sheltering Grove
Whores of the Bulk and the Alcove,
Great Ladies, chamber maydes and Drudges,
The Ragg Picker, and Heiress Trudges,
Carrmen, Divines, Great Lords, and Taylors,
Prentices, Poets, Pimps and gaolers,
Footmen, Fine Fopps, do here arrive
And here promiscuously they swive.

– From Rochester, 'A Ramble in St James's Park', March 1673[1]

After dark the Royal Park of St James's became a playground where all ranks of society mingled and all manner of libidinous appetites were catered for. It was a perverted paradise frequented by sauntering voyeurs and overheated exhibitionists alike. One moonlit night early in the year of 1677, however, the idlers and the gawpers and all those busy speculating in the currency of sex were treated to a spectacle the like of which had never been witnessed before. Two beautiful young women wearing eye masks and loose flowing silk nightgowns suddenly appeared on a silvered square of lawn as if out of nowhere. The taller woman was around thirty years of age, with long curling black hair, full red lips and large pale breasts, which she did not attempt to hide from the general view. Her companion was much younger, slighter in figure, her hair a light brown, her mouth pert and simpering, her manner pretending to a modesty that it did not in reality possess. The universal amazement at their first appearance was quickly followed by a sharp intake of breath as both women produced naked rapiers that had been hidden beneath the voluminous drapes of their skirts. They then proceeded to parry and thrust at each other's bosoms with a great show of skill and zeal. The crowd cheered and clapped and shouted encouragement and blinked to confirm that what they were seeing was really taking place. It was like a play, except they were not in a theatre and it was not at all clear whether these women were acting or intended to fight each other to the death. Many of their moves were both accomplished and daring. It seemed as if at any minute blood must be spilled, for they wore no steel vests or buff waistcoats. And then it was all over. The two fencers lowered their swords, took their bows and disappeared into the shadows as quickly as they had materialised in the first place.

In order to understand the background to this performance it is necessary to unravel the recent machinations of Ralph Montagu, for while Elizabeth had been languishing in her bed either pregnant or ill, Montagu had been busily weaving schemes of such devious complexity it was almost inevitable he would end up entrapping himself.

Around the time of the unhappy birthday party, that is January 1676, Montagu had imported Hortense, Duchess of Mazarin, into England, with the idea of pimping her to Charles. Providing Charles with an entertaining new mistress, who remained in part at least within the control of the provider, had long been a most convenient way of increasing one's power at court. Hortense, who had formerly been the object of Joscelyn Percy's brief passion, was at something of a loose end. Her most recent protector, the Duke of Savoy, had just died, so she was more than willing to fall in with Montagu's plans.

From the moment she landed at Torbay the Duchess had caused quite a stir. She was dressed as a man and had a handsome young black boy in attendance. Black boys were a popular fashion accessory at the time. Louise de Kérouaille, one of Charles's current favourites, was painted by Mignard with a pretty 'blackamoor' offering her a cornucopia of pearls.

Hortense may have been intended as a new plaything for Charles, but the conscientious Montagu thought it best to try her out first. 'Monsieur de Montagu, who had a mind to arrange an affair between the King and Madam de Mazarin, has himself fallen into her toils,' wrote Courtin, the French ambassador in London, to Louis XIV.[2] It is difficult to imagine Montagu falling into anyone's 'toils' if he didn't perceive some advantage to himself in doing so, but clearly it suited Courtin to portray Hortense as the predator. To begin with Hortense lodged with Montagu's sister, Lady Ann Hervey, in Covent Garden. According to Courtin, Madame Hervey was 'the most intriguing and the cleverest woman in England'.[3] According to Rochester her most formidable attribute was her 'long clitories'.[4]

Hortense did not work out quite as intended. She very quickly showed more interest in seducing the aging King's illegitimate fifteen-year-old daughter, Anne, Countess of Sussex, than the King himself. Anne was another of Barbara Palmer's offspring and had been married at an early age to Baron Dacre. Subsequently she had spent little time in his company, other than what it took to get her pregnant.

Hortense and Anne were soon spending their afternoons playing shuttlecock and battledore together in the grounds of the King's apartments in Whitehall, and when they were exhausted with these innocent pastimes they would chirrup at the caged sparrows and chase the ubiquitous spaniels. To begin with it all seemed girlishly charming and sweet. When they started taking fencing lessons together, dressing up in tights and lace shirts and thrusting their épées at each other, one or two courtly eyebrows were raised in amused disapproval, but no one thought fit to intervene. It didn't end there, however. Hortense was always one for pushing the boundaries of what was considered acceptable behaviour. Before very long she and her new young protégée, who was by now expecting her first child, were dressing up in masks and stealing off to St James's Park. Anne was evidently finding it all very exciting, until her outraged and bemused husband decided to put an end to her fun and packed her off to his family's ancestral home at Herstmonceux Castle, well away from the dangerous influence of Hortense. Anne, incarcerated in the country, fell into a deep gloom, lost her baby, and spent her days kissing a small portrait of Hortense in a frenzy of passion. The portrait was probably similar to the one that had got Joscelyn into such trouble some six years previously. Her behaviour continued to deteriorate until she became so wild and unmanageable her mother decided the only thing to be done with her was to send her to a nunnery. Conflans in France was chosen, and the depressed and hormonally unbalanced Anne was promptly packed off there.[5]

Barbara was constantly back and forth across the Channel, but not just to oversee her wayward daughter's convent education. Part of her reason for visiting Paris so often was to develop her friendship with Elizabeth Wriothesley. Montagu and Elizabeth spent much of their time there, as he was still ambassador. Montagu had already made it clear to Barbara that the marriage she so desired between her son Fitzroy and Bette could only be achieved through the good offices of both himself and his wife. 'I make no doubt but the daughter will declare for marrying where the mother pleases and not where the grandmother desires,'[6] he wrote. According to Montagu, Bette had several times stated very positively, in front of her mother, 'she will never marry but where her mother will have her'. So Barbara set about befriending Elizabeth, and Montagu explained to his wife that his own political career was dependent on Barbara's good opinion. What he did not tell his wife was that he was proposing to strengthen his hand still further by having an affair with Barbara. So Barbara and Ralph added each other to their long lists of lovers.

To begin with it all appeared to be going rather well. The burgeoning friendship between the two women was progressing nicely until one day Elizabeth called round on Barbara only to be refused entry by a footman. Elizabeth was bemused. She explained that there must be some mistake, because she had a prior appointment to meet with the Duchess. The footman continued to insist that she leave a note and call back some other time. Elizabeth did not appreciate being treated in such a high handed manner and asked to speak with the Duchess in person. The footman answered that that would be impossible. When asked why, the astounding reply was that the Duchess was busy with Monsieur Chattillean.

Elizabeth was insulted. When the incident was related to Montagu, he was furious, not because of the slight to his wife but because of the insult to himself. A few enquiries told him that Monsieur Chattillean was Barbara's latest young lover. He went straight round to see Barbara and did 'expostulate very roundly with the Duchess for her licentious course of life with the said monsieur'.[7] He claimed that her behaviour 'brought disgrace to the children his Majesty had by her'. Barbara, who was notorious for her temper tantrums, 'returned all upon him with rage and contempt, and 'twas his only care to get well home'.

Montagu would have been well advised to leave it there, but he didn't. Through the agency of a nun he managed to get hold of some of Chattillean's letters to Barbara, which 'abounded with gross and unseemly things in the trade of love'. Some of them also showed 'disrespect to his Majesty'. Montagu decided to forward them on to Charles. Barbara hurried back to England to put her side of the story.

Meanwhile Lady Anne, with her mother's permission, had transferred from the convent at Conflans to the more agreeable surroundings of the Convent of the Immaculate Conception, in the rue de Charenton, Faubourg St Antoine. This was where Barbara herself resided when she was stopping in Paris, and she had just spent some considerable sums of money on the fabric of the building to make it more comfortable for her own visits, including a new staircase, a revamped kitchen, and wainscoting in the refectory, which all came to 280 pistoles.[8] Paris and its environs were full of these small convents that had set up over the past few decades, most of them financially precarious and heavily dependent upon the patronage of some wealthy individual hoping to book their place in heaven by making some timely donations. Unfortunately for the nuns of the Immaculate Conception, Montagu decided to avenge himself by seducing the young Countess Anne in her mother's absence, beneath their roof. This ill-judged move suggests that Montagu must have been very piqued at finding himself thrown over by Barbara for the younger and indisputably more handsome Monsieur Chattillean.

When Barbara returned to Paris in the summer of 1678 and discovered what was going on, she was incandescent. She wrote to Charles in a fury:

> I never in my whole lifetime heard of such government of herself as she has had since I went into England. She has never been in the monastery two days together, but every day gone out with the ambassador, and has often lain four days together at my house, and sent for her meats to the ambassador; he being always with her till five oclock in the morning, they two shut up together alone.[9]

Barbara's annoyance is perhaps understandable, but her hypocrisy in her subsequent treatment of her daughter is simply breathtaking. She sends the unhappy Anne off to yet another convent, this time Port Royal, safely outside Paris, where a Jansenist regime specialised in fastings, mortification of the flesh and rigid seclusion. She insists that 'she carries no servants with her', and that 'she stirs not nor receives no visits whatsoever without a letter from me to the Abbess. For where she is now all people visit her, and the Ambassador and others carry consorts of music every day to entertain her.'[10] Having safely disposed of Anne to a music-free environment, she writes to Charles telling him that Montagu 'has neither conscience nor honour ... and has several times told me that in his heart he despised you and your brother ... you were a dull governable fool and the duke a wilful fool'.[11] She described how Montagu was in the habit of imitating Charles's manner of speaking before the French courtiers, much to everyone's amusement, and how he boasted that he could lead both Charles and his brother 'by the nose' because he had bribed their favourite astrologer to make predictions that favoured his own interests.

When the ever-eloquent Montagu tried to give his side of the story to the King in person, Charles was not amused. 'His Majesty did, as it were casually, meet ... with Mr Montagu, who, beginning to enter on the story of my Lady Cleveland, His Majesty told him he knew already too much of that, and bade him declare what affair of state it was that made him quit France without leave.'[12] The silvery-tongued Montagu, for once, was at a loss for words. He found himself promptly banned from the Court, struck from the Privy Council and removed from his position as ambassador in Paris.

It seems that the only person on either side of the Channel that believed in Montagu's version of events was his long-suffering wife. Elizabeth wrote to him from Paris: 'I did believe her [Anne] innocent of all was said of you.'[13] But even Elizabeth's patience was running a little thin. 'Sure there was never a more vexatious business, but I will say noe more. Pray God send we may meet quickly, Yours for ever.' Elizabeth's forbearance has a quiet dignity, but among the chattering gossips in London, her continuing fondness for her errant husband was regarded as nothing more than simple-minded foolishness. The acid Countess of Sunderland, writing to Henry Sidney, remarked on how 'ill favoured' Montagu was to look at, and added spitefully that nevertheless 'his wife calls him her pretty dear and kisses him a thousand times a day'.[14]

One thing was now certain. Only the successful outcome of the

Fitzroy–Bette alliance could rehabilitate Montagu in the eyes of the Court, and since his downfall it was going to be entirely dependent on Elizabeth to accomplish this feat, in the teeth of fierce opposition from the Dowager Countess.

Etching by Van der Vaart of Lady Bette's betrothal portrait by Peter Lely

16 ⤜

THE STUDIO OF PETER LELY

This makes me reflect how arts and buissness are like contrarys
... an art fills a man's life and thought, and he can no more
endure buissness, than a man of buissness can endure the minute
fantosmes of an artist.

– Roger North writing about Peter Lely in *Notes of Me*[1]

E arly in the year of 1679, Bette hurried beneath the pillared
colonnades of the newly built Covent Garden on her way to
an important appointment. She was now almost twelve years old
and she was going to sit for her betrothal portrait by the celebrated Peter
Lely. When her grandmother had been a child this entire area had been
nothing but pasture and orchard. It was her aunt's family, the Russells, who
had developed it into three blocks of elegant terraced houses, 'fit for the
habitation of gentlemen and men of ability'.[2]

Lely's studio was situated at the north-eastern corner of the Piazza. It
was a substantial building which also served as an art gallery and a private

home. When Bette first visited, its appearance must have struck her as both ghoulish and entrancing, rather like entering into a giant mausoleum that had been temporarily converted into a draper's shop. It was littered with white plaster hands, severed from the body, and jointed but headless dummies wrapped in gorgeous fabrics. Everywhere she looked there were great swathes of brilliantly coloured silks and satins, damasks and calicoes, tiffanies and velvets, as well as the usual pictorial props: anchors leaning against walls, stuffed linnets in cages, urns on tables, metal breastplates reclining on squabs. Even more disorientating than this profusion of strange objects was the venomous smell of arsenic sulphides mingling with Venetian turpentine.[3]

The studio was a manufactory of art works, rather than a studio in the nineteenth-century romantic sense of the artist's garret. The client was required to sit for only a minimum of time, with the bulk of the painting fabricated afterwards. Lely employed nearly a dozen assistants, all accomplished technicians in their own right. There was Jan Baptist Jaspers from Antwerp, whose particular expertise was in painting the rich materials that adorned the female clients. He was a genius at both sheen and shadow. Then there was Pieter van Roestraton, who did those parts that required the most meticulous brushwork, the gems, the buckles, the musical instruments. Mr Henry Lankrink was the foremost for flowers. Lely himself did the faces. And then there were the menials like the muscular John Young, who ground all day long the pigments for the production of the colours, the ochres and the indigos and the ultramarines, and who had the biceps that went with his particular occupation.

It was a room of noble proportions, not just to accommodate the large number of people constantly coming and going, but also the bewildering quantity and variety of equipment: the easels, straining frames, tempering knives, spatulas, ivory palettes, shells for mixing colours, porphyry grinding stones, chalks, pencils and brushes. Picture frames were stacked everywhere, both carved and plain, finished in gilt, leatherwork and ebony. There were great chests of linen, sacking, flaxen cloth, and canvas of various weaves, some coarse and rough, others pumiced and sized with animal glues until they were as smooth as glass.

Lely utilised a variety of clever techniques both to speed up production and to give the finished product that unique lustre his clients coveted. He was an expert at building up layers of paint, which became thinner and more transparent as he laid them one upon the other, creating subtly veiled tones and muted shades. He developed a method of applying these layers without waiting for the previous one to dry. When rival artists tried to prise out of him his secret, he answered evasively that it was a technique handed down to him by the great van Dyck himself. He finished his paintings with a thin wash of oil, which he smeared with the ball of his hand and which afterwards he blotted with bread. He used flicks of his brush to apply white highlighting to intensify the luminosity of bare skin, and deployed minute brown hatching to deepen the shadows. In the words of the antiquarian George Vertue, Lely had a 'conceiled, mysterious, scanty way of painting'.[4]

Bette's betrothal portrait shows her seated, looking towards her right, holding white blossoms that she has just picked from a potted orange tree that stands beside her. The white flowers are symbolic of her chastity, an age-old device, but the orange tree itself is a recent innovation, reflecting the current fad for exotic plants that could be grown in the new hothouses. Her eyes are the colour of celadon. Her hair is a dark red, meticulously curled around the nape of her neck but allowed to fall loosely behind one shoulder with a cultivated lack of formality and restraint. She wears a striking vermilion red dress. It is low-cut, ruched, with a tracery of muslin around the neckline and pretty loops of pearls which emphasise her surprisingly developed breasts. In contrast to the dress, her skin is the white of white lead touched with rose madder. Her nose is long and thin in the approved manner, delicately drawn but with just that touch of aloofness and disdain, preventing what might otherwise have been rather too pert and sweet a look.

The style of Bette's dress is typical of the loose shifts draped in the Roman manner that women of the Restoration period adopted to have their portrait painted in. Such draperies bore little resemblance to the dresses women would actually have worn. These antique wraps were meant to emphasise the timeless beauty of their sitters. 'Fantastic nightgowns fastened with a single pin',[5] was how Horace Walpole summed up their erotic appeal. But there was more to them than that. They were also a statement of social superiority. Persons of high standing could entertain, and even conduct business, while lounging on their beds in loose nightclothes. It was only the lower classes that needed to be properly turned out. For Lely, there was also an important economic advantage to be had from this insistence on his subjects adopting a style of 'loose, airy undresse'.[6] There was much less detail in these great swoons of gorgeous satin than there was in some of the intricately patterned garments that were actually worn. This was another device that enabled him to achieve a quicker turnaround on the product.

Lely was one of those highly accomplished Dutch artists who had come over to England because there was no work for them in Holland. Like most immigrants, they were not universally loved. 'Lusty fat two legged cheese worms'[7] was one less than entirely appreciative description. But their services were much in demand. Lely had first arrived in 1642, just after van Dyck died, and he promptly took over from where van Dyck had left off. As a young man he had clearly been handsome, but he soon displayed the seediness of a spoilt and fallen cherub. He was openly disdainful of financial affairs. In the words of his friend and first biographer Roger North, he was 'averse to businesse & loathly drawne to do anything but paint'.[8] But this was probably something of an artistic affectation. By the 1670s he had certainly built up a most enviable business. Such was his popularity that he was able to charge £60 for a full-length portrait, almost twice what some of his accomplished competitors were able to command. Even more important, he was able to produce the finished product in less time than any of his rivals.

It is noticeable that in the many gossipy references to Bette, both in the newspapers and in private letters, there is never any mention made of her as a beauty, unlike her mother, whose name can hardly be uttered without having the word beauty attached to it. Perhaps no one could see beyond the money. Perhaps the wildly melodramatic events that were so soon to overtake her life distracted from such comment, made it almost an irrelevance. It may also have had something to do with the contemporary prejudice against red hair and freckles. The former was considered unfortunate, though there were precedents, most notably Queen Elizabeth. The latter were an unforgivable blemish, to be covered up at all costs.

Lely's portraits were intended as a recognisable likeness of their subject, but were also to transform the sitter into that ideal of female beauty that was dominant at the time: the eyes sleepy, the nose aquiline, and a little swelling of extra flesh beneath the chin. It was a look that came straight out of the Renaissance. Agnolo Firenzuola had laid down all the necessary components in his book *On the Beauty of Women*, published in 1548. Not all Lely's sitters were entirely happy, however, about the way in which their distinctive personal attributes were cleverly transformed into this archetype of female glamour. Dorothy Temple, the woman who was to help Bette run away from Thomas Thynn, was clearly in two minds about the result. She wrote to her lover and future husband William Temple: 'I cannot tell whether it be very like mee or not though tis the best I have ever had drawne for mee and Mr Lilly will have it that he never took more pains to make a good one in his life. And that was it I think that spoiled it.'⁹ Dorothy was both intelligent enough and honest enough to admit that although this art was flattering, it was not entirely truthful.

In her portrait, Bette conveys a youthful innocence. Her cheeks are still plump, the mouth full but not too obviously pouting, the eyes wide open. But the gaze is impassive, its meaning elusive. Is this the innocence of a child or the insolence of a murderess? There were plenty among her contemporaries who were soon to think the latter.

Bette left no record of what she thought of her own betrothal painting. Of rather greater immediate concern to her was the all-important question of just who it was she was getting betrothed to. That detail had still to be decided. Her grandmother had made it clear to the world that she intended to dispose of Bette just as soon as she was old enough to be married, which would be her twelfth birthday. But quite where her great fortune was to be bestowed was still a subject of ongoing wrangling between the various interested parties. In recent months the Dowager Countess had cooled somewhat on the idea of Lord Ogle and the Newcastles. She had asked her brother, the Earl of Suffolk, to open up negotiations with the Marquess of Winchester. The Ormondes also were approached in connection with their eldest son, James Butler. But the Ormondes quickly withdrew. In December of 1678 the Marquess decided to 'let it fall with all the thanks that can be expressed to the younger Lady Northumberland, and without making a journey to the market at Petworth'.¹⁰ The reference to a market at Petworth is very barbed. Evidently the Ormondes did not like the bidding process that the old lady was busy fostering. Her grandmother had pretty much put Bette up for auction, best offer to be received by her twelfth birthday.

And then at the last minute came a letter from King Charles. Barbara, realising that Montagu was now going to be of little assistance to her, had prevailed upon Charles to make a direct approach. The letter is dated 10 February 1679, Whitehall:

... I understand that the treaty that was on foote for the Marquis of Winchesters son (when you writ to my L'd Suffolk) is at an end, I hope that my modesty in staying to see the issue of that will engage you not to treate with any other, till first you know what I shall offer; my earnestnesse for this, is, that (besides my inclination to oblige your family) your civilite to me in this affair, will give me more frequent opportunity particularly to serve you, which I assure you is the real desire of, Madame, your affectionate friend, Charles R."

Syon House, Isleworth in the late seventeenth century

17

SYON HOUSE

As a Daughter is neither to anticipate, nor to contradict the will
of her parent, so (to hang the balance even) I must say she is not
obliged to force her own, by marrying where she can not love.

– Richard Allestree, *The Ladies Calling*, 1673[1]

Syon House, glimpsed through the early morning mist lying low
amid the water meadows of the River Thames, possesses a dream-
like, fantastical quality. It is a castle out of a fairy-tale book for
children. Partly this is an effect of the symmetry and neatness of its proportions. It is almost perfectly square, with four diminutive towers, one at
each corner. Partly it is an effect of the luminous whiteness of its stonework. But Syon is no chimera or Victorian Gothic fantasy. The external
structure was built in the late sixteenth century, and it has been preserved
almost unchanged from that time to this.

It was situated so that it could be conveniently approached by water,
and that is most probably how Bette arrived for her marriage. She can

be imagined lying back among richly embroidered Turkey-work cushions beneath the crimson canopy of the Percy barge, rowed by four lusty oarsmen, a small sail hoisted. The blades of the oars plash the wind-ruffled waters in perfect unison. They are emblazoned with the Percy badge, dating from the Crusades, of a crescent moon. The apple orchards are coming nervously into blossom and chaste daffodils show beneath the hedgerows. A crescendo of trumpets announces her arrival, causing a colony of rooks to rise in the air and flap their wings in raucous applause.

Bette alights on the river bank to the east of the house and is assisted into a carriage, lined with crimson velvet, that is waiting for her there. She enters Syon through the great wrought-iron gates set between white stone pillars. Her route is strewn with rushes in the time-honoured manner. She is wearing a satin dress patterned with vermilion flowers. She had purchased the fabric just a few weeks beforehand. The bright colour was appropriate for a bride. There was no requirement to wear white. The rich material was acquired through the agency of a Mr George Potter, a senior member of her personal retinue. Less than two years later this same Mr Potter accepted the promise of £500 from Mr Thynn to provide some very unsavoury services. But all the scandal and misery of the Thynn affair still lay in the future. For the moment, this was a scene of rare innocence and happiness.

On 27 March 1679, Bette married the fifteen-year-old Henry Ogle, son and heir to the Duke of Newcastle, at Syon House. She had just turned twelve years of age. The Dowager Countess had given the King's letter very short shrift. As for Montagu's boast that Bette would never go against her mother's wishes, it proved to be hollow. Not that the Ogle match had been plain sailing. According to Frances, the Duchess of Newcastle, her husband only 'submitted to the many harsh conditions' in 'the articles of marriage' at 'his son's desire',[2] suggesting that the youthful Henry Ogle felt genuine affection for Bette and was determined to make her his bride against all obstacles.

The financial terms imposed by the Dowager Countess for winning Bette's hand were tough. The most unusual clause of the marriage treaty was that any children of their union were to be called Percy rather than adopt the Newcastle family name of Cavendish. This was not so much an early blow for feminism as a reflection of the Countess Howard's obsession with her own lineage.

Lord Ogle was not without his detractors. 'My Lord Ogle does prove the saddest creature of all kinds that could have been found fit to be named for my Lady Percy' was the Countess of Sunderland's cutting verdict.[3] He was generally agreed to be short for his age. The portrait of him in the possession of the University of Nottingham shows him aged about six, wearing a red coat over a pink jacket, pale and delicate in appearance. According to Frances Cavendish, Henry Ogle was 'well known for one of his age to be of very extraordinary parts and understanding'.[4] But then she was his mother, so hardly unbiased. Whatever the truth about his appearance, he clearly wasn't as good-looking as his now vanquished rival George Fitzroy, who was described by Evelyn as being 'extraordinarily handsome and perfectly shaped'.[5]

Judging by the £2,000 the Duke of Newcastle 'gave his son for clothes and liveries and other charges about his marriage',[6] the ceremony at Syon was a sumptuous affair. This marriage had, after all, taken the Newcastles eight years of hard negotiation to bring to pass. It was only to be expected that they would wish to celebrate it in a fitting and memorable manner. After the formalities of rings and vows, there would have followed a lavish feast. Dunstable larks marinated in a sweet Sauternes were popular. Roasted pigeons, boiled lobsters, lamprey pie and stewed carp were also eagerly devoured. Jasmine-yellow gloves made from the finest dogskin were given away as presents to the guests. Money was distributed to the poor. Most importantly of all, toasts were drunk to the health and prosperity of the newly-weds. As the guests became more intoxicated so attempts to make the bride and groom blush increased. Openly lewd talk of sex was quite acceptable in Court circles. Attached to Bette's wedding gown would have been the usual love knots of blue ribbon, and part of her bridal duty was to remove them one by one and present them to her friends and relations as mementos of the occasion. Everyone complimented her on her appearance and demanded a bridal kiss. For once she was the centre of attention.

The celebrations reached a climax when the gouty and sentimental Duke presented his new daughter-in-law with her special wedding present. It was a pearl necklace that had cost the outrageous sum of £3,000. There must have been a sharp intake of breath among the assembled company as the father of the groom pinned the lustrous baubles about Bette's slender neck. The Countess Howard's sharp eyes must have glinted with a mixture of avarice and conceit as she admired how the pearls lay on the fair skin of her granddaughter. She was mighty fond of pearls herself, and it was she, of course, who had stipulated the sum to be spent, as just one of the many preconditions before she would finally give her permission for this marriage.

Later came the fiddles and the jigging, and when the company finally tired of such heated activity there came the moment for putting the young bride and groom in the same bed together to symbolise their union as man and wife. When the Duke of Monmouth, aged thirteen, married Anne Scott, aged twelve, 'they did bed for form's sake that night, but did not stay together, being young',[7] according to one of the wedding guests, Lord Wemyss. If Lord Ogle did take his young wife to bed, 'for form's sake', there would have been plenty of spectators in the bedchamber with them to observe and cheer them on. It was an opportunity for throwing stockings over shoulders, and drinking the marriage posset, a concoction of milk, wine, sugar, eggs, cinnamon and nutmeg, designed one would have thought to make the bridal couple vomit rather than increase their potency. The bedding ceremony was essentially an opportunity for more coarse jokes from the bystanders rather than for sexual intimacy between the newly-weds.

There was one notable absentee from the guest list. Bette's mother was not there to give her blessing. Elizabeth was obviously furious with Bette for marrying without reference to her own wishes. An angry exchange of words followed between mother and daughter. The nature of this family discord can be glimpsed in a letter written by Rachel Russell, Bette's aunt, to Bette herself on 1 April 1679. Bette had evidently written to her aunt appealing for her assistance in appeasing the anger of her mother. Rachel's response is somewhat stiff: 'My Lord of Essex, on Saturday morning, sent me your Ladyship's letter. In it I find the change you have made in your condition. You have my prayers and wishes, dear Lady Ogle, that it may prove as fortunate to you as ever it did to any.'[8] Not exactly fulsome congratulations.

Rachel then goes on to say that while she will do her best to effect a reconciliation, it is up to Bette to make the main effort on this front – 'But, surely, Madam, it must be chiefly your own act; and you cannot pursue, in my opinion, so commendable a design too eagerly. No applications can now be too earnest to obtain her pardon, nor could have been to have prevented the misfortune of her displeasure, whose tender kindness you can not but be convinced of.' According to Rachel the reason that Elizabeth was so bitterly opposed to the marriage with Lord Ogle was not because she had any objection to Lord Ogle per se, but because she felt Bette should have given more consideration to the claims of other competing suitors:

All her advice could have no other aim at end but your being happy; and reasonably concluding the freeness of your choice was likely to make you so, she could not think your avoiding to see so many, alike qualified to make their addresses to you, was the way to make you impartiall in your judgement (as you say, in your letter, you believe you have been).

It seems most unlikely that this was a truthful explanation on Elizabeth's part as to the true nature of her opposition to the Ogle alliance. It is much more probable that she saw the forcing through of the Fitzroy marriage as the best chance she had for rehabilitating her disgraced husband. Nor can it have helped that Lord Ogle was the choice of her mother-in-law the Countess Howard, whom she loathed.

The real interest of Rachel's letter, however, is in the small glimmer of light it provides into Bette's own thinking about her marriage, which otherwise remains almost entirely opaque. Bette clearly believed that she had made an informed and wise decision in accepting the offer from Henry Ogle. It was not exactly a declaration of passion, but then passion was considered to be a suspect emotion that threatened the proper exercise of reason. It is also evident that Bette had not enjoyed being constantly paraded before every new potential suitor and wanted to put an end to the whole unhappy charade as quickly as possible. She may have only just reached marriageable age, but she had already been touted around for years, and the subject of her future husband had been a constant topic of conversation.

The aunt's letter ends with a refusal to follow some specific request that Bette has put to her. 'I can not make use of your argument to her, not thinking it of force to persuade her to what you desire.' It is frustrating not to know what that argument consisted of, but in Rachel's opinion what was now necessary was for Bette to beg for forgiveness: 'Your own constant solicitation, which will, I hope, prevail with her good nature' was what she advised. Poor Bette. She comes across as a dutiful and serious-minded young girl, anxious to please all those that surrounded her, her mother, her grandmother, her aunt and her new husband. It was hardly her fault if others had their own agendas.

Petworth Manor as it was in 1679

18 ⁀

PETWORTH MANOR REVISITED

More in their coach than at home, and if they chance to keep the house an afternoon, to have the Yard full of Sedans, the Hall full of footmen and Pages, and their Chambers covered all with Feathers and Ribands.

– Sir Charles Sedley, *The Mulberry-Garden*, 1668,
on the character of the contemporary young woman[1]

It was an odd situation. They were man and wife, yet they were both still children. The convention was that they would not be sexually intimate until Bette was fourteen. The usual procedure was to send the boy off on a Grand Tour of Europe, but Henry Ogle had already done his Grand Tour and did not seem particularly eager to repeat the experience. Instead he went to live with Bette at Petworth Manor, where it was intended that the young married couple should be under the constant guidance and protection of the Dowager Countess.

Bette may not have been sharing a bed with Henry, but the business of beds was clearly on her mind. She had no sooner arrived back at Petworth than she set about acquiring 'a fine suite of white bedfeathers containing 80 falls and 4 bunches of fine rich white down for the top springs',[2] as well as a new bedstead, rising tester, curved headboard and boarded bottom. In addition she bought 'a very fine large thick fustian quilt and a very fine Holland quilt, 4 pairs of large Spanish blankets, a pair of down pillows, a down bolster, and 7 yards of Portugall matt'. The bill from Mr Cooke, the upholsterer, came to a total of seventy pounds and three shillings. It was all finished with a tasteful blue damask counterpane, 'after the newest fashion'. Bette evidently felt that her changed status required a change of bedroom furnishings.

Only one of Henry Ogle's letters has survived. It was written some time in May 1679, shortly after his marriage, and its skimpiness and formality suggest that Lord Ogle was not a natural letter writer. The handwriting is well formed but tentative, and there are numerous crossings out. He expresses himself as being well pleased with the treatment he has received at Petworth: 'Dear Father, I am by God's blessing and your great goodnesse arrived here where I find everything tendes so well to my future happinesse that I shall endeavour to deserve God's blessing and yours with your good opinion by my dutiful obedience to you and to show you all the days of my life that I am your most dutiful son, Ogle.'[3] That is the totality of it. Other than his being a devout and dutiful son, it doesn't tell us much.

It is similarly difficult to penetrate the mind of the twelve-year-old Bette. None of her letters have survived from this period. But there is one route into the inner workings of her head that is most revealing. It is tucked away in the laboriously handwritten ledgers of her personal accounts.[4]

Bette was evidently fond of both writing and drawing. She bought numerous quires of Dutch paper, 'large quarto, small quarto and post', together with 'a bunch of Dutch pens', ink and a sand box. Like most young girls she also loved new clothes, and she was forever buying yards of yellow prunella or cherry mantua or fine blue French crepe. She had a penchant for silver and gold ribbons, braid and lace, as well as snail-dyed fringes of black or purple, silk girdles and Roman gloves. She had a dress made of white silk with gold and silver flowers, the ground scarlet and gold, and silver galleon for the skirts. It was just one of many. She wore scarlet velvet slippers. There was nothing puritanical about her taste in clothes or colour.

Nor was her dressing table neglected. During the summer of 1680 she acquired comb boxes and powder boxes, patch pots and pin cushions. She bought 'brush heads all matted and chafed'. There were new ewers and basins and Japanese porringers with covers and Japanese candlesticks. There was a large new looking-glass in a wooden frame and another smaller mirror. The bill for one year's purchases of boudoir accoutrements came to just under £155, a colossal sum.

It was not all self-indulgence. The accounts are also littered with small acts of charity. She gave half a crown to 'Goody Thorps girl' and five shillings to a 'poor woman'. Mrs Brooks, Mrs Brooks's girl and Nurse Burbridge were all remembered, and the bell-ringers of Petworth were given small gratuities. She disbursed £199 in gifts after her marriage.

But the real treasure in these accounts is in the lists of books that Bette purchased during 1679 and 1680, the years of her brief marriage to Henry Ogle. The selection is impressive both in its range and quantity. It included a number of religious and philosophical works, such as *A History of Philosophy, The Beauty of Providence, Tillotson's Sermons, The Life of Christ, The Life of the Apostles, Cane's Lives of the Fathers, The Prodigal Son* and *The Duty of Man*. This last item was ordered 'in quarto and quaker fashion'. Bette was clearly deeply and sincerely devout. She also, as a good Protestant and Anglican, bought a copy of Burnet's *History of the Reformation*, Part II. Presumably she had already read Part I. As well as being a devotee of religious works she was a passionate reader of the classics. She bought two different versions of Ovid's *Epistles*, one bound with gilt leaves, and a volume of Horace's *Poetry*. It seems that Dr Mapletoft had been industrious in his care of her classical education.

It is, however, the contemporary works that Bette purchased that tell one more about her character. She liked the *Poems* of Mrs Philips, who was much in vogue at the time and was a great celebrator of the value of tender and close friendships between women. Bette bought two different editions of her works, one costing nine shillings and the second ten shillings. Somewhat surprisingly, she was quick to purchase Bishop Burnet's *Life of Lord Rochester* as soon as it came out. The deathbed confessions of a notorious rake may not immediately seem the most proper reading matter for a twelve-year-old girl of impeccable upbringing, but it was a best-seller, and once again Bette bought two copies from her bookseller of choice, William Pott. She also had a fondness for accounts of famous historical trials, purchasing *The Tryall of Lord Stafford*, and *Raleigh's Life and Trial*. This particular interest is a little ironic, since she was soon to be closely involved in another trial that was also to be published and become a great cause célèbre, 'The Trial of Count Konigsmark'.

Bette was fluent in Greek and Latin, with a passionate interest in both history and philosophy. This was unusual for a girl in this period. The education of upper-class women had gone through a brief golden age during the previous century, but it was at something of an all-time low during the reign of Charles II. The general view was that there was little point in teaching women anything very much, as their only interest was to 'polish their Hands and Feet, to curl their Locks, to dress and trim their bodies'.[5] A little light French, singing and dancing, and perhaps some drawing, were permissible. James, Duke of York, had his two daughters taught such accomplishments but nothing more. Grammar, rhetoric, logic, physics, mathematics, geography, history and most other languages were considered a waste of time and potentially harmful. The joke that did the rounds was that 'one tongue was enough for a woman'.[6] The fear was that education would make a woman proud and then 'she would be so masterly there would be no living with her'.[7]

There were a few lone voices arguing against this limited view. Basua Makin in her *Essay to Revive the Antient Education of Gentlewomen* argued in favour of teaching the classics and pointed out that some understanding of mathematics was useful when it came to keeping household accounts. She argued 'had God intended women only as a finer sort of cattle, he would not have made them reasonable'.[8] The eccentric Margaret, Duchess of Newcastle, was also a great believer in the virtue of female education. She wrote plays and poems and was the first woman to attend a meeting of the Royal Society, much to the general ridicule of most of the other participants. It is perhaps from her that her grandson Henry, of whom she was very fond, acquired his own love of reading. It is known from a letter of his mother's, that he took with him to Petworth £300 of books. Books were expensive during this period, but even so this amounts to a fairly substantial library. Part of Henry and Bette's mutual attraction must have been based on their love of the written word. It seems probable that he read books along with his wife, and this explains Bette's fondness for buying two copies of certain items.

The 'Inventory of everything at Petworth' carried out in 1680 recorded that Bette's closet, within the withdrawing room, contained a 'shelf for books' as well as 'a little low gilt chair and a brotadilla cushion'. In her poem 'Mundus Muliebris: Or, The Ladies Dressing-Room Unlock'd', Mary Evelyn, John Evelyn's daughter, makes fun of these new-fangled bookshelves so much coveted by fashionable young ladies as an adornment to their boudoirs:

An hanging Shelf, to which belongs
Romances, Plays, and Amorous Songs;
Repeating Clocks, the hour to show
When to the Play 'tis time to go,
In Pompous Coach, or else Sedan'd
With Equipage along the Strand . . .

It is witty and pointed, and with that reference to the Strand it could almost have been aimed at Bette herself, who famously inhabited the largest house of all at the top. But it is noticeable that Bette buys no plays, or French romantic novels or books of erotic songs, and nor does she frequent the theatre. Indeed, most revealingly, during her short marriage she resides quietly with her young husband in the Sussex countryside a great distance from the giddy social whirl of London.

Bette and Henry's life together was not entirely sedentary. From Henry's accounts it is evident that he spent much of his time riding, hunting and driving around in his coach – conventional stuff for a young man of wealth and status. Bette too was passionate about riding. She used to arrange for her favourite mount to be transferred from Petworth to Syon, and back again, when she moved between her houses. It all sounds very innocent and idyllic. Then, after eighteen months, Henry fell ill. He ran a high temperature for several days and was confined to bed. The doctors were called. Perplexed as to what was wrong with him, they named it 'The New Disease'.[9] Within three weeks he was dead. Bette was thirteen and a half and promptly dubbed 'the Virgin widow'. Her husband was dead and her marriage portrait had not yet been completed. Peter Lely was still working on it in his studio in Covent Garden. That same miserable November of 1680 Lely also dropped down dead. He suffered an apoplexy while putting the finishing touches to her image. It was one of those unlucky coincidences that were later to add to Bette's reputation as a femme fatale, a woman who quite literally brought death and destruction in her wake.

PART THREE

1680–1681

Longleat in the late seventeenth century

19

LONGLEAT

Her six running wounds in her hand and arm in four or five days
were dried up, the bunch in her breast was dissolved in eight or
ten days of which now is no sign; her eye that was given for lost
is now perfectly well, and the girl in good health.

– *The Protestant Intelligence*, Friday 7 January 1681[1]

The family and friends of Peter Virnill, the beadle who was hacked to death when summoned to the brothel at Whetstone Park, were not the only people that Thynn managed to upset during his short and undistinguished career. In 1678 he had got on the wrong side of a Mr Trevor, a man of far greater standing and substance than Virnill. Thynn had enjoyed a liaison with Mr Trevor's daughter and it was generally rumoured she was 'with child by him'.[2] She was one of the Queen's ladies-in-waiting, but it was not considered appropriate for her to continue in that capacity once her pregnancy began to show. She withdrew from the Court into the country, which was the customary procedure for young unmarried women in her condition. There it was possible to give birth to the child and quietly dispose of it afterwards, usually to a poor relation. In the case of Mistress Trevor it appears she may have left her withdrawal rather too late to maintain complete discretion. Charles remarked: 'had she stayed much longer she had been delivered at St James's'.[3]

The delay was doubtless occasioned by the belief that Thynn was going to marry her. But Thynn's intentions had never been serious. Her seduction was all part of a vicious game hatched between himself and Monmouth. When Thynn eventually disowned her, and also denied that the child was his, an outraged Mr Trevor challenged him to a duel. Whether it was ever fought is not clear. It would have been in character if Thynn had declined to give Mr Trevor satisfaction.

Thynn had quite a talent for making enemies. Shortly after the Trevor affair, in his usual pig-headed and insensitive manner, he made the serious mistake of incurring the wrath of the two most powerful men in the land, King Charles and his brother, James. Thynn saw himself more and more as a major political player, and in this capacity he had started openly backing the Protestant Duke of Monmouth as the natural successor to the throne, rather than the Catholic James. Monmouth was the darling of the Exclusionist Party and was attracting huge crowds whenever he appeared in public. The shouts and the wild rhetoric naming him as the next king were becoming an addictive refrain. Nor was his claim to the throne entirely spurious. He was undisputedly Charles's eldest living son, and there was of course that persistent and embarrassing rumour that Charles had in fact gone through some kind of marriage ceremony with Monmouth's mother, Lucy Walter, his mistress from those early days when he was still living in France.

Whatever the truth of the marriage scandal, Charles had absolutely no intention of legitimising Monmouth. Apart from other considerations, Charles's close and secretive alliance with Louis XIV would have been destroyed overnight. James, Duke of York's insistence on making a public declaration of his Catholicism was awkward, and made his eventual succession to the throne much more fraught than it might otherwise have been, but despite these drawbacks, James was still Charles's favourite to succeed him.

On 22 January 1680, Thomas Thynn made his first public blunder into the political arena. He handed, in person to Charles, a petition from his Wiltshire constituents which was full of their grumbles and complaints. Charles was furious. He suggested to Thynn that he and his co-signatories 'might make better use of their time in minding their own affairs and for his part he would mind his', and then he gave full vent to his anger. He 'told esquire Thynn in particular that he did not think a gentleman of his fortune and estate would have concerned himself in anything that looked so like rebellion'.⁴ These were strong words indeed from the habitually casual and cynically amused Charles. Thynn was clearly a little disconcerted by the force and intensity of Charles's response. He asked for the petition to be returned to him. Charles refused. He told Thynn that he would take care of it himself and promptly departed into another room. There were immediate repercussions, the most serious of which was that Thynn was forbidden access to Nell Gwyn's house, which was Charles's way of declaring him persona non grata.

Neither Monmouth nor Thynn was intimidated by these attacks. Monmouth was now quite openly campaigning for the succession. In the summer of 1680, backed by Thynn's money, he embarked on a ceremonial tour of the West Country and drew large crowds of supporters wherever he went. He might have been conversationally inept and brutal in his habits, but he said what the people wanted to hear, namely that he would espouse the cause of Protestantism and redress their wrongs. The harsh economic climate played into his hands. A contemporary newsletter remarked on the problem of unemployment in the serge-making industry: 'Taunton and other adjacent Fanatick places of trade . . . have let fall 500 poor persons occupation . . . so that they begin to be mutinous.'⁵

The tour culminated with a triumphal celebration at Longleat House. It was a handsome place, with its four large stone-mullioned bay windows across the front and eight towers crowned with cupolas. Jan Siberechts' painting of 1675 shows the south front covered with climbing roses. The serried ranks of servants wore orange livery. It was a fitting palace for a future king to lay his head.

Details of the visit are scanty, but Monmouth no doubt would have approached along the London Road with the deer park on his left and dense woods to his right. He can be pictured riding the tall grey Arab stallion that Thynn had presented him with some time back. He cuts a proud figure with his spurs glinting and a bright feather in his hat. Some of his admirers reach up to touch him. Good fortune can be had from the smallest contact with such hallowed flesh. News of the miraculous cure of Elizabeth Parcet, much trumpeted in the pages of the *Protestant Intelligence*, has spread like wildfire. The power to heal the sick and lame was still believed by the credulous masses to be an attribute of divine kingship. So

Monmouth passes through the main gates of Longleat and up the gravelled drive, fountains cascading on both sides. Thynn greets him, wearing
his 'tawny coloured padisova coat' with the 'embroidered pantaloons' and
the seven-yard-long gold-fringed scarf for which he was famous.[6]

It is Dryden who best sums up this royal progress:

> Fame runs before him as the morning star,
> And shouts of joy salute him from afar.
> Each house receives him as a guardian god
> And consecrates the place of his abode.
> But hospitable treats did most commend
> Wise Issachar, his wealthy Western friend.[7]

Wise Issachar was, of course, Thomas Thynn. Dryden seems to have had
a higher opinion of Thynn's intelligence than his fellow poet Rochester.

Charles observed these antics from afar and with increasing fury. Thynn,
on the other hand, emboldened by Monmouth's triumph, now opted to
place himself right at the forefront of the growing lobby of discontent
that was gathering momentum throughout the country. In June 1680 he
was one of a group of Parliamentarians who demanded that James, Duke
of York, should be put on trial as a Papist. It was hardly surprising that
shortly afterwards Thynn found himself deprived of his command of a
troop of horse in the Wiltshire Militia. It was the only position he held
which was at the disposal of the Crown. Battle lines were being drawn.

Karl Johann, Count Konigsmark

20

THE PLAZA MAYOR, MADRID

These feasts are fine, great and magnificent, 'tis a noble sight and costs abundance. One cannot give a just description of it, it must be seen to be well understood.

Madame D'Aulnoy, *Travels in Spain*, Letter no. X,
Madrid, 29 May 1679[1]

t some point during August 1680, Count Konigsmark had arrived back in England. A newsletter dated 17 August recorded the event:

Last Saturday arrived at Windsor the famous Swedish General, Count Konigsmark, having in this time of peace got leave of his master to come for England with intention to serve as a volunteer at Tangier. The Count was well received and it's said, since there appears not any likelihood of action at Tangier, he intends to reside here some time.[2]

The item is not entirely accurate. Konigsmark was not a general, he was only twenty-one years of age, and he was more German than Swedish. But the details hardly mattered. What caught everyone's attention at Court was his luxuriant long blonde hair.

Since his previous visit to London he had spent most of the intervening years at the Court of Louis XIV in Paris. He now returned a grown man with an enviable reputation for daring deeds of gallantry and wild romantic escapades. Fabulous tales of his European adventures were soon going the rounds, the most recent example of which related to his heroics in the bullring. He was clearly adept from an early age at mythologising his own life story and creating the Konigsmark legend, but he was also fortunate to have the skilful assistance of the author Madame d'Aulnoy. It was she who memorialised him for future generations in her book *Travels in Spain*.

In May 1679, the eighteen-year-old Charles II of Spain married Marie-Louise d'Orléans of France. As part of the wedding celebrations, there was to be a magnificent display of '*Taurise*'. The Royal Palace in Madrid was situated on the crest of a hill towards the south of the city, overlooking the pretty valley of the River Manzanares. It was built there to take best advantage of the south-westerly breezes, for during the summer months the heat was insupportable. The tall rooms were hung with dark velvet drapes and shuttered against the fierce sunlight. Fountains played in the shadowy courtyards in a vain attempt to keep the air cool and moist. The Manzanares dwindled to a trickle. The joke was that the citizens of Madrid would be well advised to sell the fine bridge that had been built across it and buy some water with the proceeds. No person of quality ventured out of doors until the late afternoon.

The new young King was a poor physical specimen, his body small and twisted, his face marred by a flaccid mouth and the genetically elongated and oddly angled chin that signified a Habsburg prince. He was said to be happiest in the company of his dwarfs. There was much secret debate among his doctors as to his sexual competence and he conspicuously failed to father a child.[3] But he was fond of watching bullfights.

Ceremonial bullfights were traditionally held in the Plaza Mayor, which was directly beneath the palace walls. The Plaza was surrounded on its remaining three sides by tall houses built on pillared arches. Beautifully wrought gilt balconies adorned the façades of both palace and houses, and on bullfighting days these balconies were crowded with distinguished spectators, diplomats, nobles, wealthy merchants, beautiful women. Ordinary citizens sat on tiered benches below, supported on temporary scaffolds.[4]

Soon after dawn on the appointed day, 22 May, dozens of water carts dragged by mules arrived in the Plaza. Their contents were sprinkled upon the ground in an attempt to lay the dust, which would otherwise rise in great clouds, choking the audience and obscuring their view of the anticipated carnage. Branches of thyme and other wild herbs were strewn on the ground so that the more the hoofs of the bulls pounded, the more the air was filled with aromatic scents. The bulls selected to take part had been specially bred in the mountains of Andalusia and were noted for their wildness and ferocity. In springtime they had been herded from their grazing lands and driven along the streets of Madrid into a prepared holding pen at the gate of De la Vega, where they were branded with hot irons and had their ears slit.

By two in the afternoon the protective palisades had been erected and the square cleared of sightseers. By four the balconies were filling with spectators and the warm-up acts had commenced. A professional gladiator engaged a particularly well endowed beast, with coloured ribbons denoting its lineage tied to its horns, for the audience took an erudite interest in bull genealogy. Afterwards a wretched peasant was placed upon a lean and deformed horse, fit only for the knacker's yard, and entered into the contest for the general amusement.

The main item was reserved for the evening. Six young amateur toreadors had been selected from among the grandest families of Europe to perform 'Taurise' before the royal couple. It was a truly glittering occasion. No fewer than three thousand flambeaux shone from the golden balconies around the square. There was a crescendo of trumpets and the young toreadors made their solemn entry. Their horses were magnificently canopied and splendidly harnessed. They were accompanied by mules loaded with *rejones*, the lances thrown at the bulls' sweating flanks. These were about five feet long, made from dried fir wood and elaborately decorated. The ironwork of their points was polished until it shone. The mules themselves were covered with black velvet cloths, the same colour as the tunics of the combatants. Individual family arms were embroidered in gold.

The Comtesse d'Aulnoy in her book expended considerable quantities of gushing ink in her description of the gallant toreadors:

> They had plumes of white feathers, mixed with colours, and hat-bands of diamonds. They had scarves, some white and others crimson, blue or yellow, embroidered in gold. Some wore them round their waist, others over one shoulder, others about their arm; these last were narrow and short. Without

doubt, the scarves were presented by their ladies, for they fought to please them, and to show there was no danger they would not face for their diversion. They also wore black cloaks which wrapped them about but the ends being thrown behind them left their arms free. They wore white buskins, with long gilt spurs, which have only one point, after the Moorish fashion.[5]

It was evidently almost as much a fashion parade as it was a display of physical prowess.

The Comtesse, who came to Madrid in the retinue of Marie-Louise, described the proceedings in a letter to a cousin. She was particularly excited because one of the combatants, Count Karl Konigsmark, was wearing the scarf belonging to a young female friend and relation of hers. She does not name this friend, referring to her only as a 'titulada of Castile'.

After the parade, there followed a further flourish of trumpets, and the six young toreadors approached the King's balcony and made low bows of obeisance. The King in return gave them his permission to fight along with his blessing, and then the crowd roared '*Viva, viva, los bravos Cavalleros.*' At that point twenty steaming-nostrilled, ground-pawing, pent-up young bulls, their bodies flaming with fire from the lighted paper darts that had been stuck into their flanks, were released into the arena. In the melee that followed Konigsmark was severely injured in the leg. His horse came off far worse and had to be removed from the combat. Konigsmark chose to continue the battle on foot and in the words of the ecstatic Comtesse d'Aulnoy:

A very beautiful Spanish Lady made several signs, in all likelihood to encourage him; but his ardour did not seem to need any spur, and though he had lost a great deal of blood, and was forced to lean upon one of his servants, who held him up, yet he advanced with great fierceness, sword in hand, and made shift to give the bull a great wound on the head; then, turning himself towards the side where the young lady sat, for whom he had fought, he kissed his sword, and suffered himself to be led away by his attendants, half dead.[6]

It was all marvellously dramatic. Handkerchiefs were thrown into the air and there were chants of '*Victor, victor!*'

The Gardens at Syon in the seventeenth century

21

THE WILDERNESS

Nor is there certainly anything more agreeable then after the Eye has bin entertaind with the pleasure & refreshments of Verdures, the fragrant Flowers, the christall Fountaines and other delicious and sense ravishing objects, to be unexpectedly surprised with the horror and confusion of naturall or artificiall Rock, Grotts, Caverns, Mounts, & Precipices well represented.

– John Evelyn on the delights of the Wilderness Garden,
Elysium Britannicum[1]

Lord Ogle was buried in the Percy family tomb in St Mary's Church, Petworth. Bette's father and her grandfather had been interred in the same dark vault. Bette wore a black crepe mourning gown, with black mantle, hood and cap. The entire village turned out to pay their respects, together with the servants of the house. It was a dark, gloomy day with tempestuous winds from the west.[2] Late-flowering roses were strewn upon the coffin. The clump of beech trees that stood upon the small rise of land close to the stable block shook their ragged limbs like beggars seeking alms. A single repetitive bell tolled beneath a leaden sky.

After the formalities were over, Bette withdrew to her closet and probably wept into her brotadilla cushion. Her tears would have been heartfelt, for all the evidence suggests that she had loved her young husband. They had lived together for nearly two years. She must have felt cheated, even though this was an age when sudden death was ever present. She had the poems of Katherine Philips by her side for consolation and she had been well schooled in the virtues of patience and submission to the will of the Almighty, but the pain of his absence remained.

Life about the estate went on as usual. John Weekes mended the coping wall that surrounded the asparagus garden. A new cider press was set up in the brew house. The women's stool room was whitewashed. And Thomas Marshall built a new bridge at Hammer Pond.³ Soon after the interment, the Dowager Countess removed both herself and Bette to Northumberland House in London. Petworth in winter could be relentlessly dreary.

When spring came, grandmother and granddaughter relocated again, this time to Syon House. Here Bette enjoyed wandering alone in the area termed the Wilderness. Wildernesses were much in vogue. It was the less formal area of the garden towards the outer boundary, but still within the protective walls of the estate. It was intended to be more natural in character, with hidden glades, secret bowers and sudden surprising vistas, instead of everything being laid out in one sweeping view. To this end it made use of labyrinths and mazes, caverns and mounds, and running streams. The Wilderness was a place for reading poetry and listening to birdsong and for reflecting upon mortality. Statues of ancient heroes and even tombs were considered to be an appropriate adornment. The painting by Hendrick Danckerts in 1675 of the Wilderness at Ham House, situated close by Syon, shows a sunlit grove bordered by tremulous aspens with ten carefully arranged classical statues on white plinths, half hidden among the trees. In Evelyn's telling phrase it was a place for 'solitudes and retirements'.⁴

But Bette was not entirely given over to melancholy musings. At other times she preferred more vigorous activity and rode her horse along the farm tracks to neighbouring villages. She had her asses and her donkey sent to her from Petworth, along with her caged songbird. Gradually she resumed the pattern of her old life and habits.

It wasn't long before the marriage merry-go-round started up again. The Earl of Shrewsbury called at Syon House and Bette was favourably impressed. But when relatives of the young Earl later broached the subject of a possible marriage, the Dowager Countess wasted no time in ruling it out of all consideration. Bette was not happy with such highhandedness and was rash enough to remonstrate with her grandmother on the Earl's behalf. At this the old Lady had one of her notorious tantrums. 'She did use and utter some expressions and words against the said Earl and his friends and what were such vilifying expressions as you know or have heard,'[5] was how Bette later described her grandmother's reaction. It seems the Dowager Countess was somewhat foul-mouthed. Her word was nevertheless law. She 'did forbid all further pretences and applications to be made or received by the said Earl which was accordingly observed'.

Other offers of marriage came thick and fast. Overtures were made on behalf of Lord Cranborne, the eldest son of the Earl of Salisbury. His future income was estimated at £15,000 per annum and there were expectations of further legacies above and beyond this sum. Representatives of Lord St John made approaches. He was heir apparent to the Marquess of Winchester and was in expectation of £12,000 per annum in land tenements and hereditaments, besides the promise of a great personal estate. Lord Haughton, son of the Earl of Clare, also put his name forward. He had an expectation of £9,000 a year. The Dowager Countess had no difficulty finding fault with all these proposed suitors. Either the young man himself was debauched, or the title to the estate had defects, or the relations were vulgar, or the friends insupportable. Certainly none of them were fit matches for the Lady Bette.[6] There was no great pressure of time. The year of mourning was far from being out. The passing of a complete year was not just a formality. It was a very pragmatic way of ensuring that the widow was not pregnant with the child of her deceased husband, for a child would entirely alter the property rights. It was generally accepted that Bette's marriage had never been consummated, but they had lived together for eighteen months, and these things were difficult to prove beyond all doubt except through the passage of time.

The Dowager Countess now let it be generally known to the larger world, that she put:

> so great a value and esteem upon the honour extraction dignity and wealth
> of the person of the said [Lady Bette] that she thought and so did declare
> that she knew no match in England worthy of or fit for her and did desire
> some of her friends and acquaintance to think and consider of some foreign

prince to be husband for her and thereupon some discourse being had with her concerning such foreign prince she the said Countess declared that none but a Sovereign Prince should be accepted to be a husband of the said [Lady Bette] and no cadet or younger brother of any house whatever.[7]

It is hardly surprising that when Mr Thynn first threw his hat into the ring his offer was treated with 'great scorn and contempt' by the Countess. His £10,000 a year was not so extraordinary, and there was the embarrassing scandal of Mistress Trevor, not to mention his reputation as a waster and a rake, and now a troublemaker at Court. There was also another matter more damning than any of the foregoing. He might live in a grand house, and fritter away his cash, but at bottom he was nothing more than a commoner. With this in mind his application for Bette's hand in marriage was little more than an impertinent joke. Bette, a direct descendant of the Emperor Charlemagne, was hardly going to be married off to a plebeian.

The only contender for Bette that spring who managed to get over the first hurdle of the Dowager's approval was the most honourable Charles, Duke of Somerset.[8] This young man had only succeeded to the latter title by virtue of his older brother having been stabbed to death during a drunken brawl in an Italian tavern while he was engaged on that necessary rite of passage for all those with pretensions to civility, the Grand Tour. This piece of unexpected good fortune was understandably embraced with enthusiasm by Somerset, and he was now anxious to capitalise on it still further by making a brilliant marriage.

When he first requested that he might be admitted as a suitor, the Dowager Countess was moderately encouraging. She invited him to return to England to meet with Bette, for he was then in France. She also gave him permission to write to her. At the very least he might make a useful bargaining chip in negotiating with some scion of royal blood. But then quite suddenly the Dowager Countess changed her mind and told the Duke's friends to send him an express and prevent his coming across the Channel. No reason was provided and it was in any case too late, for the Duke had already arrived at Dover. He was, however, refused all access and any further communication with Bette was forbidden.

The reason for the Countess's change of heart did not become fully apparent until later that summer. Meanwhile Bette found herself virtually a prisoner in her own home. She was used to riding her horse, by herself, or with just a maid in attendance, across the open heathland that surrounded Syon. Suddenly this freedom was forbidden her. She used to walk through the woods and the hay fields that surrounded the estate. This liberty was also taken away. Even the Wilderness was placed out of bounds.

Having previously enjoyed unusual amounts of freedom, Bette suddenly found herself placed under virtual house arrest. She was forbidden all company and refused permission to make visits. She had no one to commune with except her caged songbirds. The reason given by her grandmother for imposing these draconian new rules was that a plot had been discovered against her person. 'There were designs and practices afoot to steal her away and force her to marry against her will.'9 The man behind this so-called plot was Mr Henry Brouncker.

The ruins of the old Carthusian priory in the Deer Park at Sheen

THE HOUSE OF MR BROUNCKER

a pestilent rogue, an atheist, that would have sold his King and Country for 6d almost.

– Samuel Pepys on the character of Henry Brouncker[1]

Henry Brouncker was generally regarded as brilliant but dissipated. He lived, with only his servants for company, in part of the ruins of a Carthusian priory called the Mansion House. It was situated in the Old Deer Park at Sheen, only a short distance from Syon House. Bette must have frequently passed the abbey during her walks and rides through the neighbouring countryside and observed the collapsed stonework covered in ivy and the neglected tombstones. It was a suitably Gothic setting for a man of such satanic reputation as Brouncker.

John Evelyn once dined at the Mansion House. There were few important houses in the south of England where he had not either dined or visited. He noted in his diary under 27 August 1678: 'I dined with Mr Henry Brouncker at the Abbey of Sheene formerly a monastery of Carthusians.'

Evelyn was intrigued to take a look at one of the original cells where a monk had lived out his solitary life. He was always drawn to places of retreat, tranquillity and quiet study, even while he was busying himself in his social whirl. He was not so taken with Mr Brouncker. He described him as 'a hard, covetous, vicious man', while acknowledging also that 'for his worldly craft and skill in gaming, few exceeded him'.[2] Brouncker was notorious for his fondness for orange-seller girls and was in the habit of taking them back to his decayed mansion house for orgies.

The Countess Howard had a more particular reason for objecting to Brouncker. She told Bette that she had received information that he had entered into a secret pact with Barbara Palmer, Duchess of Cleveland, to abduct her and force her into a marriage with George Fitzroy against her will. This idea was not so preposterous. The abducting of wealthy heiresses, with or without their consent, was becoming an increasingly popular shortcut to acquiring a great fortune. Rochester famously seized Elizabeth Malet from her coach with the intention of forcing her to marry him. Being Rochester, it was not very well planned and he was soon arrested and thrown in the Tower. Not long after this, however, he succeeded in persuading her to elope with him. She had the requisite fortune, which he proceeded to spend on wine and general dissipation. For most of their married life he insisted on her living in the country while he debauched himself in London.

The sad fate of Bridget Hyde provides another exemplary tale of the perils faced by a vulnerable young heiress. Bridget was the stepdaughter of Robert Vyner, merchant banker and Lord Mayor of London. She was endowed with her own considerable fortune and Vyner had run into liquidity problems, having extended far too much credit to King Charles with little prospect of seeing it paid back any time soon. Vyner's proposed solution to his cash-flow difficulties was to marry Bridget off to Lord Danby's second son, Viscount Dunblane. Danby liked the idea because it absolved him of any need to finance his younger son. Vyner liked the idea because Danby, in his role as Charles's first minister of state, promised to prioritise Vyner's outstanding bills on the Exchequer.[3]

There is a charming portrait of the Vyner family, painted by John Michael Wright, which shows little Bridget, aged eleven, clinging to her mother's arm, silk ribbons dangling from her shoulders, a visual echo of the leading reins of childhood, from which she is just emerging.[4] Robert Vyner is seated on the right of the painting looking every inch the successful plutocrat in his loose silk gown. It is a portrait that celebrates domestic harmony and family values. All would have gone well if a certain John Emerton had not abducted Bridget shortly after the painting was completed and forced her to undergo a form of marriage ceremony, solemnised before a rogue priest called John Brandling. At first it was generally thought that the validity of the marriage would be quickly overturned. 'The parson who played this prank is in custody and owns enough to make the marriage void,' was the gossip.[5] But then Danby, who had always been loathed by the House of Commons for his supposedly pro-French sympathies, was impeached by the House for intimidating Brandling 'not to declare the truth'. The Court of the King's Bench compounded Danby and Vyner's difficulties by awarding John Emerton temporary possession of Bridget Hyde's estates until the ecclesiastical courts could determine the validity or otherwise of the supposed marriage. The situation was at stalemate, and while the outcome was awaited, Bridget was returned into the care of her family.

In 1678, while still awaiting the verdict of the Ecclesiastical Court, Bridget was abducted a second time, on this occasion at pistol-point by a soldier of fortune calling himself Henry Wroth. Wroth was quickly arrested and Bridget freed before she came to further harm. In July 1680, the Ecclesiastical Court finally pronounced its verdict, deciding in favour of the legality of the original Emerton marriage, even though it had been carried out without the consent of the girl's mother, her stepfather or the girl herself. No wonder Daniel Defoe in his tract *Conjugal Lewdness or Matrimonial Whoredom* was to rail against a system by which 'a gentleman might have the satisfaction of hanging a thief that stole an old horse from him, but could have no justice against a rogue for stealing his daughter'.[6] The recent verdict in the Bridget Hyde case must have struck a chill into the Dowager Countess's heart. To think that any adventurer could abduct her precious granddaughter, go through some trumped-up ceremony with her, and then she, Bette's legal guardian, would lose all control over the Percy fortune, was a truly terrifying scenario.

The 1680 decision was not quite the end of the Bridget Hyde story. Her abductor John Emerton showed no great interest in enforcing his conjugal rights. What Emerton wanted was for Danby to buy him off, at which point he would renounce the marriage. Negotiations to this end were under way but their progress was too slow for Danby's son, Viscount Dunblane. He pre-empted the situation by running off with Bridget (her third abduction) in April 1682, marrying her in the church of St Marylebone and getting her pregnant by July. Danby's hand was now forced, and he stumped up the necessary 20,000 guineas to buy Emerton off. The following year the Court of Delegates, ever pragmatic, reversed its previous ruling, and declared the original Emerton marriage null and void. This should have paved the way for a happy ending, but happy endings were few and far between for heiresses in Restoration England. Dunblane proceeded to run through Bridget's money in the time-honoured manner, and left her 'in such misery and want, that she hath been forced to part with all her plate, and even her wearing clothes for bread'.[7]

The Dowager Countess described to Bette all the potential threats to her safety in lurid detail. The situation at Syon became still more tense when it was reported that a man, possibly sent by Brouncker, had climbed over the garden wall during the night with a view to seizing Bette and dragging her away. His actions had only been foiled by the vigilance of the servants who intercepted him. Bette was understandably terrified. Syon had become both a prison and a torment. She asked her grandmother whether they couldn't remove themselves back to Petworth. 'She always liked Petworth well and desired to go thither.'[8] She could ride her horse there freely and do whatever she liked without these constant constraints and threats from malign neighbours.

The Countess angrily rejected this request to move house, for private reasons of her own, that Bette, at the time, had no way of understanding. The Dowager Countess 'fell into a very great passion and was very much offended'[9] is how Bette described her grandmother's response. She told Bette bluntly that removing to Petworth was out of the question. And so the sinister shadow of Henry Brouncker continued to loom large over Bette's nightmares.

Welbeck Abbey in the late seventeenth century

23

WELBECK

I believe him of all men living at this time the most to be pitied, his thoughts being so very much fixed upon making his family great and by this sudden blow all his hopes are irrecoverably blasted.

– George Savile to his brother Harry Savile, speaking of the
Duke of Newcastle, on learning of the death of
Lord Ogle, 1 November 1680[1]

I f the atmosphere at Syon was oppressive, the mood at Welbeck Abbey, home to the Duke and Duchess of Newcastle, Henry Ogle's parents, was far grimmer. They had lost their only son, their great hope for the future. But it wasn't just his death that grieved them. Beneath the sorrow there was also a corrosive bitterness and anger directed at the Dowager Countess Howard. The Duke remained tight-lipped, pacing his terrace in solitary silence or fitfully busying himself with the grooming of his beloved horses. Frances Cavendish, Henry's mother, was far less restrained in her suffering. She felt that she owed it to her husband and to the memory of her son to speak out. She started work on an extraordinary document that she entitled, 'The Sadd and Miserable Case of Henry Duke of Newcastle'.[2]

Frances was fond of writing letters. During the happier years that had led up to the marriage of Henry Ogle and Bette, she had bombarded Countess Howard with communications of the most extraordinary and excessive sycophancy, even by the standards of an age in which flattery was something of an art form. But the 'Sadd ... Case' is very different in both tone and purpose. It is a long and savage attack by a mother defending the posthumous reputation of her son and the wealth of her husband, both of which she believes to have been put in jeopardy by the outrageous behaviour of the Countess Howard.

She begins by rehearsing the details of the original financial agreement that had been reached between the two great aristocratic families of the Percys and the Cavendishes, in relation to Bette's marriage. The Duke had given Bette a necklace worth £3,000. He also gave his son £2,000 to cover the cost of his clothes, liveries and other charges to do with the wedding. In addition he settled an annual payment of £3,000 a year on his son to cover his living expenses while at Petworth, £2,000 of which was to be paid as a 'jointure', which meant that should Lord Ogle die before Bette, the £2,000 would continue to be paid to her for the rest of her life, or until she remarried. In return Bette was to bring to her husband a 'portion' of £20,000, but this sum was only to be paid over if she bore him no children. In the event of Lord Ogle's death half his property in plate, jewels, and other 'quick' goods was to go to Bette and the other half to his father, the Duke. The £20,000 'portion', which was now triggered, because Bette had, of course, borne no children during the marriage, was to be similarly divided, which meant that the Duke should receive £10,000.

So far it was all very clear and straightforward. Frances considered that these financial arrangements were punitive, but she accepted that they were what had been agreed between the two sides. She remarks revealingly that she and her husband would not have submitted to them had it not been for her son's eagerness to marry Bette: 'The said Duke ... at his son's desire submitted to many harsh conditions as by the articles of marriage does plainly appear.' The conditions were indeed harsh, but Frances did not quarrel with them retrospectively.

The problem arose over the issue of the debts that Lord Ogle had supposedly run up during the eighteen months that he had been living at

Petworth. These debts were to be paid off by the Percys, but the total of the debt was then permitted to be subtracted from the value of Lord Ogle's estate at the time of his death. If this estate was insufficient to pay off the debts, then the £10,000 of the 'portion' that was to go to the Duke was to be reduced until sufficient monies had been retained to pay off the total of the debts. According to Countess Howard, Lord Ogle's debts were of such an enormous size that the value of all his personal possessions was wiped out, together with the entirety of the £10,000 of the 'portion'. In short, the Duke was to receive nothing, but would have to go on paying the £2,000 a year 'jointure' to Bette.

Frances was furious. She makes the very reasonable argument that the Dowager Countess herself 'was wholly trusted with the Earl of Ogle and his fortune til he and his Lady were in condition and years of age to manage their fortune'. She adds that if they had continued to spend at the rate they had been accused of spending, then they would soon have run through the entirety of both their estates. She informs the Countess that when Lord Ogle lived at home at Welbeck he was given by his father an allowance of only £200 a year for his clothes and other expenses, 'and was so provident that he saved considerably out of it and was not one penny in debt when he was married'. She also makes the telling observation that 'the said Countess did never let the said Duke understand that the Earl of Ogle was any way expensive or did at all go into debt'. In short she believes the whole thing has been cooked up to swindle her husband out of the money that is owed to him. 'I look upon all this debt as a cheat put upon us by servants and tradesmen and the indulgence of my Lady Northumberland [Countess Howard] to them.' She doesn't exactly accuse the Countess herself of being in on it, but she comes pretty close.

It is noticeable that throughout this long diatribe against the wrongs that have been inflicted upon her family, Frances repeatedly goes out of her way to absolve Bette from any blame. 'For the lady her person, her birth, her goodness, her wit understanding and affection to her husband is not to be found in any that I ever knew but herself and she deserves all the good we can say of her.' In the circumstances this is a glowing testimonial. Further on, Frances states that she is confident that had Bette been of an age to have control over her own fortune, she would have paid herself any debts that were genuinely owed by her late husband. This rather suggests that Bette too was not comfortable with her grandmother's claims that her husband had run up these enormous debts.

Towards the end of 'The Sadd … Case', Frances gets tough. She threatens the Countess with legal action. 'I much wish these differences may be composed according to reason honour and justice and not come to a suit because it will reflect so much upon the Countess of Northumberland and the trustees and servants belonging to them.' She then lays down her terms. The personal estate of the young Lord Ogle, that is the plate, jewels etc., she is prepared to forgo. But she wants the entire £10,000 'due upon the portion', without deduction for debts. She is prepared to have it yearly set against the £2,000 that the Duke will still have to continue to pay annually to Bette in respect of the 'jointure', until the full £10,000 figure has been reached.

She then reiterates her threat, stating that if it does come to a lawsuit she is confident that 'all that hear his [the Duke's] sad case will pity him and blame the injustice and cruelty is showed him by the grandmother, trustees and servants of the widow'. She finally adds that Bette's own estate is also being damaged by these extravagant claims of debt, which of course is true, and concludes with a powerful rhetorical flourish: 'those who ought to appear her Protectors will appear her Devourers which will be no honour to them and make others take warning by our harms.'

There was no court case. The Dowager Countess must have lost her nerve and backed down. What there is, is an interesting list compiled on the third anniversary of Lord Ogle's death of his outstanding debts. It was drawn up by a Richard Mason and comes to under £500 in total. The largest single item is £196-18-00 owed to Thomas Battin the sadler. The vintner at the Goate Taverne was owed £1-6-00. Mr Mason thought the bill of Mr Wiseman the surgeon might be reduced from £70-00-00 to £50-00-00. His only service had been 'the knitting off of a coachman's leg' and the 'letting of the servant's blood'. This is all very different from debts amounting to well over £10,000.[3]

The implication of this for the Dowager Countess was that Bette's £2,000 a year 'jointure' would not be coming in to the Petworth coffers as a cash payment as she originally had hoped. It would now simply be offset against the £10,000 owed as part of the 'portion'. The Dowager's urgent need of cash, however, remained undiminished, and she was soon to turn to far more desperate means of acquiring it.

Bette's grandmother, the Dowager Countess, as a young woman[1]

24 ～

MAJOR BRETT'S HOUSE, RICHMOND

Huffs, Hectors, Setters, Gilts, Pads, Biters, Divers, Lifters, Filers, Budgies, Droppers, crossbytes . . . and they may all pass under the general and common appellation of Rooks.

– Names for gamesters, taken from *The Compleat Gamester*,
an anonymous pamphlet printed at The Gun at the
West End of St Paul's Church, 1680

T he first warm days of summer arrive. Pleasure boats slide lazily past Syon's imposing wrought-iron gates, firmly locked against intruders. There are painted gondolas on the river, men in livery rowing and elegant women leaning back among velvet cushions. The sound of their laughter carries across the water. Jewelled fingers are pointed towards Syon's white towers and there is gossip about Lady Bette Percy and her terrifying grandmother, who guards her as a dragon guards its treasure.

It is not difficult to guess at the kinds of conversations that rippled across the smooth surface of the water. There is much amused speculation as to who it will be that will catch the great fortune next time. Someone asks why it is that Bette has not been seen in public for so many weeks. Someone else suggests that she must be big with child, for that is the usual reason for seclusion from the world. Others sneeringly remark that such a thing is impossible. After all, such an ugly and deformed creature as the late Lord Ogle would never have been capable of begetting a child. The conversation drifts. A gallant strums on a guitar. The name of Count Karl Konigsmark is mentioned, accompanied by appreciative giggles from the ladies, hiding their faces behind their fans. He is said to be back in town after performing great feats of chivalry in the bullring at Madrid. It is rumoured that he intends a tilt at Lady Bette himself. Some say he has already made an advance upon her which Bette has welcomed. Of course he does not stand a chance. The old lady will never allow her granddaughter to marry a foreigner unless he also happens to be a crown prince. Perhaps this is the true reason why Lady Bette is being kept under lock and key. It is to protect her from Count Konigsmark's advances. Konigsmark is undeniably very handsome with his beautiful blonde hair and nordic blue eyes. Little wonder Bette's head has been turned.

Bette meanwhile increasingly chafed against the restrictions that had been imposed upon her. She had done nothing wrong, and yet even visits to the Wilderness, where she used to sit and read the poems that she and Henry had once enjoyed together, were now forbidden. All these precautions were supposedly for her own safety, but they left her feeling lonely and cut off from the world beyond her windows. She was fourteen years old. She had already been married. She had enjoyed the independence and respect that the status of marriage brought her. Yet now she was being treated like a child again, a child that could not be trusted to go anywhere by herself, or choose her own friends or select her own entertainments. She was not even allowed to decide which of her many residences she might wish to live in. She asked her grandmother repeatedly why they could not transfer to Petworth, where she would be safe from Mr Henry Brouncker and his evil plans, but the Countess Howard would not hear of it. They had large numbers of visitors coming that summer. Their guests would not wish to be buried deep in the Sussex countryside, miles from anywhere. Bette suspected that the true reason the Countess refused to go to Petworth was that it was not so convenient for her gambling parties. All the old lady ever thought of these days was playing endless games of Beast and Ombre.

Gaming for increasingly high stakes had become all the rage in certain circles of Charles's Court. *The Compleat Gamester* describes the new addiction as 'an enchanting witchery, gotten betwixt idleness and avarice: An itching disease, that makes some scratch the head, whilst others, as if they were bitten by a tarantula, are laughing themselves to death'.[2] The Countess Howard was one of the smitten. Elizabeth Wriothesley, writing to her sister Rachel Russell, described the old lady habitually staying up until midnight, or one in the morning, night after night, and then making appointments with the likes of Lord Suffolk or Lord Scarsdale to start playing all over again the following day at noon. She was evidently in the grip of a growing compulsion, but at the same time, like many addicts, she feigned a total lack of interest in the entire business of gaming. She told the world: 'she cannot endure it.'[3]

In the light of what was shortly to occur it seems very probable that the Countess was losing larger and larger sums of money at the card tables. According to one source she had already been forced to sell her prized pearl earrings to the King's latest mistress, Louise de Kérouaille, for three thousand guineas to pay off some of her gaming debts, so great had they become.[4] There were always rumours, of course, but it was certainly the Countess's burning desire to acquire more pearls that was to be the trigger of a series of events that quickly spiralled out of all control.

Barbara Boyle, Bette's Irish cousin, came to stay. Barbara was several years older than Bette and her head was full of little except her future husband. The two girls shared a bed. This sharing of beds by young unmarried women, even women of high social standing such as Bette, was common. Barbara's company was better than nothing and the situation at Syon underwent a further improvement when Barbara's sister, Katherine Boyle, invited both girls on a visit. The Countess, surprisingly, was persuaded to relax her decree against excursions.[5]

Katherine Boyle was married to the dashing Major Brett. They lived at Richmond, which was only a short coach ride from Syon, or even more delightfully, a cruise down the river. Major Brett was typical of a new breed of entrepreneur that Charles II's reign had helped create. He had a variety of business interests and sinecures, including a logwood concession from the Crown which gave him sole rights to import hardwoods from Bermuda. In 1673 he obtained the highly profitable office of Excise Commissioner. Four years later he was a partner in a lucrative naval victualling contract. He was an astute opportunist with a sharp eye for a fast dollar and like the Dowager Countess he had a penchant for gambling. He had once won 2,900 guineas in a single session with Sir Basil Firebrace. Firebrace accused him afterwards of playing with false dice, but it was a difficult matter to prove and Brett was acquitted. Brett was not entirely respectable. In many ways it is surprising that the imperious Dowager Countess was prepared to entrust her precious granddaughter into his company. But Brett's wife was the old lady's niece and the Major had an easy charm and was adept at flattery.[6]

The first visit was a resounding success. Life within the Brett household was far more informal and relaxed than it was at Syon. There followed further visits, and during one of these an interesting new guest was presented to Bette. He was called Thomas Thynn. Bette was told he was ten years older than her. In fact, the difference in their ages was twenty years. Bette was familiar with his name because he had already put himself forward as a prospective suitor some months beforehand and had been unceremoniously turned down. The Dowager Countess had been particularly scornful of his application. His presumption had been considered laughable. But now, quite inexplicably, and only a few months later, his preposterous approaches were being smiled upon by all and sundry.[7]

Bette had never met Thynn in person before, but he was probably an old friend of Brett's, for he owned a small house in Richmond where he kept his pleasure barge.[8] His clothes were very extravagant. He had a penchant for grey beaver hats trimmed with gold lace and tight-fitting breeches in pink mohair. But there were other aspects of Thynn's character and appearance that were of more doubtful attraction. The petulant droop of his lower lip was not becoming, and his disconcerting habit of remaining wordless for prolonged periods of time could be most unnerving. Bette was assured that she should not take offence at his occasional protracted silences. She was told he was fearsomely intelligent, if at times a little taciturn.

The unpleasant stories about Thynn's treatment of Mistress Trevor were still circulating. According to those in the know, it was Monmouth who had first tried to seduce the pretty Mistress Trevor, but she had rejected his advances on the grounds that he was already a married man. Thynn and Monmouth found her logic so risible that they contrived a plot between them to revenge their masculine honour and teach her a lesson in the realities of the world. Thynn, who was not married, declared to her his passion. Mistress Trevor was naïve enough to believe him. After debauching her, he promptly abandoned her.[9]

It is unlikely that these rumours reached Bette's ears, at least not in the early days. The Boyle sisters, no doubt, linked their arms through hers, and as the three of them walked upon the gravelled terrace at Richmond, over-looking the silvery snake of the river, they reassured Bette she had nothing to fear: Thynn was an honourable and trustworthy man.

The parties and the boating trips and the dancing continued. None of this banter and intimacy was particularly surprising. What was very odd was that the Dowager Countess raised no objections. Before long, Bette and Thynn were meeting together regularly. Thynn made some effort to ingratiate himself with Bette, for he deigned to sit down to a variety of silly games with her. He even agreed to play at Cross Purposes, which was Bette's favourite.[10] One person whispered a question into the ear of a second. A third person tried to guess the right answer to the question and whispered it into the second person's other ear. The question and the answer were then both declared out loud. The absurdities caused much hilarity.

Soon there was talk of marriage. To start with the chattering was mainly between her cousins. Barbara was getting married very shortly to Major General Arthur Chichester, 3rd Earl of Donegall. Wouldn't it be fun if Bette got married as well? Bette was, at first, happy to join in so long as it was all conducted at the level of a delightful game. But when the proposal grew more serious she began to lose her nerve. The year of mourning for her first husband was not yet out. It didn't seem decent to be getting married to a second before the full year had lapsed, and she wasn't yet certain how much she really liked this Mr Thynn, with his foppish clothes and his sneers and his silences.

Then more of the Dowager Countess's relatives arrived. They descended upon Syon like a flock of carrion crows, all feasting at Bette's table, making free with her largesse. The Dowager Countess's sister, Lady Orrery, came. She was mother to Barbara and Katherine. Then a third Orrery daughter put in an appearance, Lady Elizabeth Powerscourt. They were all soon singing in unison the virtues of the admirable Mr Thynn. Even the Dowager Countess, after previously dismissing Thynn as being nothing but an upstart and a commoner, had mysteriously changed her mind about him. It was discovered that he was after all descended from the Botevilles. They were not exactly up there with the Percys or the Howards, but they were not exactly nobodies.

One evening Lady Powerscourt took Bette to one side and explained to her, in motherly tones, that she would never be secure from the threat of abduction and rape until she had remarried. That was unfortunately how the world was these days. A young woman with a fortune was simply not safe in an unmarried state. This was a powerful argument with Bette. The constant fear of abduction was both terrifying and stultifying. It seemed that she would never regain her independence and freedom of movement until she was someone's wife. The Dowager Countess, meanwhile, continued to find good reasons why all the other suitors that put themselves forward were not to be countenanced. They were not even to be introduced. Perhaps after all Mr Thynn was her best option.[11]

In the middle of May it was formally agreed, between Richard Brett on behalf of Mr Thynn and the Dowager Countess on behalf of Bette, that a marriage contract should be drawn up. As had previously been the case in negotiating the marriage with Lord Ogle, Bette's interests were to be supervised by Orlando Gee, who had been a business adviser to the Percys for many years, and also by the Earl of Essex, Bette's eldest male relative. However, matters were not altogether straightforward. Gee and Essex made the necessary enquiries of lawyers and 'did not like the said particulars of the said Mr Thynn's estate'.[12] Thynn, it transpired, was only a tenant for life of Longleat, and therefore 'could neither make provision for younger children nor give any security for her [Bette's] great estate'. It was also claimed that Thynn had several large debts that he had recently incurred pursuing various 'great schemes'. Orlando Gee so disliked what he saw that he refused to communicate any further with Thynn's lawyers on the subject of the proposed marriage contract and washed his hands of the entire business. Essex too was unhappy. He objected to the secrecy that was being imposed and felt that at the very least the consent of Bette's mother should be obtained.

Despite these serious objections a contract was still drawn up by Thynn's lawyers, agreed to by the Dowager Countess and formally solemnised in a ceremony held at Mr Brett's House on 26 June. Bette was present, but she does not appear to have been a very willing participant. Both Bette and Thynn declared themselves 'free from all other matrimonial contracts'.[13] In Bette's case this was certainly true. Henry Ogle was dead. Thynn's situation was less clear cut. Mistress Trevor, it was rumoured, was preparing to object. But the business of Mistress Trevor was not raised. Thynn later testily claimed that he had already gone through the whole annoying story of his supposed betrothal to Mistress Trevor and that everyone was satisfied as to his innocence in that affair.

According to Thynn's account of what happened on that day, he and Bette both swore their intention to marry each other and no one else. After this declaration they both kissed the Bible and then kissed each other. There were 'several persons of honour and great quality'[14] present and afterwards everyone congratulated them and 'wished them much joy and happiness together'. In fact, the only other people present were the Bretts, the Powerscourts and Lady Orrery. Countess Howard did not attend.

Bette's recollection of the occasion bore little similarity to Thynn's. She described how she tried to grab a copy of the contract out of Thynn's pocket. She was concerned at not being familiar with the detail of its contents. Thynn physically prevented her from getting hold of it. She was told that the contract was a legal matter only and she, being a minor, need neither sign it nor trouble her head over it. It is unlikely that either Essex or Orlando Gee had spoken to her directly about their misgivings, but it seems quite possible that some faint rumble of their concern had reached her. She was clearly suspicious of the contract's contents and was beginning to panic about what was happening to her.

A few days later she told Barbara and Katherine that she did not want to go ahead with the marriage after all. At this point Bette had merely entered into a civil contract to marry on particular property terms, but the marriage itself had not taken place and so the contract was not yet binding. Once again it was Lady Powerscourt who was given the task of persuasion. She had a private word with Bette and told her firmly 'that she always observed contracts to be very unfortunate if marriage did not soon follow them'.[15] The precise nature of the misfortune that would befall her was not spelt out in the legal depositions that later followed, but presumably it was something along the usual lines of the girl's reputation being damaged. She would be branded as both a jilt and a flirt.

The Nuptial Bed

25

LADY KATHERINE'S BEDCHAMBER

Pray deare do not fail to come to Richmond and come away quite from Mr Thynn and you shall see by God's help we shall live comfortably together.

> – Anne Singer to her husband Richard Singer, Thynn's steward,
> suggesting he resign from his employment[1]

On 14 July 1681 there was much rushing up and down of staircases within the Brett household. Lady Katherine's bedchamber was being hastily prepared for a makeshift marriage ceremony. Windows were flung open, flounces arranged, ribbons hung from bedposts. All that was necessary to make a marriage legal and binding was that it should be conducted before a willing Anglican priest. The ceremony itself could be held anywhere. The willing priest in this case was the Reverend Richard Jenkins. He had arrived hot and sweating the previous evening, stinking of horses and cheap taverns. He had been summoned by an urgent message from Mr Thynn and had promptly ridden post-haste from the village of Frome in Somerset, where he was the minister. He had previously been Thynn's chaplain at Longleat and he owed his present incumbency entirely to Thynn's good will.

In the various affidavits that Bette subsequently made to the court she never fully explains what it was that made her go through with this ceremony when she already had grave doubts about the man she was marrying. The most likely explanation is that she was coerced into it by all those that surrounded her. The game of courtship had reached the point where she did not feel she could decently turn back. She was terrified at what she was about to do, but she was even more terrified at the thought of what would happen to her reputation if she did not now go through with it. The interfering Lady Powerscourt was present at the wedding, with her dire warnings about what happened to girls who balked at the last minute. Major Brett was there, winking and laughing and relating his usual bawdy jokes. Barbara and Katherine Boyle were there, busily whispering and giggling and telling Bette how pretty she looked. Lady Orrery was there, giving little smiles of encouragement. But strangely there was no sign of the Dowager Countess. She had come to the house with Bette in the Percy coach, but her mood had been somewhat strange and withdrawn. Then quite suddenly she had disappeared.

It was later suggested to the judges of the Court of Arches at Lambeth Palace, the judiciary body that decided upon the legality or otherwise of marriages, that the use of Richard Jenkins as the officiating priest was clear evidence that even if this marriage didn't involve actual physical force, it was all stage-managed in a very underhand manner. This was, after all, the marriage of a fourteen-year-old girl, a great heiress, to a much older man, on property terms that she had not been allowed to see, terms which had been rejected by her advisers, without any of her close relatives being in the room with her. Only a priest who was in the pocket of the main beneficiary, namely Thynn himself, would have been prepared to give his blessing to such self-evidently dubious proceedings.

Thynn, of course, hotly disputed this version of events. He argued that this particular minister had been selected only because Bette was so anxious that the wedding should remain a secret until her year of mourning for Lord Ogle had expired. For this reason, and this reason only, it had been necessary to choose a minister who was not known to anyone in the locality; 'some trusty honest person that lived at some distance in whom they might repose confidence to keep the marriage concealed until the said year of her mourning' was how Thynn's lawyers put it.

The Reverend Jenkins indicated to the assembled company that proceedings were about to begin. The weather was clammy and overcast with occasional drizzle. Thynn crossed the room and stood to the left of Bette. Bette took him irritably by the hand and moved him to her right side. It appeared he was so foolish he did not even understand the proper protocols. Thynn was later to make much of this small incident. He related it to the court as clear evidence that not only was Bette a willing participant in all that took place, she was in fact in charge of how they disposed themselves before the priest. It does suggest that she maintained a certain self-possession. But it doesn't prove that she was not under enormous external pressure to proceed with this marriage.

The ceremony took its usual course. Their vows were sworn upon the Book of Common Prayer: 'I Thomas take thee Elizabeth to my wedded wife, to have and to hold from this day forwards, for better for worse, for richer for poorer, in sickness and in health, to love and to cherish, till death us do part, according to God's Holy Ordinance, and thereto I plight thee my troth.'[3] Bette swore the same vow with the inclusion of the words 'to obey'. When the minister came to reciting the section 'with all my worldly goods I thee endow', Thynn did 'lay upon the Common Prayer Book one hundred pieces of gold guineas or thereabouts with some silver mixed therewith. And the said Lady Ogle did take all the said gold and silver from off the said book, and put it into her handkerchief and took it away and kept the same and disposed thereof according to her own will and pleasure.'[4] Such was the custom of the time, although in some variants the gold was stuffed down the bosom of the bride's dress, rather than decorously removed in a handkerchief.

Once the formalities were finished an elated Major Brett was very keen that Thynn should close the deal by having sex with his bride there and then. His suggestion was greeted with a chorus of approval from the other guests. 'The said Lady Ogle after the time of the pretended marriage in question was desired by Captain Brett and others to bed with the said Mr Thynn'[5] is how the court staidly recorded the proposal. Bette did not consent. She later asserted 'she absolutely refused so to do'.[6] Thynn also appeared to be indifferent to the prospect. Bette, a few months later, was at pains to make it crystal-clear to the court that 'he [Mr Thynn] never did lodge or live with her and so much he doth know and hath confessed'.[7]

The Dowager Countess did not put in an appearance. She remained skulking in some lower room. According to Chaloner Chute, writing to the Countess of Rutland, the old lady had absented herself so that 'she may jesuitically or fanatically deny several things that would be asked of her'.[8] In other words she wanted to distance herself from the whole sorry business and pretend that it had nothing to do with her. This may well have been the case. It is equally possible that she was actually overcome with remorse at what she had allowed to happen and could not bring herself to witness the outcome.

Bette was later to claim that within a matter of only a few hours of the ceremony being concluded, she experienced an intense wave of revulsion over what she had allowed herself to be talked into. Back at Syon, in the privacy of her own bedroom, she broke down and told Barbara Boyle that 'she had a very great dislike and aversion' for Mr Thynn. She did also 'complain to her with great trouble and passion that her friends had betrayed her and used several other expressions to the like effect and purpose'.[9]

A few days later matters unravelled further. Barbara and Bette came suddenly together into a room where the Dowager Countess was seated. The old lady had something in her hand which she had been fingering with affection, but which, immediately the girls entered, she tried to hide. The Countess was embarrassed. She placed the objects in a bag and a little later she requested Barbara to remove them for her and 'to carry them into another room or to put them in some draw or box of her cabinet which the said Lady Barbara did'.[10] As Barbara was removing these mysterious objects a pearl necklace fell out. Bette said nothing at the time. She was too shocked and confused. But a couple of days later she confronted her grandmother about the pearls, 'at which the said Countess seemed to be much surprised and in disorder'.[11] The clear inference of this odd episode was that the Countess had acquired a new pearl necklace from the largesse of Mr Thynn. It was with these dearly coveted pearls, as well as a cash payment said to be as much as £7,000, that he had bought her acquiescence to the marriage.

Widespread bribery had been Thynn's modus operandi to secure the Bette marriage right from the beginning. On the 17 December 1680, less than seven weeks after the death of Lord Ogle, a bond had been signed between Mrs Potter, a member of the Percy household, and Thomas Thynn in which Thynn agreed to pay her £500 in return for her services in 'promoting and procuring a marriage between him and the Lady Ogle'.[12] The money was to be paid over within ten days of the marriage taking effect. If Thynn failed to pay the money on time then he was liable to pay a £1,000 penalty to her husband, George Potter. The marriage itself was to be 'the only consideration' for the payment of the bond.

Unfortunately, the surviving court papers relating to this case do not specify exactly what Mrs Potter's services were, and why Thynn was prepared to pay so much money for them. Bribes by unscrupulous suitors sometimes involved a cash payment to the chambermaid to leave the appropriate bedroom door unlocked. There is no suggestion that anything of this nature was being proposed by Mrs Jane Potter, who was anyway not a maid of any kind, but a woman of far more considerable standing. She may have been a housekeeper. Her husband was probably an assistant steward, involved in the management of the Percy estates. There is evidence in the Petworth accounts of a George Potter in 1680 being paid for carrying out a variety of small commissions on behalf of Bette, including the purchasing of teapots.

Whatever Jane Potter claimed she could do for Thynn she clearly failed to deliver on her promise, since Thynn's initial overtures were rudely dismissed. But he was not deterred by this early failure. It wasn't long before he was informed by his friends that Major Brett was 'a likely person' and so he 'applied to him' for assistance.[13] Brett, with his extended family connections, was in a position to deliver both access and influence. His house at Richmond was very handy as a trysting place. His wife had the car of the Dowager Countess. And from his coterie of gambling cronies he had very probably heard that the Countess Howard had recently incurred some sizeable gaming debts. It was not out of the question that the old lady could be brought to the negotiating table. As Bette's lawyers were to put it, 'did not the said Captain Brett and his Lady then and before take upon them to have a great power in ordering the Lady Ogle in the way of her marriage'.[14]

As it happened, Thynn was not Brett's first choice of suitor. The Major knew how keen Barbara Palmer, the Duchess of Cleveland, was to secure Bette for her son George Fitzroy, and it was to Cleveland that Brett first offered his services. But these negotiations did not prosper. Perhaps Brett could not persuade the venal Duchess to part with sufficient cash to make it worth his while. He was always mindful 'that in case the same did take effect [the marriage] he would have good advantage to himself therein'.[15]

Some time around April 1681, Brett decided to drop the Fitzroy cause as being a hopeless one and switched his support to Thynn. Brett's success fee was far larger than that of the Potters, and he had the good sense to obtain it up front. Thynn agreed to make over to him the lease on the rectory of Thame in Oxfordshire. 'And the said Mr Thynn, discoursing with his steward [Richard Singer] about the Major's credit in the Lady's family, and the way to engage him, said, I have no money but I will give him land.'[16] Officially Brett agreed to pay £3,650 in consideration for the rectory, but in reality nothing was ever paid, nor was it ever intended that it should be. The lease was Brett's reward for services rendered.

By the time of his marriage to Bette, Thynn was getting in very deep. He had already run up debts with numerous London finance houses. Bankrolling Monmouth's political aspirations had proved extremely expensive, even for a man with an income of ten thousand a year. He was gambling a lot on securing Bette's enormous fortune to defray his own heavy outlays elsewhere. There is evidence that some of Thynn's creditors were running short on patience. Thynn's brother-in-law, John Hall, had already been called upon to head them off.

There was a curious sequel to the business of the various bribes Thynn made to secure Bette's hand in marriage. Mrs Potter was most put out that she was never paid her £500. She pursued the matter against Thynn's executors through the courts for the next fourteen years, until it was finally brought before the House of Lords on 11 January 1695. The judges did not dispute the existence of the contract, nor did they concern themselves with the issue of whether or not the Thynn–Bette marriage was valid. They threw out Mrs Potter's application 'Because such bonds to Matchmakers and Procurers of marriages are of dangerous consequence, and tend to the betraying, and often times ruin, of persons of quality and fortune'.[17]

Mercury treatment of syphilis

26

MADAME FOURCARD'S
HOUSE, LEATHER LANE

Rub-a-dub-dub
Three men in a tub,
And how do you think they got there?
The butcher, the baker,
The candlestick-maker,
They all jumped out of a rotten potato,
'Twas enough to make a man stare.

– Seventeenth-century nursery rhyme[1]

Early in the year 1678 Harry Savile booked himself into Madame Fourcard's establishment in Leather Lane, situated just off Hatton Garden and close by the White Hart Inn. He had come for the cure. Madame Fourcard's was much recommended, but the process was neither cheap nor quick. A residency of up to six months could be required in the most severe cases, always presuming that the patient lived that long. Savile had syphilis. The symptoms involved widespread skin rashes, pustular boils in the groin, fever, headaches, chronic fatigue, aching limbs and hair loss.

The regime was a tough one. Daily hot baths infused with wine and mercury were mandatory. Their purpose was to purge the body of 'Pocky Herpes, Tettars, Ringworms, Serpigo, ulcers, gums, nodes, tophs, warts and the like'.[2] These baths were alternated with periods of fumigation inside specially constructed wooden tubs. The patient was stripped naked, wrapped in towels and placed inside the tub with a simple stool to sit on. The tub was raised up above the ground with a grid for a floor. Below the grid were heated coals on which cinnabar was thrown. The cinnabar fumes rose upwards through the tub and were vented at the top. 'Let him endure it so long as he can endure it without fainting'[3] was the recommendation. When the patient reached the point of collapse he was removed, wrapped in warm sheets, and carried to a 'warm place and put into a warm bed to sweat for three or four hours more'. Mercury baths and mercury fumigations, combined with mercury pills and mercury plasters, induced continuous salivation. Dr Sydenham calculated that the average patient should spit or drool two quarts of saliva every twenty-four hours. In addition daily injections of 'aqua regulata' into the penis 'with a proper syringe for the part' were considered beneficial. Even the sanguine Savile seemed a little perturbed at what was required of him. He wrote to Rochester: 'I confesse I wonder att myself at that masse of mercury that has gone down my throat in seven monthes.'[4]

Rochester knew all about Madame Fourcard's. He had first been a client back in 1671, the same year that he, Thynn and Monmouth had visited the brothel in Whetstone Park and murdered the beadle Peter Virnill. When Savile wrote to him some seven years later, Rochester was in pretty poor shape. He was convalescing in the country and wrote back to Savile with gallows humour: 'at this moment I am in a damned relapse brought by a fever, the stone and some ten diseases more which have deprived me of the power of crawling, which I happily enjoyed some days ago'.[5] By this time he was probably in the tertiary stage of syphilis. In it the mucous membranes are all eaten away, which is why sufferers often took to wearing prosthetic metal noses. The gums are riddled with infection, causing the breath to stink repulsively even by the none too fastidious standards of the seventeenth century, teeth fall out, skin corrodes, bones crumble, internal organs collapse, and rubbery tumours develop all over the surface of the body. A sufferer's coordination gradually fails, they begin to stumble rather than walk, the brain softens, eyesight is lost and eventually insanity sets in.

Syphilis, as a medical term, was originally used by the doctor poet Fracastoro in 1530, but it didn't catch on. Soon after the illness had first appeared in Europe in the late fifteenth century, it was recognised to be a by-product of sexual contact and before long the favoured word for it was the pox. Gonorrhoea was only distinguished from syphilis in 1879, and syphilis itself was such an elusive condition that it wasn't reliably diagnosed until 1905. So the pox was a generic term that covered all venereal conditions.

No one knew much about where this mysterious new disease had come from. The Italians called it the French disease, the French called it the Neapolitan disease, the Portuguese blamed the Spanish, the Persians pointed the finger at the Turks, the Turks accused the Christians, the Russians the Poles, and so on. It is most probable that Columbus and his crew brought back a mutated form of the illness from the women of Haiti. It goes almost without saying that the English called it the French Pox. It was all part of a general fear of the alien and the unknown.

The pox was a pervasive and determining part of Elizabethan and Jacobean culture. It certainly did not lead to universal chastity, but it was a significant underlying argument in the armoury of the puritan preacher. Women, of course, tended to get the blame for spreading it and so it helped contribute to a set of vicious and misogynistic attitudes. Many of Rochester's blackest and most bilious outpourings exhibit just this kind of bitterness.

There were numerous and widespread misunderstandings concerning the nature of the disease. It was generally thought, for instance, that women could not catch it off men but men could off women. This was very convenient for infected husbands and did little to explain how women ever contracted the disease in the first place. A particularly obnoxious belief was that a man could be cured of his condition by having sex with a virgin. The smoking of tobacco was thought to be beneficial, but then the smoking of tobacco was widely regarded as a universal panacea for most infectious conditions. Washing out the vagina with hot white wine before intercourse was also recommended by certain physicians, as was the use of Fallopio's small pouches, to be inserted after copulation, with an infusion of copper, mercury, red coral, burnt deer-horn ash, wine and guaiacum shavings.

In the second half of the seventeenth century the forerunner of the modern condom came into being. Sheaths of animal gut became popular both as a form of contraception and as a preventative against infectious disease. Their preparation involved much scraping and washing and hanging up to dry, somewhat similar to the preparation of leather gloves, and they were finished off with pretty coloured ribbons for tying around the base of the penis. They were intended to be reusable. Rochester celebrated the device in his 'Panegyrick Upon Cundums'. 'Happy is the man who in his pocket keeps a well-made cundum, nor dreads the ills of shankers or cordes or buboes dire,'[6] he wrote, but clearly, in his case, he either forgot to have one handy, or he overrated their efficacy.

Madame Fourcard's establishment had started out life as a bath house. Bath houses had been popular in the previous century. They were frequented by both sexes and quickly became synonymous with upmarket brothels. However, eventually this led to them becoming associated with the spreading of disease rather than cleansing, and their popularity waned. Adapting to the new circumstances, a number of bath houses were converted into places for curing the pox instead of disseminating it. The main agent used for achieving a cure was mercury or quicksilver, and it was deployed in prodigious quantities. The men in charge of the treatment were dubbed quacksalvers. Rochester, lying ill on his bed in his country retreat of Woodstock, replied to Savile while he was at Madame Fourcard's with a facetious piece of mock epic on the wonders of Leather Lane:

> Were I as idle as ever, which I should not fail of being if health permitted, I would write a small romance, and make the sun with his dishevelled rays gild the tops of the palaces in Leather Lane. Then should those vile enchanters Batten and Ginman lead forth their illustrious captives in chains of quicksilver, and confining 'em by charms to the loathsome banks of a dead lake of diet-drink ... Thus would I move the mournful tale along ... and this, I take it, would be a most excellent way of celebrating the memories of my most pocky friends, companions and mistresses.[7]

Batten and Ginman were two quacksalvers who plied their trade at Madame Fourcard's. Diet drink was a mercury solution that patients were required to consume. Pork, salty meats, geese, ducks, fish, cheese, raw fruits and sweet wines were all forbidden. Savile moaned about being thrown back on 'dry mutton and dyet drink'.

Mercury was a fairly obvious choice of substance for curing the pox because it had been used in the treatment of a variety of skin diseases for centuries. The joke was that five minutes with Venus resulted in a lifetime with Mercury. The treatment was repeated, several times a day, day after day, week after week. Death from the side effects was common. Heart failure, dehydration and suffocation were all quite likely, but by far the most frequent result was mercury poisoning, which if not immediately fatal could still damage the kidneys, impair the nervous system, cause weight loss, impotence, anxiety, insomnia and general mental instability. If the patient was lucky enough to survive the treatment there was often evidence that the symptoms of the disease had indeed disappeared. This was nothing to do with the mercury, just one of the usual remissions that the disease went through, but mercury took the credit.[8]

Thynn, as a member of the 'Merry Gang', had visited the same brothels as Rochester and Savile during the same period. It is almost inevitable that by the time of his marriage to Bette he too was suffering from syphilis. This helps explain Bette's sudden and intense revulsion towards him and her desperate decision to flee the country. It is certainly the subtext of a number of remarks made by third parties when they heard the news of Bette's flight. The Earl of Longford, writing to Ormonde on 12 November 1681, just a few days after Bette's departure made the pointed comment: 'It is said Mr Thynn being not then in a good condition of health easily consented to it [not to bed until the year of mourning was expired] to gain time for his cure.'[9] Two months later, shortly after Thynn had won the first round of his court battle with Bette, Lady Brunswick wrote to Lord and Lady Hatton and joked that 'Mr Thinn has proved his marriage with Lady Ogle, but she will not live with him for fear of being rotten before she is ripe'.[10]

The most telling words on this subject, however, come from Bette herself. While she was living in Holland she received a letter from the Earl of Anglesey, an old friend of her grandmother's, pointing out to her the evil of her behaviour in running away and the disgrace she had brought upon her family. He instructed her to return to England and honour her marriage vows. In her reply Bette referred to the two reasons that she had already provided for repudiating the marriage. First, that it had only been achieved through bribery, and here she particularly mentioned Major Brett, and second, that Thynn was already betrothed to Mistress Trevor. She then went on to make a veiled mention of a third reason that trumped the other two: 'if these two arguments fail me, as you conclude they will, others must be produced, but these I thought the least offensive to Mr Thynn and the fittest for me to use.'[11] This must surely be a reference to the common rumour then going the rounds that Thynn had the pox.

After Thynn's murder the Whig press went out of its way to try and rebut the rumours. *The Impartial Protestant Mercury* stated: 'whereas some malicious wicked people have most falsely aspersed him as if he had contracted some scandalous disease, never any corpse appeared sounder in all parts and particulars'.[12] But this assertion carries little weight. The physicians who examined the corpse were in the pay of Thynn's relatives, and in any case, at the time of his death he may well have been symptom-free.

Binnenhof Palace, The Hague

27 ≋

THE ROYAL PALACE IN THE HAGUE

This place being at present pretty quiet as to state affairs, my Lady [Bette] could not have come more opportunely to furnish me with matter worth entertaining you with.

– Thomas Plott to Mr Blathwayt from The Hague, 18 November 1681[1]

When Bette took flight across the North Sea her destination was Holland. Despite the blustery November weather the voyage was completed without incident. At the Hook a pilot was taken on board to help Captain Clements to negotiate the treacherous sandbanks of the Meuse River. At the port of Rotterdam, Bette and Lady Temple disembarked and travelled onwards by fast coach to The Hague. The roads were rough and in places waterlogged. They ran parallel to a network of canals busy with brightly painted lateen-rigged boats. The low-lying fields were lined with alder and willow. The whole journey from London took the best part of six days. By the time Bette reached Henry Sidney's house she was physically and emotionally exhausted. Without

Lady Temple's constant support and encouragement she could not possibly have coped.

Dorothy Temple and her husband William had a house at Sheen close by Syon. The two families frequently visited each other. It was during one of these visits that Bette must have opened up her heart to Dorothy about the secret marriage and how she had been tricked and betrayed by her closest relations. The older woman had taken pity on the girl, still little more than a child, and offered her comfort and help.

Dorothy was something of an expert on the difficulties of marriage for women of fortune in the seventeenth century. William had courted her for seven long years before he finally obtained permission to marry her. It was only then that Dorothy's elder brother, who was head of the household, considered William had achieved sufficient wealth and status to be worthy of her. During those seven years Dorothy wrote a series of love letters which after her death were published. Witty, passionate and intelligent, they have been through endless subsequent editions and are still in print today.[2]

Dorothy was no romantic. She believed that a parent or guardian should have the right to approve or disapprove of a prospective suitor and advise in the child's best interests. However, as a counterbalance the child also had an inalienable right to say no to any candidates that were put forward. She did not consider in this instance that Bette's feelings had been given sufficient weight, or that she had been well advised. Her husband had told Dorothy things about Thynn that chilled the marrow of her bones. William had been ambassador at The Hague before Henry Sidney. He was now retired from both business and office, preferring to tend his garden, famous for its orangery. He was, however, still a man of the world who knew what needed to be done and how it would be best accomplished.

As Bette prayed that night in an unfamiliar bedroom, she must have thanked God that she was safely out of England and far from the clutches of her supposed husband. The following morning the weather was damp and grey, but Bette's mood was already lighter. After breakfast, Lady Temple explained that it was her intention to pay an immediate courtesy visit to Princess Mary, the daughter of James, Duke of York, who had recently been married to Prince William of Orange. Bette was not at all keen to expose herself to the public gaze and prying questions but she accepted the need to make such a visit and agreed to accompany Lady Temple.

Bette's story of abuse and exploitation was evidently sympathetically received by Mary, for that same afternoon Prince William returned the visit, and made numerous further visits over the next few days. The presence of such a high-ranking refugee could have posed something of a diplomatic issue for the Dutch ruler. Thynn had recently become a very noisy advocate for the Protestant cause, and William was a stout Protestant, the main defender of nonconformist values in continental Europe, and engaged in a protracted struggle against the overweening ambitions of the ardently Catholic Louis XIV. Thynn and William should have been natural allies. But the astute Dutchman had no fondness for Monmouth, or his coterie of supporters, and no wish to antagonise Charles. He had his eye on the English throne for himself.

He received the two ladies with a great show of graciousness and gener-osity, and offered them more spacious accommodation in his own palace, an offer they were happy to accept. Even more importantly, William prom-ised Bette his protection. In the words of Thomas Plott, special envoy in The Hague, writing to his superior William Blathwayt, Secretary of State back in London, 'If Mr Thinne comes over he can not get her but by dint of force and then he must fight with all the prince's guards.'³ The prospect of Bette being physically seized and repatriated back into England was being taken very seriously.

The arrival of Bette and Lady Temple in The Hague in such scandalous circumstances caused quite as much sensation in the Netherlands as their recent departure had done in London. Thomas Plott's dispatches from The Hague affect the supercilious amusement of the disinterested observer. He was, however, clearly well informed regarding the details. 'My Lady [Bette] intends to keep but little company and will remain in this country until she has weathered the storm one way or another, her ladyship seeming to have a great aversion for Mr Thinne and being resolved to undergo anything before she will live with him . . . I think there's a kind of marriage between them, but he has never bedded her yet.'⁴ This question of Thynn's failure to consummate the marriage is returned to again and again by all those who write on the subject and is clearly perceived as being a weakness in Thynn's legal position. He must have regretted the omission. For a woman to sue for divorce on the basis of male impotence it was necessary for there to have been three years of sexual inactivity on the part of the husband. All the same the failure to bed her was considered to be to Bette's advantage.

Bette's spirits steadily revived. A few days after his previous letter, Thomas Plott again updated Blathwayt on the latest developments: 'My Lady [Bette] seems very well satisfied with her abode here receiving all the civilities due to her merit and quality nor will she return for England til her business be cleared one way or another though she remain years abroad. She has sent for most of her servants and intends to live very well here.'[5]

The weather continued to be dreary. It rained nearly every day. But Bette was evidently digging in for the long haul and determined to make the best of the new circumstances she found herself in. The Hague did have certain advantages over London. The air was less stinking and full of soot. The gabled buildings, painted green, red and white, and ranged along the banks of the waterways, had the prettiness and delicacy of doll's houses. They had neat yards where plump-faced young women in white starched caps with white starched aprons carried pails of water. Everything was clean and brightly polished. Even the brass nails and hinges of the doors shone.[6]

It wasn't long, of course, before a troop of new suitors was knocking at Bette's door. If Thynn failed to prove his marriage, which was beginning to look quite possible, then she would once again be on the market. 'My Lord Zuckiqueen is lately come over with his son and goes back within a few days, it is thought his business is to send good offices for a young great man's account, but the Lady is not inclined in her present circumstances to any proposals of that nature. The Prince of Nassau Stadhoulder of Vriesland is one of her admirers here, and owns himself conquered, what affect it may work upon her, time will make appear,'[7] writes the diligent Plott. In his next dispatch a week later he returns to the same theme: 'Were she at liberty to dispose of herself she would not want gallants of great quality here for besides the Stadhoulder of Vriesland, the Prince of Oostrfrise would likewise be a pretender.'[8] According to Plott, Bette was in no mood to entertain thoughts of new lovers. She was no doubt immensely relieved to be far from Thynn. 'She thinks herself happy that she has preserved her person from him and as for the estate that the law must decide.'[9] But none of that meant she was not willing to receive a secret visit from Konigsmark.

Thomas Plott makes no mention of Konigsmark's presence in The Hague, but he must have been there during most of December and the early part of January. It is evident from the original court transcripts that he and Vratz had gone from Strasbourg to Holland and it is unlikely that they had any purpose in mind other than paying a visit to Bette. Konigsmark was probably in disguise, which may explain why Plott's spies did not pick up on him. He was to use disguise on two other occasions in the near future, and in view of what he had in mind he would not have wished to advertise his whereabouts to all and sundry.

Lady Temple would never have sanctioned a meeting between Bette and Konigsmark. He had already been named as Bette's lover even before she fled England, and Lady Temple must have heard of the rumours about the two of them. But she did not, it seems, monitor Bette's every movement in the same oppressive manner as the Dowager Countess. Plott may not have picked up on the rumours but it was soon to be the common talk that Lady Bette 'had great intimacy with the Count in Holland'.[10] It would have been relatively easy for Bette to slip out of the Binnenhof Palace and enjoy a clandestine meeting with her dashing admirer.

Perhaps they skated together along the frozen Prinsessegracht Canal, lined by willow trees, snatching a few brief moments of intimacy. They move at speed side by side, arms folded. Bette's long tapering fingers, that so elegantly gather orange blossoms in Lely's picture, are now tucked inside a muff of the finest Russian sable. They execute figures of eight and their laughter mists the air. Afterwards they repair to Hippolito's Chocolate House and sip the rich, sweet concoction lately transported from the Indies. Exactly what occurred during those meetings, what hopes were expressed and what vows were made, who is to say?

Thynn meanwhile had not been idle. Bette might have put herself temporarily beyond his reach, but her property remained more vulnerable. He immediately took possession of Petworth and began collecting rents from all possible sources. Henry Sidney was dispatched by Bette's supporters to meet with Thynn and see whether some compromise solution could not be worked out, but Thynn was having none of it. Bette had made him look ridiculous in the eyes of the world. His compensation was that her property was now his to dispose of as he saw fit. The Sidney mission having failed, Bette took recourse to the law. On the 17 December, she applied to the Court of Chancery to prevent 'one Thomas Thynn Esq [who] ... hath gone about by ... undue and illegal means, contrivances and practices ... to prevail with several of the tenants ... for tythe ... on pretence that he hath married your oratrix [Bette] and that the same upon that account in her right do belong to him'.[11]

In his response Thynn did not dispute that he had taken possession of Bette's property and was collecting the rents. The only point at issue, so far as his lawyers were concerned, was the validity of the marriage, and he was busy asserting that through the Court of Arches. His choice of the Court of Arches, the ecclesiastical court, was significant. Under common law, in order to positively prove a marriage it was necessary for the marriage to have taken place inside a church and for banns to have been called, whereas under ecclestiastical law, all that was required was for the ceremony to have taken place before witnesses and a willing priest.

On Tuesday 20 December, *The Impartial Protestant Mercury*[12] reported that Bette had won the first round of the legal battle:

> The Lady [Bette] who sometime since retired into Holland and disputes her marriage with Esquire Thynn hath brought her bill in Chancery against him, and we are told obtained on Saturday last an injunction to quit the possession of her estate, until such time as the matters in controversy touching the validity or invalidity of the marriage shall be legally determined.

This meant Thynn could no longer extract money from Bette's properties. But it only bought her time. The general opinion was that the ecclesiastical courts would inevitably uphold the legality of the marriage and that Bette would then be forced to return to England.

On learning of Bette's flight her mother, from whom she had been largely estranged since her marriage to Henry Ogle, wrote to her coldly and bluntly: 'if she was married, it was best to come and live with her husband'.[13] The unspoken anxiety that was felt by both her mother and her grandmother was that she might now run off with Count Konigsmark and ruin her reputation for ever. On this issue the Countess Howard and her daughter-in-law were in rare accord. But the grandmother's credibility with Bette had been severely damaged by being caught red-handed and red-faced with the guilty pearls in her lap, the price of her betrayal. It was perhaps for this reason that the old lady, for once shamed into silence, engaged the Earl of Anglesey to plead her cause. It was not a good move. Anglesey's letter to Bette was pompous, condescending, illogical and ill-natured. Bette's feisty response pulled no punches. She not only enumerated her reasons for running away from Thynn, she made it clear she was prepared to fight him through the courts to the bitter end:

> as you declare yourself Mr Thynn's friend and think flatteries a fault, I may with the same plainness tell you that Mr Thynn may, if he pleases, trouble himself and me and we may make both our fortunes a prey to lawyers and seven years hence be where we are (except so much elder and poorer). If he like it, I am content, for in all probability myself and my purse may hold out as long as his, and it is neither humour nor passion, interest nor persuasion, but bare truth, which I cannot resist, if I would.[14]

Not all Bette's family were so opposed to her behaviour. Her uncle, Lord Essex, claimed that he had never thought Thynn was a 'competent match'[15] for Bette. On the 15 November, just a week after Bette's flight, he invited John Evelyn to take dinner with him in his town house. He wanted to put his side of the story, and what better way to disseminate it than by communicating it to the socially ubiquitous Evelyn. After the meal was finished the two men withdrew to the study, where they sat either side of a large fire. Essex admitted he had known of the marriage proposal, but explained that he had always disapproved of it and had made his disapproval clear to Countess Howard. He claimed to have been under the impression that the scheme had been dropped. He had been as shocked as anyone when he had learnt that it had gone ahead after all. He told Evelyn 'how much he had ben scandaliz'd & injur'd in the report of his being privy to the marriage',[16] and to prove his innocence he showed Evelyn a letter of Mr Thynn's in which Thynn excused himself for not communicating his marriage to Essex beforehand.

PART FOUR

1682

King Street, Westminster

LODGINGS, KING STREET, WESTMINSTER

What the bottom of the design was remains yet inscrutable.

– Impartial Protestant Mercury, 17 February 1682[1]

O n 25 January 1682 an anti-Catholic protester slipped into the Guildhall in London and slashed the portrait of James, Duke of York, cutting him off at the knees.[2] It was a violent and potently symbolic act to convince the Duke that he would not be welcome as the successor to the throne. Two weeks before this there had been a riot at the King's Head Tavern in Chancery Lane. It had been started by some 'gentlemen of the Temple'[3] well known for their radical views, and they had been supported by a crowd of watermen of similar political sympathies. When the watch arrived to restore order, one of them was hacked with a halberd, an old-fashioned long-handled axe that could also be used as a spear. He was not expected to live. The tension on the streets was gradually ratcheting up.

Around the beginning of February 1682, Captain Christopher Vratz arrived back on English soil having just spent over two months on the Continent. He was accompanied by a man calling himself Carlo Cusk, although that was not his real name. Cusk was wearing a long black periwig and a bulky greatcoat made of camlett. The large collar of the coat was turned up, partly against the cold, which was bitter, but also to shield himself from the common gaze. He didn't want to be recognised. He didn't want anyone to even know he was in the country. His real name was Karl Konigsmark.[4]

Konigsmark's use of disguise was not too professional. If he had had more sense and less *amour propre* he would have shaved off his mass of long fair hair. Most men who wore wigs shaved their heads so that the wigs fitted snugly against their scalps. He had just piled his blonde locks up on top of his head in an enormous yellow coif. The black periwig, balanced on the summit of this great mound, looked bizarre rather than discreet. Clearly vanity was an even more powerful consideration than anonymity.

Vratz and Konigsmark were met at a posting house by Frederick Hanson, a Swede living in London. Hanson was employed as the guardian of Konigsmark's brother, Philip, and acted as their general fixer. The reference to a posting house suggests the two men had entered London by coach, from one of the main port towns, in this case Harwich, since they had come from Holland. The weather had been stormy and the crossing rough. Konigsmark was pale and agitated. The pervading post-house smell of steaming horse dung and boiling mutton stew was enough to make the strongest stomach queasy. He just wanted to lie down on a bed.

On 4 February they took rooms in a lodging house situated on the corner of the Haymarket. Hanson had previously arranged the accommodation. They were waited on by a chatty and pert maid called Anne Price. Vratz now took the opportunity of making contact again with his old comrade and drinking companion Lieutenant Stern. He resumed the subject of his quarrel with Thynn and his need for Stern's assistance. The business had become more urgent. He told Stern all about how, while he was in Strasbourg, he and the friend he was travelling with had been attacked by six of Thynn's hired thugs. He related the heroic details as to how they had managed to fight them off. This story was to be Stern's justification for re-pledging his allegiance and his willingness to help with Thynn's murder.[5]

On Wednesday, 8 February, Vratz and Konigsmark left their Haymarket lodgings. The reason for the move is unclear. Perhaps Anne Price was asking too many awkward questions. Perhaps they thought that it would be advisable not to stay in any one place for too long. Konigsmark now moved into lodgings by himself in Rupert Street. Vratz and Stern moved together into rooms in King Street, Westminster.

There were a bewildering number of King Streets in London at the time, all part of the post-Restoration monarchist fervour, but the one selected by Vratz was 'a long, dark, dirty and very inconvenient passage' according to Daniel Defoe.[6] The choice of this location was no accident. The street was connected by a narrow alley to a quiet lane called Canon Row, where Thomas Thynn had his town house. From their new lodgings Vratz and Stern were able to keep a close observation on Thynn's movements.

The weather had turned bitterly cold. The skies were grey and overcast, threatening snow, and there was a persistent pummelling east wind. Vratz told Stern that the decision to murder Thynn had finally been approved at the highest level. This was good news. It meant that the gold dollars were getting nearer. The only outstanding problem was how to do it.

Initially, Vratz was in favour of using a poignard, a slim light double-edged steel knife easy to conceal beneath a jacket, and which could be deftly sunk between the ribs of an adversary while just brushing casually past them in the street. It was quick, businesslike, and involved a minimum of fuss. The more Vratz thought about these poignards the more enamoured he became with them. He summoned ink, pen and paper and spent some time drawing his ideal design to make it clear to Stern exactly what he was looking for. Stern was not enthusiastic. The poignard was not a soldier's weapon. But on Vratz's insistence he agreed to acquire a couple. At the same time Vratz suggested to Stern that he should try to locate some disaffected Frenchmen, of whom there were a large number living in London, and see if any would be willing to carry out the murder for a couple of hundred dollars. A day or so later Vratz switched his thinking to the Italian community. Slipping a dagger into another man's vitals was more of an Italian accomplishment, he decided.

Stern never got round to purchasing the poignards because the mercurial Vratz had yet another change of thinking. Poignards were not going to work. After watching Thynn's movements for several days it had become obvious that their intended victim never went anywhere except by coach. It would be impossible to get near enough to him to inflict any real damage with a blade. Vratz was also concerned about the large numbers of servants that Thynn always chose to surround himself with whenever he left the house. He didn't present an easy target to his enemies. In fact, he behaved like a man who knew full well that his life was in danger.

While this debate about the perfect method for killing a man was still going on, Vratz came back one day with 'four brace of pistols', three small sets and one large.[7] He had evidently been on a spending spree at the gunmakers. The two men spent some time admiring the different qualities of the various shooters, the fine polished wood of the handles, the etched steel, the smoothness of the improved firing mechanisms, the neatness of the pan that held the priming powder, the straightness of the barrels. Their lodgings in King Street were rapidly turning into an impressive armoury of small weapons. But there was also a drawback to pistols that Vratz did not appear to have considered. They only fired one shot at a time. And from a distance of twenty yards or more the accuracy that would be required for that one shot was very considerable. Pistols were useful in close-up combat, for waving threateningly in someone's face, but they weren't the ideal assassination tool against a man who, once outside his house, rarely left the confines of his coach.

Then Stern had one of his dreams, or visions is perhaps the more accurate description, for it came to him while he was awake. The hearing of voices and the seeing of visions in the seventeenth century was not considered to be a sign of mental instability. On the contrary they were a perfectly respectable part of normal spiritual life and believed to be a valuable prognosticator of future events. 'A very strange ominous dream'[8] is how Stern described this particular supernatural experience. Four dogs flew at him. Two were chained but one seized him by the throat. Stern recounted the dream twice, and as usual with Stern, the accounts are slightly inconsistent. In the first version he said the dream had occurred while he was in Vratz's company. Vratz, noticing that Stern had gone pale and sweaty, asked him whether he was ill. Stern told him about the vision he had just had. Vratz laughed it off, saying: 'there is no heed to be given to dreams'. In the second version Vratz was 'concerned' by what Stern said.[9] He thought Stern was implying that he was one of the dogs doomed to lead Stern into some terrible life-threatening danger. Vratz's response was to show Stern a copy of a letter from Konigsmark which empowered him to appoint whomsoever he wished to a place in his Regiment. If Stern had had the opportunity of observing Konigsmark, skulking in cheap lodgings in Rupert Street, wearing a ludicrous disguise and apparently ill, he might have been less than impressed by the prospect that was being dangled before him. But he had still not set eyes on Konigsmark. All he saw was a signature and the mention of six hundred gold dollars. It was sufficient to calm him.

It is difficult to know whether or not Konigsmark was genuinely ill. He was attended almost daily by a Dr Harder, apparently for a chest rash, but Harder may have been visiting the Count's lodgings more in the capacity of friend than physician. Konigsmark was to claim at the trial that the reason for his living in London so secretly was that he wished for his medical condition to be kept private from the world at large, 'for he would not have it known that he did take physick'.[10] Usually this would have implied that the patient was suffering from the pox. In his examination before Sir John Reresby he admitted to 'lying here concealed upon the occasion of his takeing phisick for a clap, and therefore was unwilling to discover himselfe till he was cured'.[11] But there was no evidence of him receiving mercury treatment, the standard cure, and a chest rash was anyway not a classic venereal disease symptom. Dr Harder claimed that Konigsmark had returned from service in Tangiers with 'spots all over his breast',[12] which he had acquired when becoming overheated in the service of England and King Charles, and that it was for this that he was being treated. But there is no clear evidence that Konigsmark ever made it to Tangiers. There seems to have been some confusion between Konigsmark and his own doctor as to what exactly it was he was being treated for.

At some point between 9 and 11 February, Vratz had a meeting with Konigsmark and a group of unnamed advisers. Stern was not present. The identities of those who composed this private counsel were never revealed. It would be reasonable to assume, however, that it included Hanson as well as Harder. The general opinion was that since Thynn always chose to go out in a coach with a retinue of footmen, a musquetoon would be by far the best weapon to deploy against him.

Back in King Street Vratz told Stern of this decision. Stern, awkward as ever, was not in favour of using a musquetoon. He thought it was too large, that it would be seen too easily, and that it would alert the enemy before they had had sufficient time to discharge it. Vratz, however, was insistent. They had decided on a musquetoon and a musquetoon it would be.

The musquetoon certainly had considerable advantages. It could fire a number of shots at once, so greatly improving the chance of hitting the target. It was also shorter and lighter than the conventional musket and so could be easily deployed by someone on horseback. It was the weapon of choice for both highwaymen and pirates. In Vratz's opinion it was also possible to conceal it beneath a greatcoat until it was necessary to bring it into play. Despite his misgivings, Stern finally agreed to make the necessary purchase. Vratz told him where to go for it and Stern secured a nice piece for just five shillings. The cheapness and easy availability was remarkable.

On Friday, 10 February, Vratz bought three horses. It seemed to be generally agreed at this stage among all the concerned parties that the number of attackers should be limited to three. The fewer involved, the less chance that their plans would leak out. That just left the decision as to who was going to fire the gun. Both Vratz and Stern seemed oddly reluctant to take responsibility for carrying out the actual killing. Why was this? Squeamishness? Moral sensitivity? Neither explanation seems very probable. It is much more likely that they were both looking for someone to take the blame if things went wrong. They must have realised that there was a significant chance of getting caught, in which case it would be advantageous to have a fall guy. Provided Vratz and Stern kept their hands clean they could always argue later that they had only approached Thynn's coach out of a desire to talk with the occupant and that the shooting was something that the third member of the party just took it into his head to do, entirely out of the blue and on his own initiative. This was, in fact, exactly the defence they gave when they were first arrested.

It was around this time that the name of George Borosky again entered into the frame. Among the other conspirators he was more generally referred to as The Polander. He was big, strong, dull-witted, obedient, and a good shot, all of which made him ideal material to play the hapless stooge. The Polander was a long-standing servant of Konigsmark's and the Count had sent for him some weeks back, shortly before leaving Strasbourg. The problem was he had yet to show up.[13]

Wellclose Square, Wapping, after Barbon's redevelopment

29

THE HOUSE OF THE SWEDISH ENVOY

You mince your words mightily.

– Prosecution lawyer cross-questioning Frederick Hanson.[1]

The lodgings in Rupert Street were not to Konigsmark's liking. The sea coal was of poor quality and gave out little heat. To make matters worse the chimney was blocked and downdraughts of smoke constantly filled the room with noxious choking fumes. Outside, snow was falling and the temperature dropped steadily. The streets were even filthier than usual, and the sky was a malignant, unrelenting grey. Konigsmark lay on his bed all day and all night, wrapped in his flannel shirt, coughing and shivering. He was anxious, irritable, and was not sleeping well. Each morning, long before it grew light, there was noise from the street, the raucous shouting of vendors, the constant clatter of iron wheels on flint cobbles.

Konigsmark complained repeatedly to Joseph Parsons, who owned the house, about the state of the chimney.[2] Chimneys in that condition caused fires. It needed a brush pushed up it, or even better a small boy to climb up it and remove whatever obstruction was causing the problem. The use of small boys to climb chimneys was a recent innovation. But Parsons did nothing to remedy the defects. In disgust, Konigsmark decided to change his lodgings yet again, this time decamping to St Martin's Lane.

Hanson continued to call round at regular intervals. They talked about Bette. Konigsmark was obsessed with thoughts of the girl and her money. He ranted about Thynn and his insolence and rudeness. He wanted to know from Hanson whether, if he killed Thynn in a fight, he would still be allowed, under English law, to marry Bette. Hanson didn't know the answer, but being of an obliging and deferential nature he agreed to find out.

So Hanson went to see the Swedish envoy, Mr Leinberg. There was a large Scandinavian merchant community working in London. Mainly they lived near the river, in the area of Wellclose Square, Wapping. In the early 1680s 'it was a dangerous place to go over after it was dark, and many people have been robbed and abused in passing it'.[3] In 1682 the entrepreneurial Nicholas Barbon[4] purchased the freehold of an area of narrow and evil-smelling streets and developed Wellclose into a square of elegant brick town houses.

Mr Leinberg was used to dealing with questions of tariffs on wood and copper imports and embargoes on woollen textiles. The question that Hanson desired to discuss in the privacy of Leinberg's muffled rooms was outside the envoy's usual remit. Hanson was later required in court to repeat the conversation word for word. After much evasion and fidgeting, he was finally forced to admit that he had asked 'if Konigsmark should meddle with Esquire Thynn, what the consequence might be, and if the laws of England would be contrary to him in the hopes or pretensions he might have to my Lady [Bette]'.[5] When cross-questioned further as to just what he meant by the word 'meddle' Hanson hesitated and became increasingly flustered. He eventually conceded, however, that he was anxious to know the legal implications of Thynn being killed in a duel or general 'rencounter'. A 'rencounter' was not a duel but a melee in which more than two adversaries could be involved. In reality there was little to distinguish it from a brawl or a shoot-out.[6] The ambassador's answer to Hanson regarding the marriage issue was non-committal but he promised to make further enquiries in his turn.[7]

The prosecution, understandably, regarded this visit by Hanson at such a time as a crucial piece of evidence that proved Konigsmark was all along complicit with the plan to murder Thynn. When Hanson realised which way the prosecution's questions were tending he tried to retract part of his statement. He claimed that Konigsmark had never specifically asked him to make any visit to the Swedish envoy's house, that he, Hanson, had done it entirely on his own initiative, thinking it was information, of a general nature, that the Count might just happen to be interested in. '[Count Konigsmark] never charged me, or gave me any positive order, to go to the Swedish Envoy; but he did name the Swedish envoy to me, as if he were willing to know his advice . . . so, paying my respects to the Envoy, I spoke with the said envoy about this business; and that is all I can say.'[8] The prosecution lawyers were not impressed by Hanson's slippery replies but the envoy himself was never called to clarify what exactly had been discussed.

Foubert's Academy in Swallow Street

30

MONSIEUR FOUBERT'S ACADEMY

What was his crime that thus they sought his life?
Was it because deceived by a wife?
Or was't because that he was Monmouth's friend,
He found so fatal and so sad an end?

– Anon., 'Elegy on the Most Barbarous Murder of Thomas Thynn Esq.', 1682[1]

Monsieur Solomon Foubert's Academy was originally situated on the corner of Brewer Street and Sherwood Street, close to Covent Garden. It was a new establishment and was designed to teach young gentlemen horse riding and related martial skills. It quickly acquired a good reputation and so Foubert soon moved the Academy to larger premises in Swallow Street, a quiet blind alley still known as Foubert's Place, and to be found to this day just off Regent Street. Monsieur Foubert had come to England in the summer of 1679 with his wife, son and extended family. He had previously run the Académie Royale in the Faubourg St Germain, Paris, and been the personal 'keeper of the horse' for Louis XIV. He was generally esteemed to be the ablest horseman in Europe and an expert at teaching those equestrian arts required by a cavalry officer.[2]

Evelyn described the training Foubert's pupils underwent,[3] which included galloping at a ring with a lance, flinging a javelin at the head of a Moor, discharging a pistol at a mark, and taking up a gauntlet with the point of a sword. Other accomplishments that were taught were fencing, dancing and vaulting. Foubert had supposedly transferred to London because of the increasing persecution of Protestants and the closing down of Protestant institutions in France. This is unlikely to have been true. His links to Louis XIV meant that he was far from being the typical Huguenot refugee. He also received regular sums of money, paid from a secret fund, authorised by King Charles and subsequently the Catholic James.[4]

Only young gentlemen from the very best families attended Foubert's Academy. The Duke of Norfolk, the Prince of Denmark, Lord Lansdowne, the Earl of Feversham, and Barbara Palmer's son, George Fitzroy, were all pupils. Neither the Duke of Norfolk nor the Earl of Feversham was impressive in the saddle, but Fitzroy was considered to be highly skilled. He was described by Evelyn as being both a 'bel homme à cheval', and a 'bon homme a cheval', meaning that he was both graceful in his person when sitting on the back of his horse, as well as an excellent rider. In his capacity as teacher to Europe's elite, Foubert was excellently placed for keeping a watchful eye on what the younger generation of courtiers were thinking and doing, particularly in connection to the vexed question of the succession. It is very probable that in return for those secret payments he was passing this information on to his royal patrons.

At the beginning of 1682, one of Foubert's 'young gallants' was Philip, the younger brother to Konigsmark. When Borosky the Polander arrived in London the first thing he did was send a message to Philip at Foubert's Academy.[5] Borosky had left Hamburg on 24 December 1681, but it had taken him some time to obtain a berth on a ship, and when he eventually succeeded the voyage had proved extremely rough. He was several weeks just crossing the North Sea. When he finally turned up in England he was in a badly dishevelled state. Not only was his campaign coat threadbare and disreputable-looking but he carried all his worldly possessions on his person. These consisted of something described as a 'seabed', presumably a rolled-up hammock, to which was tied a pair of old boots.[6] He also had a small portmanteau and a fifty-year-old wheel-lock gun. He looked like a typical unemployed soldier, one more refugee from the continental wars, even harder up than Lieutenant John Stern, if that was possible. At least Stern still had the trappings of gentility. Borosky had no such pretensions. He was described in court records as a labourer.

Borosky's arrival had been eagerly awaited. Such was the concern for his whereabouts, Konigsmark had daily sent Hanson to the Royal Exchange to make enquiries about the fate of the ship from Hamburg. The Exchange was the great brokerage for mercantile gossip and it was there that news of any sinkings was first heard, not always accurately. As it turned out, Borosky had not been drowned. It might have been better for him if he had been. He turned up in London on Friday, 10 February, and immediately booked into Bock's Place. It cannot be coincidence that he went to the same lodging house where Vratz and Stern had previously stopped.

As soon as news of Borosky's arrival in London was received at Foubert's Academy, Hanson was informed, but he did not go to meet the Polander himself. Instead he arranged for someone called John Wright to go on the Saturday morning, 11 February. John Wright's status is interesting. He was described in court papers as a servant to Philip, but he appears to have had far more independent status than the average servant, for he was more concerned with carrying on trading activities on his own account, than fulfilling his orders. He had a rather tetchy relationship with Hanson.

Wright met Borosky at the Cross Keys in Throgmorton Street and brought him back to west London, but the two men did not immediately enter Foubert's establishment to find Hanson. Instead they went into a tavern next door. Wright claimed that this was at Borosky's suggestion, because Borosky did not wish to appear in front of his master encumbered with all his personal baggage. Wright took the opportunity to call 'for a pot of ale'. The next thing he knew Borosky had disappeared. Wright thought that he 'had gone to make water', but a short while later Borosky returned in the company of Hanson, who asked Wright irritably why he had not arrived sooner. Wright replied that 'he had some other business . . . with some French merchants to look upon some goods'. Hanson was not impressed by this explanation. He told Borosky to pay Wright for his trouble, gather his belongings and 'go along with him'.[7]

Hanson then conducted Borosky to the lodging house in St Martin's Lane where Konigsmark remained in hiding. When they arrived Vratz was also there. Stern was not. Konigsmark told Borosky that for the next few days he would be in Captain Vratz's service and he should do all that Vratz asked of him. Konigsmark was not impressed by the sight of Borosky's threadbare coat. He remarked to Hanson: 'The fellow is all naked' and asked him to go and acquire a new coat for Borosky immediately.[8] It was a cheap way of buying Borosky's favour. Hanson was none too happy at being ordered to carry out these menial tasks. He was, after all, a tutor, not a general dogsbody. But rather than risk a rift he grudgingly performed the errand, stopping to have his dinner along the way.

When Hanson returned with the coat, Konigsmark informed him that Borosky also needed a decent sword. Hanson, who was becoming increasingly irritable by this stage, asked Konigsmark how much he was prepared to spend on it. 'Ten shillings or thereabouts' was the answer.[9] Hanson demurred. He told Konigsmark that he hadn't really got the time to go purchasing swords. He was meeting with Philip and they were going to the theatre together. But Konigsmark was insistent that Borosky needed a sword, and Hanson, yet again, ended up deferring to him. He promised that it would be delivered that same evening.

Hanson now went off to look for a sword. It was already getting dark, a miserable cold February evening. A pall of smoke hung heavily in the air and rasped at the lungs. Hanson first tried the various emporiums of St Martin's Lane, 'but could not find a sword worth even a groat'.[10] He then went down to Charing Cross to a cutler he was familiar with called Thomas Howgood. Howgood did not have an appropriate sword in stock but promised to make one by the end of the evening. Hanson told Howgood that he would leave the exact style of sword to his discretion. 'Use my friend well, and use yourself favourably, too,' he told Howgood.[11] The most important thing was to have the sword ready by that same evening. It was six thirty. Howgood promised that the sword would be ready for collection by eight o'clock. Hanson could pick it up when the play was finished.

Hanson and Philip went to watch Otway's *Venice Preserv'd*, which was running at the Dorset Garden Theatre, situated at the end of Dorset Street on the edge of the Thames. The theatre could be approached both from Fleet Street and by river via Dorset Stairs. Hanson took the road route. The building was of new construction, two storeys high, sixty feet wide, with a fine porch and an ogee dome. It was home to the Duke's Company and the mastermind behind the scheme was the actor manager Thomas Betterton.[12] Evelyn was particularly impressed by 'the new Machines ... which were indeed very costly and magnificent'.[13] These machines enabled angels to descend from the skies and other sensational tricks, as well as the shifting of the enormous scenic backcloths. The play had opened two days beforehand to a rapturous response. It was viciously anti-Whig and pro-James, Duke of York. The epilogue was a loyalist flourish, wishing James and his pregnant wife a safe voyage back to London from Scotland where they had recently been residing.

After the play was over Hanson called back at the cutler's. The sword was still not ready. Hanson was angry. He told Howgood that it was 'strange, a gentleman could not get a little sword ... ready for him in an whole afternoon'.[14] Howgood promised that it would be finished very shortly but Hanson did not wish to wait. He told Howgood to send the finished weapon round to Foubert's Academy.

Borosky spent that Saturday night at Konigsmark's lodgings, in the basement. On the Sunday morning a messenger arrived at St Martin's Lane having come from Foubert's Academy. He brought the sword and a note. The servant boy, Francis Watts, carried both items upstairs to his master and asked whether there was to be a reply to the note. Konigsmark answered that no reply was required. Watts was aged fifteen and was paid sixpence a day to wait on Konigsmark. He was also provided with his food. He worked from early morning until nine in the evening. His testimony at the trial was remarkable in its detail and totally damning of Konigsmark in its content.

Konigsmark told Watts to take the sword down to Borosky, who was still below stairs. It was a broad horseman's sword, two fingers wide. Later that same morning Konigsmark asked Watts a very odd question. He wanted to know whether it was permitted for horsemen to ride through the centre of town on a Sunday. Watts replied that it was permitted except during sermon time. Meanwhile, Dr Harder had arrived and he now escorted Borosky, wearing his new coat and equipped with his new sword, from St Martin's Lane to his own house, where Amien Berg, a servant to Captain Vratz, was waiting. It was Berg who then led Borosky to where Vratz and Stern were lodging in King Street. According to Stern's testimony Borosky arrived about noon.

Vratz was delighted with the new man. He told Stern: 'Now I have got a brave fellow.'[15] He took Borosky into a separate room and explained what would be required of him. After this conversation Vratz was even more enthusiastic. He returned to Stern and expanded further: 'This is a brave fellow indeed, for he says those that will not fight must be killed.'[16] One wonders whether Vratz wasn't deliberately riling Stern here by alluding to his own evident lack of bravery. After all, Stern could have agreed to fire the gun himself.

Under examination Borosky said that he was initially unwilling to go along with Vratz's plan. He claimed to have argued with him, saying: 'If we were taken we should come to a very ill end.'[17] He was only persuaded after Vratz told him that if they were caught he himself would take the blame, not Borosky. On the basis of this assurance Borosky concluded, not altogether unreasonably, 'that it might be here as it is in Poland, viz. Where a servant does a thing by his master's order, the master is to suffer for it, and not the servant.'[18] To clinch the deal Vratz also offered Borosky the same inducement that he had previously promised Stern, namely a position in Konigsmark's private army.

Contemporary etching depicting the murder of Thomas Thynn

31

THE BLACK BULL

Now he is a dead man.

– Captain Vratz to Lieutenant Stern[1]

T he plot to kill Thynn at last began to gather momentum. Some time after midday on Sunday, 12 February, the three assassins transferred themselves from the Three Sugar Loaves in King Street to the Black Bull in Holborn, a suitably reclusive establishment situated down a narrow alley just opposite Fetter Lane.[2]

From a strategic point of view it was an odd move to make. The Three Sugar Loaves was close to Thynn's house. From there they could track him from the moment he left the protection of his home. The Black Bull on the other hand was a good two miles away, and so useless as an observation post. To make good this deficiency Vratz left his servant Amien Berg behind in King Street. His job was to provide intelligence as to exactly when Thynn left his premises. But by the time Berg had legged it to the Black Bull with this information, Thynn's coach would have long disappeared into the greying miasma of London's narrow streets.

There must have been some overriding consideration that made this last-minute change of operational base a necessity, because otherwise it makes no sense. The most likely explanation is that the Three Sugar Loaves did not have adequate stabling for the three horses that were going to be needed and that Vratz had already purchased. It is also possible Vratz was worried that they had already become too well known in King Street and a change of locality would be helpful in preserving anonymity.

The fact that the three assassins had no difficulty in catching up with Thynn even though they were not in a position to track him from source is revealing. It indicates that they had prior knowledge of his intended destination. It is most unlikely that such information could have been picked up on the streets or obtained through tavern tittle-tattle. What it suggests is that details of Thynn's plans had already been provided to the assassins from a well placed source. In the light of later events this is very probable. Unfortunately, at their trial no explanation as to how they acquired this prior knowledge was asked for, so the identity of the informant was never revealed.

Before finally leaving the familiar comfort of the Three Sugar Loaves the conspirators had one more all-important piece of business to complete: the charging of the musquetoon with bullets. Simple enough, one might have thought. But where Vratz and Stern were concerned nothing was ever that simple. The priming of the murder weapon rapidly turned into another of those moments where the two old soldiers were unable to agree and the plot teetered on the edge of farce. Vratz wanted the musquetoon loaded with fifteen bullets. Stern argued that with so much lead shot spraying in all directions they would be in danger of killing the footmen, the driver, the postilions, and anyone else in the vicinity. Stern thought five bullets quite sufficient for their purpose. Vratz with his characteristic insouciance remarked that who else got killed was an irrelevance, just so long as Thynn was dead. In the event, it was Stern who got his way.[3]

It was Stern who now carefully wrapped the bullets in combustible rags and primed them with powdered rosin. The musquetoon was then ceremonially handed to Borosky. Before finally setting off, Vratz gave the Polander one last crucial instruction. If the Duke of Monmouth also happened to be in the carriage with Thynn, then they must not attack under any circumstances. Vratz was very emphatic about this. In spite of his generally casual attitude regarding any collateral damage to innocent bystanders, it was plainly of paramount importance to someone that Monmouth should not be exposed to harm. Such a sentiment is unlikely to have originated from Vratz himself. It is much more probable that an instruction of this nature came from a source close to the King. The fact the assassins knew that Monmouth was likely to be in the carriage with Thynn is similarly significant. It again suggests that they had inside information as to how Thynn intended to spend his final Sunday afternoon.

With the gun loaded and the strategy finally decided upon, the three conspirators left their King Street lodgings and transferred themselves to the Black Bull Inn. They did not travel together. Vratz went from Westminster to Holborn incognito inside a sedan chair. Borosky walked. Stern, who always felt most comfortable in the company of horses, fetched two from a nearby stables and brought them to the agreed rendezvous point. The third horse was being delivered by Markham, Vratz's personal tailor, who seemed to be employed for rather more than simply his ability with the needle.

Once installed in the Black Bull the three men settled down to a long Sunday afternoon of steady drinking, while awaiting news from Berg as to Thynn's movements. There was a nearly calamitous error when Markham delivered the third horse to the Blue Bear instead of the Black Bull. It was a mistake that could easily have ruined the entire enterprise. But the error was quickly rectified and the requisite number of horses was eventually ready at the right premises, saddled, fed and watered. It was now just a matter of waiting for Thynn to emerge from Canon Row.

The assassins were understandably tense. Even the super-casual Vratz comes across as being a little on edge. According to Borosky's later testimony the Captain reminded him on no less than 'five or six separate occasions'[4] that when he was commanded to shoot, he must discharge the contents of the musquetoon into the body of the man sitting in the coach. He also reminded Borosky more than once that he must ensure Monmouth was no longer in the coach with Thynn when he pulled the trigger. Under no circumstances was Monmouth to be killed.

It was just beginning to get dark when word finally arrived that Thynn was abroad. The three conspirators hastily mounted and clattered out of the Black Bull's cobbled yard. It had been a grey, misty, quiet day, but as the sun went down a north-easterly wind sprang up and the air turned suddenly chilly. It was cold enough to make a man shiver. Borosky had the musquetoon tucked under his greatcoat and each of the three men was armed with a brace of pistols. Borosky had also been equipped with a pocket pistol. There was no shortage of firepower.

The assassins hadn't got very far before they had to stop and ask a passer-by the way to Temple Bar. The evidence for this is provided in the speech of Sir Francis Wythens the prosecuting lawyer, and was not disputed.[5] It is an odd detail, since the fact that they were lost within a few minutes of setting out on their deadly mission was not particularly relevant to their guilt or innocence. It does, however, demonstrate the most lamentable lack of pre-planning.

They were evidently trying to find their way from the Black Bull to Northumberland House, which was situated at the far end of the Strand close by Charing Cross and where they had been told Thynn could be found. It was not a difficult journey to accomplish. It simply involved crossing over Holborn, riding down Fetter Lane, turning right into Fleet Street and then passing beneath Temple Bar, which marked the eastern entrance to the Strand. Temple Bar was a superb new gateway designed by Sir Christopher Wren and was a well-known landmark.[6] But why did they not know their way to it? Borosky was a newcomer and so his ignorance was understandable. Vratz probably chose to go everywhere in a sedan chair with the curtains drawn and so perhaps had an excuse for being unfamiliar with the terrain. But Stern had been living in central London for nearly six months. His confusion suggests that he did not have much of a mental grip on what was going on.

Once the assassins had succeeded in orientating themselves and were progressing southwards down Fetter Lane, they would have passed Barnard's Inn on their right-hand side, a large sprawling establishment, part of Gray's Inn courts of law. There followed in quick succession Three Horse Shoe Alley, Plough Yard and Bond's stables. They also must have passed the shop of Thompson the printer, situated next to the Cross Keys Tavern. Thompson would very shortly come to their defence in his newspaper columns, only to be hauled off to appear before the magistrates for his trouble.

When the three horsemen had emerged onto Fleet Street they must have been able to see the Temple Bar ahead of them, surmounted by two strangely plumed swans. It was dark by now but Fleet Street was still busy and there were numerous flambeaux in front of the shops casting dancing shadows. After Temple Bar they passed St Clement Danes Church to their right, and on their left hand towards the river came a succession of grand houses, Essex, Arundell, Somerset, and finally the grandest of them all, Northumberland House. Stern was wearing his small three-cornered hat. Borosky wore his new greatcoat. Vratz went bareheaded. He liked to display his dark hair, which fell forward across his forehead in two lustrous locks.

It is not entirely clear whether Thynn went directly from Canon Row to Northumberland House. A newsletter to Sir Francis Radclyffe of Dilston, written on Monday, 13 February, suggests that prior to his murder Thynn and Monmouth had been riding together in Hyde Park 'to take the air'.[7] This was possible. Riding in a smart carriage in the park on a Sunday afternoon, flirting with the young women to be found walking there, and on occasion picking them up, was an established pastime for wealthy and idle men about town such as Thynn and Monmouth. What is certain is that later that same afternoon Thynn called on Countess Howard, the grandmother of his estranged wife. Thynn's coach driver, William Ellers, and the servant boy who walked in front of the coach, William Cole, both stated that the two grandees had been visiting the Dowager Countess, and that it was shortly after they left Northumberland House that the attack took place.[8] It seems highly probable that the three horsemen had been waiting down a nearby side street until Thynn resumed occupancy of his coach to continue his journey.

The fact that Thynn was visiting the Dowager Countess is of interest for reasons other than that it was his last social call before being murdered. His motives for the visit are not given. Perhaps he simply wished to know whether the old lady had received any further letters from her wayward granddaughter. Perhaps he also wished to inform her of how the court case was progressing. He was very confident of victory.

Some time between seven and eight in the evening Thynn left Northumberland House. It was now pitch-dark, a starless night, heavy clouds moving rapidly across the sky. The link boy, William Cole, walked in front of the coach carrying a flambeau to light their way. The three horsemen followed, silently and at a cautious distance, their presence unnoticed, biding their time.

The situation was still not straightforward. Thynn was not alone. Monmouth remained in the coach with him. It looked quite possible that the two men were returning together to Thynn's house, in which case the plot would fail, at any rate for that day. But then they had a stroke of luck. Monmouth alighted at Hedge Lane, situated just past Dung Hill Mews. It was not the most salubrious address, but he had a decent lodging house and stables there.

Having dropped Monmouth off, the coach immediately turned left into Pall Mall. It had only gone a few yards further, to the point that it was abreast of a narrow little street called St Albans, when the three horsemen came riding by on the right-hand side. One of the three men grabbed hold of the bridle of the leading coach horse and shouted to the coachman: 'Stop you dog!'[9] Neither the coachman, Ellers, nor the link boy, Cole, provide any testimony as to whether or not they heard Vratz order Borosky to fire his musquetoon, but Borosky in his initial examination before the magistrates Reresby and Bridgeman was adamant 'that he fired the musquetoon by the Captain's order; and that, before he did it, the Captain bid him, as soon as ever he had stopped the coach, to fire'.[10] Vratz on the other hand claimed: 'he only intended to fight with Mr Thynn, and that the Polonian had mistook his orders when he shot him'.[11] On 15 February[12] the *Protestant Mercury* published brief details of the statements that the two men had supposedly made to the Privy Council. This was their first interrogation and it took place on Monday, 13 February, some days before the one conducted by Bridgeman and Reresby. Vratz was quoted as saying 'that he never ordered his man to fire, but took him along with him to defend him in case Mr Thynn should set his servants upon him'. Borosky's statement is almost identical to the one he made to the Justices. He said that 'his master ordered him to do it and he could not deny his master'. When asked what words his master had used, he replied: 'Be sure you fire into that coach I stop.'

As for Lieutenant Stern's actions at the crucial moment of the shooting, his testimony is full of his usual confusions and contradictions. In his *Last Confession*, made after he had been found guilty and sentenced to death, he makes much of 'the dullness of his Horse in following Mr Thynn's chariot all along Pall Mall ... for though he used the spur pretty smartly, yet he could not get him to follow close. That, and a disorder in his own mind, made that he was almost twenty paces behind when the fire was given.'[13] This is Stern in repentant mode, distancing himself from the murder and crediting his horse with prognosticatory powers. But according to Bridgeman's testimony in the witness box Stern had said: 'he was about ten yards before, and he heard the Captain say, Stop the coach, upon which he turned about, and presently saw the shot made.'[14] This is almost certainly the more accurate version. All the witnesses are agreed that the horsemen made their escape up Haymarket. This would have involved turning around, which would have left Stern at the rear of the party. Stern talks of suffering from mental confusion both before and after the murder, 'nor was he recovered of that stupidity until the second day of his imprisonment'.[15] It seems quite possible that this 'stupor' was alcohol-induced and that prison had the effect of sobering him up.

The hold-up and the shooting were over in the blink of an eye. The most competent part of the entire assassination was Borosky's decisiveness and accuracy with the musquetoon. Thynn's coachman and the postilions seem to have been stunned into a state of paralysis by the suddenness of the attack. The only member of Thynn's party who showed any initiative was the link boy, Wiliam Cole. His testimony is vivid and detailed: 'I heard the blunderbuss go off; so upon that I turned my face back, and saw a great smoke, and heard my master cry out he was murdered.'[16] Cole ran after the fleeing horsemen all the way to the top of the Haymarket shouting murder at the top of his voice. He ran until he 'was quite spent, and was able to go no further'. He reckoned the time was a quarter past eight. He didn't get a good look at the faces of the assassins but noticed that one of them rode 'a little bay horse'.[17] A pistol was later found at the scene of the shooting. It was probably the weapon that Vratz had waved in the coachman's face.

Thynn was rushed to his house and laid on the bed in his chamber. At that point he was still alive, although according to trial testimony he was already only semi-conscious. His friends and relatives were immediately sent for, and so too was Mr Hobbs the surgeon. The latter arrived between nine and ten. Hobbs later gave evidence to the Court: 'I was with him, Sir, that Night he was wounded and I found him shot with 4 bullets which entered his Body and tore his guts, and wounded his Liver, and his Stomach, and his Gall, and wounded his great Guts, and his small Guts, and broke one of the Ribs, and wounded the great bone below.'[18] Mr White the coroner confirmed that there were four holes in the right-hand side of Thynn's body below the short ribs, 'each mortal wound the breadth of one inch and the depth of some six inches'.[19]

The fact that Thynn was delirious with pain and barely conscious did not appear to stop him making an impressive deathbed speech. A few days after the shooting the newspapers were full of his dying words. *The Impartial Protestant Mercury* reported that he declared:

> he had a Loyal Heart and he kept no company but such as he verily believed wished his Majesty a long and prosperous Reign; That he heartily forgave all the world, and knew not from whence this Malice should proceed, not having given any person any provocation thereunto; that in particular he forgave the Lady Ogle and as he loved her living so he did now at his death.[20]

Speculation as to what exactly Lady Bette might need forgiveness for was soon rife.

A different version of Thynn's last words was printed in the *Loyal Protestant* by Nat Thompson. According to this account, Thynn repeatedly cried out 'Oh my belly! Oh my belly!'.[21]

Sir John Reresby, Justice of the Peace

32

SIR JOHN RERESBY'S HOUSE

Murder is as fashionable a crime as a Man can be guilty of.

— John Gay, *The Beggar's Opera*[1]

At 11 p.m. on the night of the murder, approximately three hours after the shooting, and just as Sir John Reresby was on the point of going to bed, there came a great commotion at his front door. It was a late hour for an honest citizen to be still up but Sir John had been enjoying the company of the King earlier that evening at the Palace of Westminster. He turned away from his staircase and crossed the wide hall, trailing his left foot as he moved. He was a powerful tough Yorkshireman, but he had had the limp since the age of two, when he had fallen out of a window. The defect had not stopped him leading a physically very active and accident-prone life. He was forever falling out of boats and off horses and getting into scraps and scrapes. As a young man he had been involved in frequent duels, brawls, cudgellings and fisticuffs. Now, at the age of forty-seven, he had slowed down just a little. He was a loyal servant to the

King and had become an astute operator of the political system. He had just been made a justice of the peace for Middlesex and Westminster, the nearest London had at that time to the role of police commissioner. He was also possessed of a more artistic side to his character. He played the guitar, the lute and the violin.[2]

The frantic hammering at his door continued. On going to investigate, he discovered that a gentleman had come from Mr Thynn's house in a state of great agitation. He informed him that Mr Thynn had been shot and was likely to die of his wounds. He requested that Sir John immediately authorise a hue and cry to hunt down the assassins. A hue and cry was an official warrant enabling pursuers to enter and search premises where they thought a suspect might be hiding. Moments later the Duke of Monmouth's page also arrived on the scene, requesting that Sir John go immediately to Mr Thynn's house. The page had come by coach, which was promptly placed at Sir John's disposal. The flanks of the horses were still steaming from their recent exertions in the cold night air. Sir John clearly felt he had no choice but to comply with the various demands that were being placed upon him.

As it happened Sir John already knew about the shooting. Earlier that evening he had been present when the King received news of the attempt on Thynn's life. Charles had, according to Reresby, been greatly disturbed, not so much because of the violence involved, but because of the potential political implications of such an act. Reresby later recorded in his *Memoirs* that Thynn 'being one deeply engaged in the Duke of Monmouth's interest, it was much feared what construction might be made of it by that party, the authors escaping and not known'.[3]

The *Memoirs* were compiled several years after the event and it is possible there are errors in sequencing, but in his recall of the Thynn murder Reresby appears to have a good grasp of all the detail. His account, however, raises some important questions. If news of the attack had already been brought to court while Reresby was with the King, why was Reresby not dispatched at once to investigate? Instead, he returned home and, by his own account, would have gone to bed, had not Thynn's supporters and relations put him under such pressure he was left with no alternative but to authorise a hue and cry. It suggests that Charles did not consider arresting the assassins to be a top priority. Perhaps indeed he wanted them to escape.

This wasn't the first time in recent days that Reresby had found himself in conversation with the King on the subject of Thomas Thynn. On 2 January he had dined at the home of Lord Conway, the principal Secretary of State, together with Lord Halifax, the King's first minister, and the King himself. Reresby had proudly presented to the assembled company an affidavit that had been made before him in his capacity as a Justice of the Peace, earlier that same day. The affidavit concerned a 'pre-contract between Mr Thynn and Mistress Trevor before his marriage with my Lady Northumberland [Bette]'.[4] Reresby was very aware that there were moves afoot to have the marriage to Bette annulled, 'it not having been consummated, and my Lady Northumberland having fled from Mr Thynn into Holland'. He was equally aware that Charles was in favour of this annulment, and so his production of the affidavit would be a great feather in his cap, 'at all which the Court was not dissatisfied, the husband being one that had opposed its interest, and engaged himself in that of the Duke of Monmouth'.[5] So pleased was Charles by this development that he asked Reresby to prepare for him a copy of the affidavit, which was presented to him the next day. Such involvement in the detail was most unlike Charles.

On Reresby's arrival at Thynn's house, which cannot have taken longer than ten minutes by coach, for by this time it was approaching midnight and the streets were almost empty, Sir John found himself surrounded by 'several gentlemen and Lords, friends to Mr Thynn'.[6] Monmouth was there, and so also was Lord Mordaunt, a close ally of Thynn's. Reresby immediately granted the necessary search warrants 'for severall persons suspected to be privy to the design and that might give some intelligence of the partys that had acted that murder'.[7] This is most revealing. It appears that either Thynn's friends or Sir John himself already had a pretty clear idea regarding the identity of the culprits. A search for Vratz immediately took place. The 'whoor that used to visit that gentleman'[8] was soon located and questioned. So too was the chairman who had taken Vratz from the Three Sugar Loaves in Westminster to the Black Bull in Holborn. From these two witnesses they found out where Vratz had been lodging. Constables were dispatched to the Three Sugar Loaves and Berg, Vratz's servant, was arrested. That he was still there seems very careless on the part of the conspirators.

Berg put up little resistance. He confessed both that Vratz was his master and that 'he had a quarrel with Mr Thynn, and had often appointed him to watch his coach as he passed by'.[9] Berg also helpfully provided a number of addresses where Vratz might be found. Having been left with little choice, Reresby was now anxious to play the part of the energetic and relentless law enforcer. 'At six a clock in the morning, having been in chace almost the whole night, I personally took the captain [Vratz] at the house of a Swedish doctor in Leicester Fields,'[10] he boasts with an under-standable rush of pride. This was almost certainly the house of Dr Harder, who lived in St Martin's Lane, where he had hosted meetings between the conspirators throughout the previous two weeks.

Reresby was obviously surprised to find Vratz 'in bed and his sword at some distance from him upon the table'.[11] He wisely secured the sword first and then took hold of the man, handing him over into the custody of two constables. He did not expect that Vratz would give himself up 'so tamely'. Reresby does not interpret this as cowardice, however, but rather as supreme self-confidence. He makes a point of commenting favourably on Vratz's nonchalance: 'he appeared inconcerned from the beginning, notwithstanding he was very certain to be found the chiefe actor in the tragedy.'[12] Reresby was impressed by Vratz, calling him 'a man of great courage'. Not long after Vratz's arrest Borosky and Stern were also picked up. Stern, typically, was found drinking in a tavern in Drury Lane. Exactly where Borosky was arrested is not stated.

As the assassins were rounded up one by one and the sun struggled to light up a murky February Monday morning, rumours rapidly began swirling through the streets of London. Some said the murder had been committed by a gang of tailors. Others claimed Monmouth had been killed as well as Thynn. Those that knew Monmouth to be still alive believed he had only escaped by the intervention of Providence. The most pervasive rumour, and the most dangerous to the King and his brother, was that the murder was part of a Catholic conspiracy.[13]

Reresby, who had worked all through the night, was still examining the three prisoners at his house when word came that there was to be a special meeting of the Privy Council with the King in attendance, and the prisoners were to be brought before it. Charles asked Reresby to brief him on how the arrests had been accomplished and what the prisoners had said under examination. He then examined them further himself. This was an-other example of unusual involvement on the part of the King.

So far as the public was concerned, the link between the murderers and Count Konigsmark had already been made by the Monday morning. The Tuesday, 14 February, edition of the *Impartial Protestant Mercury* carried the following details: 'A diligent search was immediately made after these inhuman assassinates and at last several of them were providentially dis-covered and seized . . . and this morning examined at Whitehall, and, as we hear, some of them confessed they perpetrated this Detestable Villainy in respect to an Outlandish Count.'[14] Konigsmark's name was already in play, but surprisingly, it wasn't until two days after the first arrests, that is on 15 February, that any attempt was made to go in search of him.

On the 15th there was a further meeting of the Privy Council at which Philip Konigsmark was brought before it and questioned. Again Reresby was in attendance. Philip admitted that his brother 'had made addresses to my Lady Ogle before she had married Mr Thyn'.[15] Bette's name was getting dragged further and further into the murder plot. Philip also admitted that his brother had returned into England, incognito, ten days before the murder, after a brief spell on the Continent. Reresby comments that this 'gave great caus of suspicion that the said Count was in the bottom of it'.[16] But the world had already been saying as much for at least forty-eight hours. The King now finally ordered Reresby to go and search Konigsmark's lodgings, which Reresby did in the company of two constables. Unsurprisingly, it was discovered that the Count had already departed two days beforehand.

Over the next few days Reresby had several further meetings both with the King and the prisoners. Vratz admitted that he had been a friend of Konigsmark's for eight years, and that Thynn had affronted the Count, by slandering him behind his back. Vratz also claimed he had taken it upon himself to be revenged on Thynn on his friend's behalf, but not with his knowledge, 'but as he then pretended not with his privitie'.[17]

Reresby was full of self-congratulation. Not only had he found out the culprits but he had successfully defused a potentially very fraught political situation, 'the phenaticks having buzzed it already abroad that the design was chiefly against the Duke of Monmouth; and I had the Kings thankes oftener then once, my Lord Halifax his, and severall other's, for my diligent discovery of the true caus and occasion as well as the authors of this matter'.[18] The true cause, it was claimed by the Court Party, was nothing more serious than a love squabble over Lady Bette. The perpetrators were Vratz, Stern and Borosky. It was all very simple and contained. Basking in this glow of self-satisfaction, Reresby rather overlooked the fact that Count Konigsmark had got clean away.

Anti-Catholic Propaganda 1681

33

NEXT THE CROSS KEYS, FETTER LANE

Will you have your throats cut ere you believe?

– Henry Care, *The History of the Damnable Popish Plot*, London 1681[1]

Charles had been right to worry about the political consequences of Thynn's murder. As soon as news of his killing broke, the 'Fanatick' party spread it about that it was all part of a Papist plot to ensure James came to the throne and that the real target had been the Duke of Monmouth. Langley Curtis, publisher of *The True Protestant Mercury*, rushed into print with a poem entitled, 'The Miraculous Escape of the Duke of Monmouth'.[2] The message was:

> We may believe it as we do our creed
> None but some hired Papists did the deed.

But Curtis did not limit himself to turning Thynn into a Protestant martyr. He also took the opportunity to throw some dirt in Lady Bette's direction:

Hard was the Fate of this most Worthy Man,
Whom first a Wicked Woman did Trepann;
And now more hard, if that he lost his life,
by MURDEROUS means of his DISLOYAL WIFE.[3]

The wicked woman mentioned here is Mistress Trevor, and the murderous wife is obviously Lady Bette. By pointing the finger at Bette, Curtis did not consider that he was distracting from the more political interpretation of the murder. Quite the contrary. This linking of the downfall of man with the iniquities of woman was calculated to appeal to the puritan extremists. Bette was just another of those treacherous whores that filled the halls of Whitehall. Curtis concluded by calling Bette a 'JILTING DRAB' and suggested that in future, as protection against the evil designs of such women:

Under our English Cloth men shall wear Buff;
A coat of mail, or armour Pistol-Proof.

Curtis did not have a monopoly over published opinion. Within hours of his broadsheet being circulated, Roger L'Estrange in his paper *The Observator* leapt to Bette's defence, 'who is as conspicuous in the world, for her Generous, and Unspotted Virtue, as for her State and Quality'.[4] He castigates Langley Curtis as 'a Despicable Scoundrel, viler than the Dirt in the Kennel'. In his defence of the Tories and the Court Party, L'Estrange makes frequent references to the horrors of the Civil War, as if to remind people that the alternative to loyalty to the King was the general breakdown of law and order. Even thirty years later the wounds inflicted by that defining experience were still very raw.

Meanwhile, the *Impartial Protestant Mercury* reported that 'both grandmother and mother have wrote to her [Bette] not to marry Count Konigsmark whom they fear has been the procatarctick [immediate] cause of this wickedness'.[5] There was a genuine fear on the part of Bette's relations that Konigsmark would succeed in escaping to the Continent and proceed directly to The Hague to take possession of his great prize.

There were some suspicious circumstances that did indeed suggest a Papist plot. One of these was the presence in London at the time of the killing of the Grand Prior of France, Philippe de Vendôme. Vendôme was the senior representative of the secretive order of the Knights of St John throughout the realm of Louis XIV. The Knights were based in Malta and had traditionally been involved in the fight against the Turks, but their remit and their tentacles spread far wider than this. They were also pledged to assist with the triumphal fightback of Catholicism throughout Europe, overthrowing Lutheran-inspired principalities and repossessing those Church properties that had been seized by apostate kings like Henry VIII. King Louis XIV and James, Duke of York, were both sympathetic to the Order's aims and closely involved with its activities. Even more incriminating than Vendôme's presence in London was his hasty departure as soon as news of the murder broke.[6]

It was vital for Charles to at least appear to be making every effort to bring the murderers to justice. On first learning of the killing, he had ordered all the sea ports to be closed in order to prevent any of the assassins escaping the country. It was an order that was unlikely to have any practical effect. There were thousands of ships moving in and out of the Thames at any one time and, without enlisting the aid of the navy, the King did not have the resources necessary to impose a blockade. In any case a blockade of this magnitude would have caused a furore among the merchant community. All that was really feasible was to spread the word and try and keep a watch on suspicious passengers.

The sailing of the Grand Prior in one of the King's own yachts around exactly the same time that Konigsmark disappeared was clearly something of an embarrassment, and to avoid any suspicion of complicity in the plot Charles agreed to send a shallop after it to check that Konigsmark had not been secreted aboard. The yacht was stopped and searched, but there was no sign of Konigsmark.

The Grand Prior connection could have been far more embarrassing for King Charles than many at the time realised. It was generally unknown that Konigsmark was also a Knight of St John. In the late 1670s, Konigsmark had left the Court of France and travelled to Malta, where he had helped the Knights in their naval war against the Turks. In this capacity he had apparently performed many daring deeds, including the taking of a Turkish ship almost single-handed. When that ship blew up, he had escaped by swimming, sword between gritted teeth, back to his own vessel. For these heroic actions he had been appointed to a special position of trust within this influential and highly secretive Order, whose roots went back to the original Knights Templar.[7] Fortunately for the Count his membership of the order was such a well guarded secret that during his trial he was able to declare himself to be a loyal Protestant,[8] a claim that went entirely unchallenged.

The printer Nat Thompson was not one to sit idly by while a fierce circulation-boosting story was in progress, centring on a sex-and-murder scandal with far-reaching political ramifications. From his premises next to the Cross Keys in Fetter Lane he weighed in straight away with a version of events that had Thynn as the one who had first resorted to violent tactics. The *Loyal Protestant* claimed that:

> about 7 or 8 weeks ago, as he [Konigsmark] was travelling betwixt Strasburgh and Metz, [he] was set upon by 5 ruffians; whether they design'd to Murder, or only to Rifle the Count, is variously conjectured, for he had in his coach 1500 French Pistoles in gold: two of the Ruffians were kill'd in the attempt, but the rest got away: the Count receiv'd a pistol shot in the back, whereof he is not yet recovered.[9]

Thompson went on to suggest that Thynn was behind the attack: 'the said Count after this Assault had some jealousie that Mr Thynn might be an Abettor thereof'.[10] The purpose of the piece was clear. It was to discredit Thynn and increase sympathy towards Konigsmark. It even offered an explanation for Konigsmark's mysterious illness. Thompson no doubt thought his piece would find favour with the King and James. Unfortunately for Thompson he miscalculated the support that Charles was prepared to extend to him, for while Charles was no doubt delighted to see Thynn dead, he certainly did not wish to appear delighted.

Thompson quickly found himself hauled up before the Privy Council. 'Thompson, who so often rejoices at the misfortunes of others, was sent for before the Council, for misrepresenting the relation of Thynn's most horrid murder, which he slubbers over after his Tory manner,' trumpeted *The True Protestant Mercury*.[11] Thompson hastily tried to mitigate the damage. In the *Loyal Protestant* of 23 February he retracted his story and admitted that it had derived largely from 'the discourse that passed about the town'. He went on to add: 'it being far from our thoughts to make any unhandsome or false reflection upon the memory of that Worthy Person, who was so Barbarously and most Villainously murdered'.[12] This half-apology was not considered sufficient. On 27 February Thompson found himself indicted at the Old Bailey.

The claims about the Strasbourg attack had done little to damage Thynn's standing and Thompson had been publicly discredited for mentioning it. There is, however, a further fascinating dimension to the Strasbourg story which 'The Fanaticks' failed to pick up on, and, as with Konigsmark's secret membership of the Order of St John, it could have provided them with far more potent ammunition. On 30 September 1681 Louis's army walked into Strasbourg and claimed it for France. Shortly after this the Cathedral was removed from Lutheran control and restored to the Catholics. By 23 October King Louis himself had arrived in the city in order to attend a celebratory mass in the Cathedral. It was around this date that Konigsmark was granted a private audience with the French King.[13] This meeting underlines just how close Konigsmark was to the key source of Catholic power in Europe and it begs the question of just what it was he was talking to Louis about, since only a few weeks later he was back in England and organising Thynn's demise. It also makes one wonder about the source of the 1,500 gold coins that were in Konigsmark's carriage when the ruffians, supposedly hired by Thynn, attacked him. It was certainly an awful lot of cash to be casually carrying around in a coach, and given that he had just met up with Louis, there has to be a strong possibility that the money had come from the coffers of the French state. This possibility is further strengthened by evidence that this was not the only occasion when the names of Karl Konigsmark and Louis were linked by gold. In January 1686, a few years after the murder, Louis awarded Konigsmark a pension of 2,000 ecus for services rendered.[14]

While the gutter press wars were raging in a fiercely partisan and personal way about the larger implications of Thynn's death and who was really to blame, the public at large were not quite sure what to make of any of it. What was growing more and more obvious, however, was that Lady Bette's reputation was severely damaged. On 18 February the Earl of Longford wrote to the Duke of Ormonde at length on the subject. He sounded an ominous warning: 'The discourse of the town is with great reflection upon my Lady Ogle.'[15] There was a growing section of society that regarded her as at best an adulteress and at worst an instigator of homicide.

Seventeenth-century waterman with boat full of passengers

34

THE HOUSE OF DEREK RAYNES
AT ROTHERHITHE

'Tis their way to be violent in all their motions. They swear violently, whore violently, drink punch violently, spend their money
when they have it violently . . . in short they are violent fellows,
and ought to be encourag'd to go to sea, for Old Harry can't
govern them on shoar.

– Daniel Defoe on the character of the seaman[1]

At about eight o'clock on the Sunday evening, the day of the
murder, a maid from a nearby house came bursting into the
lodging house where Konigsmark was staying. She was breath-
less with the sensational news that Mr Thynn had just been murdered in
his coach, and that the assassins who had perpetrated the wicked crime
had that very minute escaped up the Haymarket. She told her story to the
serving boy Francis Watts and then returned to her own household.[2]

At around 8.45 p.m. Watts observed Captain Vratz enter Konigsmark's lodgings in a great hurry. The Captain ran up the stairs and immediately closeted himself with the Count in the Count's room. When Konigsmark was later questioned in court as to the reason for Vratz's appearance that evening, within an hour of the murder, all he could reply was that he 'came to give him a visit'.[3] The boy Watts remained below stairs for the rest of that evening in what he described as the 'shop'. It seems that some kind of trade must have been carried on from the lower rooms. At about 9.30 p.m. he went off duty. Some time after 10 p.m. Hanson called on the Count. When questioned during the trial as to what he was doing there at such a time of night, Hanson explained that there was nothing at all unusual in his presence there; he always called round on a Sunday. He confirmed that Vratz was still in the Count's company. He also confirmed that there was some discussion among them about Thynn's murder. Hanson claimed he had already heard about it from the ambassador of Savoy. During the trial, Hanson was closely pressed as to what questions Konigsmark had asked him about the murder. All Hanson would divulge was that: 'the Count asked me what the people said; so I told him what I heard at Whitehall'.[4] Vratz had been with Konigsmark for over an hour at that point. It is inconceivable that Vratz had not told Konigsmark exactly what had occurred. What they both needed to know was how close the authorities were to establishing the identity of the murderers. According to Hanson, they spent the evening discussing some drawings that Konigsmark had been working on for military fortifications. Hanson was the first to leave, retiring to his own house. It is not stated at what time Vratz left Konigsmark's lodgings. He must have done so at some point, however, since he was arrested later that same night at Dr Harder's in Leicester Fields.

Monday morning was dark and misty. Street vendors were just blurred grey outlines, disembodied voices crying their ghostly wares. At around 6.30 a.m. there was a sudden excited burst of shouting outside Konigsmark's window. The boy Watts was already back on duty in his cold and dank basement quarters. He worked long hours for his sixpence a day. When he went upstairs he was surprised to find that Konigsmark was already up and dressed. He asked the boy what all the hubbub and bustle in the street had been about. Watts, who kept his ear well to the ground, explained that some men had just been arrested for Thynn's murder. Konigsmark then asked what kind of man Thynn had been. The boy answered: 'a man of great estate and well beloved.'[5] He then added that the Duke of Monmouth 'was in the coach but a little before, and if he had not gone out he would have been killed too'. Konigsmark made no further comment.

On the stairs Watts passed a stranger going up whom he had not set eyes on before. It turned out that this was Markham the tailor, one of Vratz's servants. He had come directly from Hanson's house and had been sent to inform Konigsmark that the Duke of Monmouth with several other noblemen had already called on Hanson and had been asking questions. Clearly Thynn's supporters were closing in. Konigsmark decided there and then on immediate flight. He ordered that his two portmanteaux should be fetched down from his room and placed in the first available cab. Watts's father carried them out of the house. The cab was ordered to go to Windsor and some trouble was taken to let both the father and son overhear this command. Konigsmark made quite a pantomime of it. But before he had gone very far he changed to another cab and ordered it to go straight to Rotherhithe, which was in the opposite direction to Windsor. The boy Watts remembered that Konigsmark had been wearing a black periwig and a light-coloured suit with gold buttons.

Borosky's old wheel-lock gun was afterwards found in Konigsmark's rooms. When Konigsmark was later questioned as to why he chose to flee he said 'he did to escape the fury of the rabble, who he thought would have torn him in pieces'.[6] Asked why, if he knew himself to be innocent of the murder, he did not put himself under the protection of the King, he had no answer.

That Monday afternoon, 13 February, Konigsmark turned up in Rotherhithe, a low-lying, pestilential stretch of land to the south of the river. It was an area that had been home to countless generations of sailors of every nationality. In its stinking dockyards, the inhabitants built ships, repaired ships, and then broke them up again when they became too crank and rotten to be of any further use. Konigsmark went straight to the house of a Swedish sailor called Derek Raynes. He can't have happened upon Raynes by chance. There is some suggestion that Konigsmark and Vratz had come over from Holland in Raynes's sloop and that he had been ordered to wait there until they returned. Konigsmark remained in Raynes's house from Monday through to Thursday morning, pacing up and down, not daring to show his face. There would have been little point anyway in venturing outside. The wind blew constantly from the east or the north-east making it impossible to sail out of the Thames. The weather was cold and overcast. The murky waters of the river were wreathed with pale grey mist.

Raynes was evasive and unhelpful during his cross-examination. He tried to give the impression that Konigsmark was unknown to him, but his evidence was unconvincing. He admitted to having supplied a 'stranger' with a coat, stockings and shoes for which he apparently received no payment. He also claimed that it was his understanding that these clothes were not for the purpose of disguise but because the 'stranger' was concerned he would not be warm enough on the water. The 'stranger' wanted to get to Gravesend. Later on during his examination Raynes stated that, 'as soon as I came to know he was the man [Konigsmark], I told him he should not stay in my house'.[7] But even then he did not simply throw him out. Instead he introduced him to a man called Chappel. Chappel described himself as a 'sculler', which is to say a man who rows with two oars.

By this time Konigsmark had a story prepared. He introduced himself to Chappel as an apprentice who had worked for a jeweller. 'A fellow 'prentice had fraudulently conveyed from his master a great many jewels, and other things, to several thousand pounds value; and though he was innocent, yet being the elder 'prentice, he sadly dreaded imprisonment for his partner's fault.'[8] Chappel was to be paid five shillings for every twelve hours of service. They still did not, however, go straight to Gravesend. The first day they went only so far as Deptford, the next to Greenwich, then to Greenhithe, and only on the Sunday evening did they arrive at their destination. The probable explanation for such dilatory progress is that Konigsmark wanted to arrive at Gravesend only shortly before the Swedish ship *The Hope* was due to depart. Konigsmark had at some point during the previous week made a prior arrangement to go as a passenger on this ship, but he did not want to be on board any longer than was strictly necessary before it sailed, for fear of being betrayed by one of the crew.

Meanwhile, the *London Gazette* published an offer of £200 for information that might lead to Konigsmark's arrest. Mr Thynn's heir, Sir Thomas Thynn, made a yet higher offer of £500.[9] This was a significant fortune and it probably did the trick. Not long afterwards the Duke of Monmouth received some useful information from a neighbour of Derek Raynes, who had had his suspicions aroused. According to the *True Protestant Mercury* of 21 February, Raynes's wife had been wary of the 'stranger' all along, not understanding why her husband was treating a man so poorly dressed with such respect. She had mentioned her doubts to her neighbour. It does not appear that she was actually prepared to betray Konigsmark's whereabouts to the authorities herself. It seems probable that she had been intimidated into silence by her husband and did not want to go against his will. The neighbour on the other hand was quite prepared to go straight to the Duke of Monmouth.

Gravesend in 1662 by John Moore

THE RED LYON AT GRAVESEND

A degradation to his honour and quality.

– Count Königsmark's response, on being sentenced to spend the night in Newgate
Gaol rather than the Tower, *Impartial Protestant Mercury*, 23 February 1682[1]

As soon as Derek Raynes's neighbour, another waterman by trade, informed the Duke of Monmouth about the mysterious stranger who had turned up in Rotherhithe a couple of days after the murder, the Duke dispatched a Mr Gibbons to investigate. Gibbons was described as being 'a valiant gentleman belonging to his Grace',[2] more usually employed as one of his footmen than as a detective. He was accompanied by a Mr Kid, Thynn's huntsman, so a man who was used to stalking and tracking. These two loyal servants went together with the neighbour to see what they could find out and hopefully to effect an arrest.

It was by now the afternoon of Saturday 18 February. The weather continued misty but it had become a little warmer and the wind had gradually shifted towards the south-west.[3] The larger sailing ships could now begin to edge their way towards the estuary. There was clearly no time to be lost, but Kid and Gibbons immediately ran into a procedural difficulty. To make an arrest they would need a warrant from a Justice of the Peace. They went first to Reresby's house but he wasn't at home. They then went to Bridgeman's, but he wasn't at home either. They finally got their warrant from the Recorder and promptly took a boat for Rotherhithe to interview the Rayneses.[4]

Neither Derek Raynes nor his wife was anywhere to be found, but fortunately for Kid and Gibbons, the wife's sister was in their house and she proved to be very obliging. It seems probable that an offer of a share of the bounty money must have helped to secure her cooperation. She revealed that Mr and Mrs Raynes had gone to Greenwich, by boat of course, for these were all water people. They were taking some clothing for the stranger who had recently been lodging with them, including a grey suit. Quite why Konigsmark hadn't taken these clothes along with him in the first place, or why they were considered so necessary, is unclear.

Kid and Gibbons decided to take the sister along with them and it was agreed between the three of them that she would call out the couple's names, 'Moll' and 'Derek', so as not to alarm them. The pursuers were obviously worried that if the Rayneses heard a stranger's voice they wouldn't declare their whereabouts, but remain concealed below hatches where they would be impossible to discover. The subterfuge worked, but Derek Raynes proved uncommunicative. He claimed to have no knowledge of Konigsmark's present whereabouts. He wouldn't even admit to knowing the identity of his recent lodger. At this point the neighbour who had alerted Monmouth in the first place had a word with Derek Raynes in private. Once again it is probable that the reward money was mentioned, because Raynes suddenly remembered that his one-time lodger was heading for a Swedish ship called *The Hope*, currently moored at Gravesend and due to depart the river on the flood tide Monday morning.

Kid and Gibbons went straight to the Red Lyon at Gravesend. Kid positioned himself at the back stairs of the inn, while Gibbons went to the front, where there was a landing place. The two men were very aware that there were thirteen or fourteen Swedish sailors drinking inside the Red Lyon and if it came to a confrontation they might well join in on the side of their compatriot, in which case the two Monmouth men would be completely overwhelmed. For this reason, it was decided to try and apprehend Konigsmark as soon as he set foot on land and before he had the chance to communicate with the rest of the ship's crew.

Some time between eight and nine o'clock that night, by which time it was already pitch-dark, a man came on shore. Gibbons approached him and knocked into him to try to establish his identity. 'Gave him a little kind of justle ... to see whether he had not a black coat under his campaign [coat].'[5] It appears that Konigsmark was no longer wearing the light-coloured suit that the boy Watts had observed him in when leaving the St Martin's Lane lodgings. Perhaps this was the explanation for Mr and Mrs Raynes carrying further supplies of clothing down the river, in which case they must have told Gibbons and Kid that Konigsmark was now wearing a black suit.

Whether the jostling alarmed Konigsmark isn't clear, but he turned away from Gibbons and walked back towards the water's edge. He began to remonstrate with the watermen who had just brought him ashore, asking why they were taking so long to stow their boat. It seemed he wanted them to accompany him past this threatening stranger who had just bumped into him. Undeterred, Gibbons waited until Konigsmark approached a second time and then seized his man tightly by the arms. Konigsmark shouted out, thinking he was being robbed. Gibbons announced that he was there as the King's messenger and had come to arrest Karl Konigsmark. At this mention of his name the Count apparently 'gave a little start'.[6] His sword got in a tangle and dropped between his legs, and at the same time his periwig fell off his head. In a situation of one-to-one combat with the doughty Mr Gibbons, the hero of the Madrid bullring and the sea battle against the Turks seems suddenly to have been somewhat physically inept. But the story was reported from Gibbons's point of view and he had no reason to be sympathetic to Konigsmark.

At this point Kid showed up and the two of them manhandled Konigsmark away from the tavern. The Swedish sailors made no attempt to get involved on Konigsmark's behalf. News of the arrest, however, spread rapidly through the small and close-knit seafaring community, and within minutes a crowd had gathered. The people 'were very rude and very rugged',[7] in Gibbons's blunt words. Kid and Gibbons, having made their arrest with impressive competence, now found themselves having to protect their prisoner from a mob seemingly intent on tearing him apart. They managed, with some difficulty, to get Konigsmark safely to the Mayor's house, where he was searched. There, they found in the Count's pockets seven to eight pounds in money and 'two pieces of Polonian Sassages'.[8]

Konigsmark's response to being captured was neither surly nor aggressive. He opted instead for charm. 'With the mayor he was very ceremonious and said he was glad he had fallen into the hands of gentlemen.'[9] After he had been interviewed, he was returned to the Red Lyon, where he spent the night under guard. He distributed some drink money among the soldiery. The following morning he tried to ingratiate himself with Gibbons with a similar display of genial good manners, asking for his name and telling him 'he would come to give me thanks for my civility after his trouble was over'.[10] But Gibbons was not to be won over. In response to Konigsmark's ingratiating overtures he replied bluntly that a good friend of his had been killed and 'a more particular friend and master'[11] had been nearly killed. Konigsmark's reply is very revealing. He says to Gibbons: 'I don't think they would have done any harm to the Duke of Monmouth.'[12] This begs the question as to quite how Konigsmark knew what the assassins' intentions were in respect of Monmouth. Konigsmark was to be closely questioned on this point at his trial. His only explanation was that he overheard the general opinion of the people saying among themselves that the murderers would not attack the coach until Monmouth had left it. But this was not the general opinion of the people. Quite the opposite. Most ordinary people believed that Monmouth had been the prime target.

Gibbons showed himself to be a subtle inquisitor as well as a tough and determined vigilante. Konigsmark was anxious to know what people were saying about him, and in particular what Vratz, Borosky and Stern might have said. Gibbons told him 'that the Captain [Vratz] had made a confession',[13] even though Gibbons knew very well that this was not the case. Konigsmark responded dismissively: 'I do not believe the Captain would confess anything.' He was clearly very confident of Vratz's loyalty, but why? Was it simply a matter of soldierly bonding or was it because he knew Vratz would stay silent out of self-interest? Vratz's steadfast refusal to incriminate his master has been interpreted as gallantry on his part, but there was actually very little in it for Vratz to incriminate Konigsmark. It would just have meant that the two of them would hang. If on the other hand Konigsmark got off, then there was always the chance he might be able to wangle a pardon for Vratz as well.

Towards midnight that same Sunday, just as the flood tide was starting, a file of heavily armed guards arrived to escort Konigsmark back to Whitehall. Kid went with him in the boat. There wasn't room for Gibbons. Once again Konigsmark's mind runs upon what the other arrested men had been saying about his own role in the killing. When Kid told him that Borosky had confessed everything and 'wept mightily' Konigsmark lost some of his sangfroid and was visibly upset. 'With that, my Lord seemed very much concerned, and took up his clothes and bit them, and sat awhile up, but was very much discomposed, and then desired to lie down.'[14] Konigsmark might be confident of Vratz's loyalty but he certainly wasn't sure of Borosky's.

It was nearly dawn when the fiery beacons atop the tallest ramparts of the Tower of London came into view. Soon after the Tower came that treacherous section of the river that flowed under London Bridge, where many small boats had been tipped over in the swirling currents and come to grief. A half-moon could be glimpsed between the fast-moving clouds. The wind was against them but the tide was still in their favour, although shortly it would begin to turn. Konigsmark started to question Kid somewhat anxiously about how comfortable the lodgings were in Newgate. He also began muttering about how the whole affair was a 'stain upon his honour' but he would be able to wipe it clean 'with one good action in the wars'.[15] This reference to 'the stain upon his honour' was something the prosecuting counsel were to return to. They suggested it was tantamount to a confession of guilt.

The boat finally drew up at Whitehall Steps. It was the best part of ten miles from Gravesend. The rowers steadied their craft by flattening their oars and the helm was secured to a post. It was just beginning to get light. The spires of the abbey were silhouetted in the distance against a pale sky. There were two files of the King's musqueteers lined up on the quayside to escort Konigsmark to his cell. The authorities were taking no chances. Some of the guards carried lighted flambeaux. The reflections created jagged patterns where the water lapped the oozy mud. News of the arrest had travelled widely and there was already an enormous crowd gathered at the water's edge, all eager to get a glimpse of the murderer. The press was so great that the gates to Scotland Yard had been shut, 'to prevent the great recourse of the Mobile which ran thither upon hearing of the news'.[16]

On his arrival at Whitehall, Konigsmark was kept under guard in the lodgings of Secretary Jenkins until the afternoon. He was then examined by the King and the Privy Council, Sir John Reresby being among those present. By this time Konigsmark appeared to have recovered his self-possession. Sir John, at any rate, was suitably impressed. 'He appeared before the King with all the assurance imaginable, was a fine gentleman of his person, his hair was the longest for a mans I ever see, for it came below his wast.'[17] Reresby remarks that this initial examination was 'very superficial', but Konigsmark was later taken before Lord Chief Justice Pemberton and Bridgeman the Attorney General, with Reresby again being present. They examined him until eleven o'clock that night. Pemberton was to be the presiding judge at the trial and it seems somewhat extraordinary that he should have been permitted a lengthy interview with the prisoner beforehand. Konigsmark made no admission of possessing prior knowledge of the murder.

At the conclusion of his examination Konigsmark was committed to Newgate Gaol. He immediately complained about being sent to Newgate, considering it beneath his dignity – 'the reproach of being sent to so infamous a place was worse to him than death.'[18] He asked to be transferred to the Tower. His request was refused. He was told 'it was the proper place for that crime he was suspected to be guilty of'. Still unhappy, 'he begged leave ... to write to the King'. Again he was refused; 'it was then too late to disturb his Majesty, it being then past eleven o'clock'.[19]

He was kept in the Press Yard in the house of Captain Richardson, the prison governor. A succession of foreign ambassadors visited him there, by far the most important among them being the ambassador for France. It was generally expected that these foreign dignitaries would 'intercede with his Majestie for his pardon'.[20] When Reresby spoke with the King on the evening of Tuesday, 21 February, seven days before the trial took place, he found the King 'was willing Count Konigsmarke might come off'.[21]

Newgate Prison as it was in 1681

36

NEWGATE

**It is a most fearful sad, deplorable place, hell itself in compar-
ison can not be such a place, there is neither Bench, Stool, nor
Stick for any person there, they lie like swine upon the ground,
one upon another howling and roaring, it was more terrible to
me than this death.**

– Colonel Turner before his execution in 1663 requesting
that conditions in Newgate should be improved[1]

B y the time of Konigsmark's arrest, Vratz, Stern and Borosky had
already been languishing in Newgate for the best part of a week.
It was a forbidding and dreary edifice built from bleak grey stone.
As new prisoners the three men had been taken first into the Keeper's
Lodge, which was situated on the opposite side of the road to the main
bulk of the prison. It was here that the initial business was done between
the new inmate and the Governor. The prison was run as a franchise and
the Governor was free to extort as much profit from his 'customers' as he

could. Vratz had cash about him and Stern, even if he was short on ready money, probably still had some possessions worthy of pawning. Both men were able to secure superior accommodation in the Press Yard, which was technically an extension of the Governor's own quarters. Borosky on the other hand was almost certainly less fortunate. He probably ended up in the same level of cell as Letitia Wiggington of Ratcliff, who had been inside just a few months earlier and had complained bitterly that she had nothing 'but bread and water ... and my flesh black and blue from lying upon the boards for want of a bed'.[2] Once inside Newgate, money could buy you most comforts, from superior food to a fire in the hearth. William Robinson, who became Governor in 1700, even charged male prisoners sixpence for admittance to the female quarters for the night.

After the booking-in process had been completed, the prisoner was escorted across the road by means of a footbridge over which was formed a closed arch, so that in appearance it resembled the Bridge of Sighs, and from which there could be no escape by jumping. There were now various rituals that it was as well for the newcomer to comply with, the most important being the custom of buying existing inmates a round of liquor. This was called paying 'chummye' or 'shine'. If a man refused, he was dragged off by the prison bullies to a place topically nicknamed 'Tangiers', where he was stripped of his clothes and beaten.

Defoe, who was personally familiar with the inside of Newgate, provides the best description of the novitiate's experience in the words of his heroine Moll Flanders:

> 'Tis impossible for me to describe the terror of my mind, when I was first brought in, and when I look'd round upon all the horrors of that dismal place: I look'd on myself as lost, and that I had nothing to think of, but of going out of the World, and that with the utmost Infamy; the hellish noise, the Roaring, Swearing and Clamour, the Stench and Nastiness, and all the dreadful croud of Afflicting things that I saw there; joyn'd together to make the Place seem an Emblem of Hell itself, and a kind of an Entrance to it ... These things pour'd themselves in upon my Thoughts in a confus'd manner, and left me overwhelm'd with Melancholy and Despair.[3]

During the first few days of his confinement, between committal and trial, the new inmate was interviewed privately by the Prison Ordinary or Chaplain. The purpose of the interview was to give the prisoner the opportunity for a full and complete confession of the crime, including details of any accomplices. Again it is Moll Flanders who provides the best description of the average prison chaplain:

> The Ordinary of Newgate came to me, and talk'd a little in his way, but all his divinity run upon Confessing my Crime, as he call'd it, (tho' he knew not what I was in for) making a full Discovery, and the like, without which he told me God would never forgive me; and he said so little to the purpose, that I had no manner of consolation from him; and then to observe the poor Creature preaching Confession and Repentance to me in the Morning, and find him drunk with Brandy and Spirits by Noon; this had something in it so shocking, that I began to Nauseate . . .⁴

The Ordinary at Newgate, when Vratz and his companions walked through the door, was Samuel Smith. He may well have been anticipating a lucrative commission, for the assassins had rapidly achieved huge notoriety. If he was fortunate enough to be able to extract a confession and then publish it, he would be guaranteed an instant best-seller. Unluckily for Smith, Thynn's relations had far grander ideas. They did not want any old prison chaplain to be entrusted with this most delicate of tasks. They wanted the best man in the kingdom for the job, and there was little doubt about who that man was. It was Gilbert Burnet.

Burnet was a fleshy-faced pugnacious Scot with a protruding lower jaw and fiercely intelligent eyes. He was already a celebrated theologian and historian, having recently published the first two parts of his famous *History of the Reformation*. He was also a charismatic and beguiling preacher. His biggest coup to date in the eyes of the general public was persuading that notoriously decadent atheist, the Earl of Rochester, to convert on his deathbed. Burnet's published account had been a runaway success. The thirteen-year-old Lady Bette had bought two copies, reading it along with her young husband, Henry Ogle, during that idyllic and chaste year they spent together at Petworth before all her troubles began. Little can she have imagined at the time that she would very shortly be the unwilling focus of attention in another Burnet blockbuster.

The True Confession genre for criminals and reprobates was highly popular in the late seventeenth century. Burnet, with his love of gossip and keen eye for self-promotion, must have seen in the Thynn murderers a further chance for enhancing his already considerable reputation as the divine with almost miraculous powers of persuasion. His only small difficulty was that although he was fluent in Latin, Greek, Hebrew, French and Dutch, his High German was rather on the weak side. It was for this reason that he enlisted the help of Dr Horneck, a German-born proselytising minister attached to the Savoy Hospital, a large sanatorium originally intended for the succour of the sick and poor, but which had largely fallen into disuse. It stood where the Savoy Hotel now stands. Horneck also had a reputation for delivering powerful hell-fire sermons that were highly effective in inducing sinners to repent of their evil ways. He was later to become a founding member of the Society for the Reformation of Manners, a rather sinister organisation aimed at the suppression of brothels, prostitutes and general lewdness. They employed a network of informers to assist them in stamping out such iniquities, but the focus, as always, was on the whores rather than their clients.

Burnet and Horneck's first visit to Newgate was not a success. They went on Thursday, 16 February. There was a cold wind from the east which howled through the iron bars of the prison and mingled with the shrieks and caterwaulings of the inmates to create a dreary cacophony. Vratz was uncommunicative. 'He was unwilling to enter into much discourse with us,' as Burnet put it. He simply stuck to his original line that he had only ever intended, 'to fight with Mr Thynn' and Borosky had 'mistook his orders when he shot him'.[5] Stern was equally unhelpful. He admitted to being present at the shooting but claimed that he had never had any intention to murder anybody. Borosky was more penitent. He 'expressed great sorrow for what he had done'.[6] He also claimed that he had only acted under orders from Vratz. But Borosky's testimony, so far as Burnet was concerned, was the least interesting of the three. Borosky had little choice but to admit he had carried out the shooting.

Burnet returned to the prison most probably on the following Monday after Stern had made a full statement to Reresby and Bridgeman and shortly before Konigsmark was also committed to Newgate. He found Stern to be a completely changed man: 'wonderfully touched'[7] was Burnet's term. Stern was now more than ready to confess. Indeed, he wouldn't stop talking. He told Burnet that 'he hated himself so much that he was glad to do everything that was lawful'. He wanted to be made a public example, to help others avoid the dangers of sin. He had begun furiously reading his favourite book, *Dilheren, His Way to Happiness*,[8] and when he wasn't reading he was writing his life story. He slept only a few hours a night, towards dawn. He confided to Burnet that 'if his writing should become public in Germany or in other places where he had been, he was confident that many might read it, who would know for what reason he had writ many passages in it ... and would understand his meaning'.[9] Stern was suddenly a man with a mission. He was enthralled with the idea of posthumous fame.

Burnet listened, probed and made careful notes. They spoke together in French which, Burnet remarked, Stern had a good command of. Stern admitted to having been a Papist but now 'detested the idolatry he saw in it'.[10] He admitted to having made the mistake of believing that 'if a man was honest and good he might be saved in any religion'. He now realised that 'Popery [was] but as a contrivance of priests for governing the world'.[11]

Stern described to Burnet his mental state on the day of the murder as being like a man acting in a state of trance – 'though he was not drunk, yet he was like one drunk'.[12] Even the gunshot had not awakened Stern from his stupor. He did not fully regain his wits, he said, until the second day of his imprisonment.

Stern then confided to Burnet that he had argued with Vratz about the best weapon to be used for killing Thynn. He had preferred a pistol but Vratz had insisted on a musquetoon. When Stern enquired why, Vratz had answered him it was because the Count's private counsellors had decided upon it. Vratz had then named to Stern the three men who composed that counsel, and Stern now passed on these names to Burnet.

Later that same week, in a further interview, Stern retracted these names, because he was concerned that when Vratz had mentioned these men he had only done so to deceive him and that he might be inadvertently libelling them. Burnet regarded this as evidence of Stern's new scrupulousness of conscience.[13] It seems unlikely, however, at this point, when the conspirators were still anticipating a successful outcome to their plot, that Vratz would have felt any need to lie.

Burnet was delighted with his progress. He was almost as enthralled with his new convert as Stern was with his confessor. He promised the Lieutenant that he would see to it that his confession was published after his death, for there was never any question of Stern being pardoned. Vratz meanwhile continued to be laconic and unbending. He was left mainly to Horneck because he claimed to understand only High German.

In the relationship between Burnet and Stern there is an interesting parallel with the experience of Moll Flanders, who also discovered the comfort of confession not from talking 'to the Ordinary of the Place', but to a minister from outside the gaol:

[his] honest friendly way of treating me, unlock'd all the sluces of my Passions: He broke into my very Soul by it; and I unravell'd all the Wickedness of my life to him: In a word I gave him an Abridgement of this whole History; I gave him the picture of my Conduct for 50 years in Miniature. I hid nothing from him, and he in return exhorted me to a sincere Repentance ...[14]

Defoe clearly subscribed to the theory current at the time that the truth would necessarily reveal itself however abhorrent it might be:

This necessity of nature is a thing which Works sometimes with such Vehemence, in the minds of those who are guilty of any atrocious villainy; such as secret murther in particular, that they have been oblig'd to Discover it, tho the Consequence would necessarily be their own destruction.[15]

By the day of the trial, however, Vratz had still not succumbed. On the subject of Konigsmark's involvement he remained stubbornly silent, maintaining that he had all along acted entirely on his own initiative.

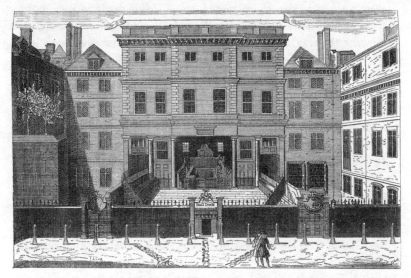

The Sessions House as it was in 1681

37 ⌒

THE SESSIONS HOUSE I

... the Count, in the opinion of all mankind, at that time and since, was the most guilty man; yet the care taken to punish the less guilty, as Stern and Borosky, was in order to let the most guilty escape, for I think both Stern and Borosky might and would have been good witnesses against the Count, if the Court would have permitted it ...

– Remarks upon the Trial of Count Konigsmark
by Sir John Hawes, 1689[1]

On the morning of Tuesday, 28 February, the four prisoners were brought in chains from their prison cells into the Sessions House, situated in Old Bailey Street, immediately adjacent to Newgate. The original courtroom had burnt to the ground in the Great Fire but had quickly been rebuilt. It was now a three-storey stone building with sash windows to the upper two floors. On the ground floor, where the court sat, there were galleries for spectators. The front of the ground floor was open to the air, which was considered to be a healthier option than an enclosed room. The judges and barristers had no wish to breathe the fetid and contaminated stench that the prisoners inevitably exuded after a period of confinement in Newgate's cells. One in four prisoners died of typhus before being sentenced. The open-sided structure also enabled a crowd to gather outside, if there was insufficient seating in the galleries to accommodate everyone who wished to be present. In many respects the trial process was more like street theatre than a court of law.[2]

It was a filthy morning, heavy rain pushing in from the west. This did not stop enormous numbers from gathering long before the opening of the proceedings. The Thynn murder had been the talk of the town for weeks. Now everyone wanted to lay eyes on the monsters or heroes that had perpetrated such a cold-blooded and daring crime. Thynn's relations and Whig friends were well represented among the onlookers. They occupied places of honour on the raised benches. But there were a good number of Tories there as well.

The accused were brought in one by one, Captain Vratz swaggering and smiling, playing to the gallery as always, Lieutenant Stern, head bowed and making a great show of penitence, Borosky, tall, confused and uncomprehending, 'dull witted'[3] according to the acerbic Sir Nathaniel Johnson. Johnson was a fervent Royalist, devoted to the cause of James, Duke of York, who rewarded him well when he came to the throne a few years later. He attended the trial supposedly as an interpreter, but behaved throughout as if he were Count Konigsmark's personal defence lawyer, even though counsel for the defence were not permitted at felony trials at this time, the accused being required to answer for themselves.

Count Konigsmark was the last to be led into the dock. In the grey light of morning he did not appear to be quite the glamorous Adonis that rumour had promised. He was somewhat short of stature, and his complexion was pale and pockmarked, but at least his hair did not disappoint.

The prisoners were secured in what was called the bail dock, a kind of holding pen at the back of the courtroom. Spikes on the irons attached to their legs prevented any possibility of escape. From here they could be fed into the interrogatory dock as and when required. Proceedings started solemnly enough. The Clerk of the Court requested all four men to hold up their hands as their names were read out. Borosky was described as a labourer, Stern and Vratz were called gentlemen and Konigsmark was dignified by the term esquire.

Next came the business of swearing in the necessary interpreters. Nathaniel Johnson and a Mr Craven were already present in that capacity, but Konigsmark was not satisfied. At first he wanted two or three more, and then he wanted three or four more, 'to be sure that no mistake is made'.[4] A Mr Vanbaring was called for by the Count but he failed to appear. Later a Mr Vandore did make an entry. Whether there was some confusion over names or whether the two men were different entities is not clear. Eventually it was agreed that Konigsmark could speak in High German and Vandore and Johnson would translate. A member of the Thynn family shouted from the gallery that Konigsmark spoke perfectly good English and should make his statements in a tongue that could be comprehended by all present, but this suggestion was ignored. It is odd, however, that Konigsmark wasn't at least made to speak in French, a language he was fluent in, and which was generally understood by the English upper classes at this time.

Having got his way over the business of interpreters, Konigsmark then requested that he should be tried separately from the three principal felons, and that he be given a further two or three days to prepare his case more thoroughly. Pemberton refused to allow this, but agreed that when appropriate it would be made clear to the jury that his situation was distinct from that of the other three defendants. Konigsmark was not satisfied with this concession and continued to insist on being tried separately, until Justice North, another of the three presiding judges, the third being Baron William Montagu, finally lost patience, and turned to Nathaniel Johnson and desired that he would explain. 'Look you, pray will you tell him, when the trial is once begun, the jury can neither eat nor drink til they have given their verdict. That is the law, and we can not change the law; therefore we can not allow him what he desires. He knows what he is accused of and has known it a good while, and has had time to prepare himself.'[5]

If the business of agreeing interpreters and courtroom schedules was problematic, the swearing in of a jury rapidly turned the whole legal process into a farce. It had already been agreed, as a concession to the foreign nationality of the defendants, that half the jury should be composed of Englishmen and the other half of men from overseas. Konigsmark then upped the stakes by demanding, through Johnson, that no Poles, Papists or Danes should be included, on the basis that his father had fought against all three groupings. Extraordinarily, Pemberton was prepared to indulge Konigsmark's wishes in this respect, but misheard the precise nature of his request. He instructed the under sheriff who was responsible for the composition of the jury to call only French and no Dutch. It was pointed out a second time that it was the Danes not the Dutch whose towns had been burnt by Konigsmark's father. Then Konigsmark took exception to anyone with a name that might suggest that they were of Walloon origins, because the Walloons 'have always been against the Swedes'.[6] Even with the English jurors he proved himself very picky. He used his right of peremptory challenge against Henry Herbert and he wasn't too sure about Richard Paget, asking to take a closer look at him. Paget passed inspection and was finally allowed to be sworn. And so it went on with one juror after another.

When the jurors had finally been agreed upon, the formal indictment was read out:

> You the said Charles George Borosky, alias Boratzi, Christopher Vratz and John Stern, the prisoners at the bar . . . feloniously and voluntarily, and of your malice aforethought, did make an assault upon Thomas Thynn . . . And you Karl John Konigsmark, the other prisoner at the bar, stand indicted for that you, before the murder and felony aforesaid, did, of your malice aforethought, move, invite, counsel, persuade, and procure the said Borosky, Vratz and Stern to do that murder . . .[7]

From the outset of the trial it was fairly evident to everyone that Vratz, Borosky and Stern were all going to be condemned. All three had admitted to being present at the scene of the murder and Borosky had admitted to firing the gun. Although Vratz claimed that Borosky had gone beyond his orders, and Borosky and Stern claimed they had merely done what had been commanded of them, it was obvious that these arguments would not be sufficient to get them off the charge that they were facing. It was Konigsmark who was the real focus of everyone's attention.

It is significant that in his opening address Sir Francis Wythens, one of the counsel for the prosecution, focused primarily on Konigsmark's role in the murder. He summed up the main issue before the court succinctly enough:

> These persons [Vratz, Borosky and Stern] not having any appearance or any reason whatsoever for any particular quarrel with Mr Thynn, but the Count having some disgust to him, upon terms that the witnesses will tell you by

and by, and they being related to the Count, we must leave it to you to judge whether these gentlemen did it [the murder] singly and purely upon their own heads, or whether they were set upon it by the Count.[8]

Sir Francis first set about proving to the court that the three 'principals', as they were called, were indeed the same three men who had been present at the murder. For this purpose, William Cole, the link boy who had carried a flambeau before the coach, and Ellers, Thynn's coachman, were the first witnesses called. But although they both confirmed that three men had been involved, neither of them could positively identify the culprits. This was not an insuperable problem. Sir Francis had the written statements of the two justices Bridgeman and Reresby, which confirmed that all three men had confessed to being present at the scene of the crime. Sir Francis prepared to read the magistrates' statements, but before he could get a word out Lord Chief Justice Pemberton interrupted, suggesting the prosecution should first provide some evidence of Thynn's wounds. So Dr Hobbs, who had attended Thynn on the evening he was shot, was called instead.

Dr Hobbs testified that he had found Thynn 'shot with 4 bullets'.

Pemberton wasn't quite satisfied with this. He wanted to know whether the bullets were iron or lead.

Hobbs answered: 'two of them, the little ones, may be Iron, for one of them went through a thick bone, and yet there was no impression on it'.[9]

Pemberton then held up one of the bullets between his fingers. 'And this that has the impression. You think that that might be done against the bone?'

'Yes,' replied Hobbs.

'Was this left ragged on purpose to do the more mischief?' asked Pemberton.

Hobbs thought that it might have been.

'[And] this that is left at the end here. Would this be more mortal than another bullet, or harder to heal?'

'No, but as they take up a greater space in flying,' answered the obliging Dr Hobbs.

'Would not the raggedness hinder the healing?' insisted Pemberton.

And so their exchange went on. Lord Chief Justice Pemberton appeared to be morbidly fascinated by the forensic details of the damage done to Thynn's flesh by the entry of the four bullets. But it was all irrelevant.

The exact construction of the bullets and the nature of the injuries they caused had no bearing on the guilt or innocence of the various parties involved.

Eventually Justice Bridgeman was called. Bridgeman started to read his statement, which recorded the details of his interview with the three principal murderers shortly after their arrest. This statement was crucial because it was here that Stern and Borosky had both testified as to Konigsmark's involvement. But Pemberton immediately interrupted again. He told Bridgeman to limit himself to what he knew of the facts relating to Borosky only. Any reference to Konigsmark was ruled out of order: 'Speak only as to himself [Borosky]; for it is evidence only against himself,'[10] that he was allowed to communicate. In other words, because Borosky was also on trial for the murder of Thynn, he was only permitted to incriminate himself and nobody else.

The rules of evidence in murder trials at this time were highly rudimentary, but even so Pemberton's interpretation of them was suspect. The Judge, Sir John Hawes, commenting retrospectively on the Konigsmark trial in 1689 remarked:

> The Chief Justice was blameable that he did not ask the Lieutenant and Polander, what they had to say for themselves, which was always done before, and since, that time, and ought to be asked of every prisoner ... if they had been asked they would have said as they did before their Tryals to the Justices of the Peace, who committed them ... that Count Konigsmark put them upon doing what they did.

Hawes was of the opinion that 'a man may give evidence which accuses another of the same crime, whereof he is indited, if it doth not tend to acquit himself'.[11]

Sir Francis Winnington, the senior lawyer for the prosecution, was not at all happy that Stern's statement to the magistrates was not being allowed. He protested: 'My Lord, his confession is entire, and we can't separate it.'

But Pemberton was adamant: '... we must direct what is just and fitting. His evidence can charge nobody but himself, and that is the reason I would not have the examination read.'[12] This was to prove most problematic for the prosecution, for it meant that the two main witnesses against Konigsmark, namely Stern and Borosky, were not going to be allowed to provide any evidence against him, nor was anyone to be allowed to quote anything these two men might have said relating to Konigsmark.

Pemberton then wanted to hear Vratz's version of what had happened. Vratz claimed not to understand anything that was said to him in English, and so Craven was called to put the questions to him in French, a language that Vratz apparently now understood, although he had previously refused to converse with Burnet in French. Vratz stuck to his original story, namely that he had taken it upon himself to fight with Thynn, after Thynn had insulted his master, Count Konigsmark. He had only brought Borosky and Stern along with him in case it had turned into a general rencounter (scuffle) and he had trouble escaping. He reiterated once again that Borosky had fired his gun without his authorisation. When pressed upon the nature of the insult that Thynn had made, Vratz stated that Thynn had called his master a 'Hector'. He also admitted that this insult had been delivered eight months prior to the shooting and that he had never actually himself spoken to Thynn. It all sounded extremely weak.

Stern was the next to take the stand. The evidence he had previously given in his deposition to Sir John Reresby, namely that Vratz had offered him large sums of money if he could 'find a man that would kill Mr Thynn',[13] was disallowed and therefore had to be retracted. He admitted to being present at the shooting but claimed he was there simply as Vratz's second in a proposed duel. As for Konigsmark, he was not mentioned.

There then followed another tussle between one of the counsel for the prosecution, Sir Francis Winnington, and the judges North and Pemberton, over exactly what was and was not permissible evidence. Winnington wanted it stated in open court who it was that had assisted Stern in loading the gun.

Pemberton intervened: 'Why that is no evidence against anybody.'

'But my Lord,' said Winnington, 'it was delivered to the Polander charged, and we desire to know who loaded it.'[14]

Justice North now attempted to mediate with an absurd compromise proposal. 'That is no evidence; yet the question may be asked, and then the jury may be told it is no evidence.'[15]

Pemberton was quick to point out the problem with this tactic. 'But we must not let the jury be possessed by that which is not evidence.'

North ignored this advice from the senior judge and asked the interpreter Craven to put the question to Stern: 'Who helped him to load the gun?'

The answer came back: 'The Captain and I did it together.'

Pemberton let this pass, perhaps because it was obvious by now that all three men were heading for the gallows anyway.

The Bench

38

THE SESSIONS HOUSE II

Pemberton is as great a rogue as his predecessor.

– Calendar of State Papers Domestic[1]

It was already late afternoon before the court got round to what was the main interest of the day, the guilt or innocence of Count Konigsmark. The first witness called by the prosecution was Hanson. He testified that Konigsmark had returned into England a couple of weeks before the murder and when he first met him at the posting house he was in the company of Vratz. He related how Konigsmark had come incognito, calling himself Carlo Cusk. He confirmed that Konigsmark had lived very privately and that he had changed his lodgings frequently. When pressed on the nature of the business the Count had come on, Hanson said he was not told of it. Hanson admitted, however, to having seen Vratz in Konigsmark's lodgings shortly after the murder took place. Hanson also admitted that he had called on the Swedish ambassador to find out what Konigsmark's position would be concerning marriage to Lady Bette if he had already 'meddled' with Thynn. Finally, Hanson confirmed that it was Konigsmark who had sent for Borosky, and that on the latter's arrival in England he had been directed to Konigsmark's lodgings, where he had been equipped with a new sword and greatcoat and where he had spent the Saturday night immediately prior to the murder.[2]

All of this vital evidence was extracted from Hanson in English. This posed a problem because half the jury did not understand English. Pemberton suggested that Hanson should now repeat what he had just said, but this time in French. The prosecution immediately objected that this would allow Hanson to gloss over the crucial detail without anyone being able to keep a check. 'There is a great deal of difference when you examine a man with the hair, and where you examine him against the hair; where you find it difficult to make a man answer, you will pump him with questions and cross interrogate him, to sift out the truth,'[3] said Williams, one of the prosecuting lawyers, jumping to his feet.

Pemberton suggested that Williams in that case might like to examine him in French, but Williams knew 'none but pedlar's French', and requested the use of an interpreter. Pemberton was resistant but Lord Justice North finally persuaded his fellow judge to concede to the request on the grounds that, 'if there be two ways to take, 'tis best to give that which gives satisfaction to all persons'. So Hanson went through his evidence again, this time in French.

After Hanson, the next witness was Dr Frederick Harder, Konigsmark's physician. Harder admitted to accompanying Borosky from Konigsmark's lodgings to his own house in Leicester Fields. From Leicester Fields, Vratz's servant Berg had taken Borosky to meet with Vratz at the Three Sugar Loaves. At first Harder claimed that this had all taken place on the Saturday morning, but later he conceded he was in a muddle as to which day of the week it had happened. He also confirmed that Vratz had been present in Konigsmark's lodgings at nine o'clock on the Sunday evening, that is within an hour of the murder being committed.[4]

There was a moment of levity when Williams, during his cross-examination, started flirting with the young maid Anne Price, who had worked at the lodging house in the Haymarket where Konigsmark had first stopped. Lord Chief Justice Pemberton was not amused. 'We are now upon the life and death of a man; pray let us have those questions asked that are serious; not such light things as are permitted in ordinary cases.'[5] The serving boy Francis Watts, Derek Raynes and the sculler Richard Chappel were all called in their turn, together with Kid and Gibbons, to give evidence relating to Konigsmark's flight and subsequent capture. None of it made it look as if Konigsmark was an innocent man.

It was late in the day by the time Konigsmark finally took the stand. He made his answers through interpreters in a smooth and assured manner. He began by explaining that he had come into England to buy horses, with a view to sending them over to the Continent in connection with the siege of Strasbourg, about which there was much talk. Borosky had been brought over to help with the horses. Konigsmark's brother Philip was called on to confirm that a bill of exchange for a thousand pistoles had been sent into England for this purpose. Philip stood up and complied, although he also admitted that only one horse had actually been bought. It did not seem to occur to anyone to make the point that this money could equally well have been imported in order to pay the assassins for their work. As for the siege of Strasbourg, Konigsmark had known it was all over some time before he returned into England, but the court had no way of knowing this and Konigsmark did not choose to enlighten them.

Konigsmark was then pressed on the question of his conversation with Hanson regarding Hanson's visit to the ambassador. At this point the smooth-tongued Nathaniel Johnson took over answering the questions, supposedly in his capacity as translator, but in reality as an unappointed defence lawyer. According to Johnson, Konigsmark had no memory of any conversations with Hanson concerning enquiries of the Swedish ambassador. When questioned on the subject of the boy Watts's testimony about the Count asking him whether it was legal to ride in the streets on a Sunday, Johnson was scornful. Why would the Count ask 'a scullion boy ... when he himself over and over again has rid to Hyde Park on a Sunday, as many persons of quality do'.[6] Again, no one made the point that the question at issue was not riding in the Park but on the streets of Westminster, and that Borosky and Stern were anyway clearly not men of quality.

Nathaniel Johnson then made the extraordinary request to address the court concerning some private information he had recently acquired about the Watts boy. He informed the jury that Watts had told him about an offer of employment he had received from the Thynn camp, an offer that Johnson construed as being a blatant attempt to corrupt him to their cause. This statement predictably enough provoked an outcry from Thynn's family members sitting in the gallery, and Sir Francis Winnington for the prosecution at once stood up and made the point: 'We observe what a sort of interpreter Sir Nathaniel Johnson is; he speaks more like an advocate than an interpreter; he mingles interpreter, and witness, and advocate together.'[7] It was a reasonable enough retort and the Lord Chief Justice set Johnson's remark aside, but the damage had been done, the smear had been made.

Pemberton now asked Konigsmark to explain why Vratz had come to see him so hot on the heels of the murder taking place. The Count could only reply that 'he came to give him a visit'.[8] The weakness of this answer caused a renewed uproar in the gallery and it was some time before the crowd settled. The Count was then asked why Borosky needed to be furnished with such a strong sword. It was left to Johnson to provide the answer: 'he [Konigsmark] says all servants of gentlemen in Germany wear such broadswords'.[9] Pemberton asked Johnson whether he had ever visited Germany. Johnson promptly replied that he had done and that he could confirm the truth of this statement. Next came the question why, when Borosky had been brought over to help the Count purchase horses, he was given into the custody of Vratz the day after his arrival. Konigsmark explained that hostilities not developing as expected meant that he no longer had need of Borosky, and it was a common thing in Germany to give servants away if they were no longer needed. Again Pemberton consulted Sir Nathaniel Johnson as to the truth of this statement and Johnson was once more quick to confirm it: 'Yes, my Lord, it is very frequent in Germany to give a servant away if there be no use of him, for these Polanders are like slaves.'[10] Johnson was now being utilised by Pemberton more in the role of an expert witness than as an interpreter.

There followed some discussion concerning what Konigsmark knew of Borosky's character before he imported him into England. It was clearly important for the defence that Borosky should have been generally thought of as a man of good reputation before he had inexplicably taken it upon himself to kill Thynn. Johnson had thought of this. A man named Russell was in court to testify to the fact that the German merchant who had dispatched Borosky was a man of excellent character and would not have sent him had he had any doubts about him. As if this in itself was not sufficient, Pemberton once again consulted Nathaniel Johnson as to this German merchant's credit. Johnson readily complied. 'I know him to be a man of considerable estate and credit,'[11] he answered. The third of the judges, Baron Montagu, who had been largely silent until now, was prompted by this exchange to express some surprise that Borosky, having such a good reputation, should so suddenly have become evil. 'He could not be so ill a man at the first dash,'[12] he remarked. But his comment was lost in the general uproar and a spat that ensued between Johnson and the lawyer Williams about the latter's lack of any military background. Johnson equated this with a lack of integrity.

The Count was finally permitted to address himself directly to the jury on his own behalf. He was told by Pemberton 'not [to] be too long'.[13] He spoke first in French and then German, and Nathaniel Johnson provided the translation into English. His speech had nothing to do with the murder. He talked instead of how he was a Protestant and how glad he was that he was being tried in a Protestant country. He spoke of how his father and grandfather had fought for the Protestant religion in Germany. He declared that he was 'very ready, upon all occasions, to serve the King of England; and that he loves the English nation'.[14] He made no mention of his membership of the Catholic secret society, the Knights of St John.

The final words of the proceedings were left to Pemberton, and he addressed himself to a point of law on which he claimed the prosecution lawyers had misled the jury:

> It hath been said by the Counsel, it will be all one whether it (the Murder) were with the knowledge of Count Konigsmark or not. Now, I must tell you gentlemen the law is not so: for, if a gentleman has an affront given him which he does seem to resent, if any of his servants officiously, without acquainting him with it, out of too much zeal and too forward a respect to their master's honour, will go and pistol and kill him that they apprehend has affronted their master, he not knowing of it, it will not charge their master with any guilt at all.[15]

All true, of course, but nowhere in the printed accounts of the trial is there any suggestion that the counsel for the prosecution had claimed any different. The prosecution's argument was that it was simply unbelievable that Konigsmark was not only complicit in the murder plot, but was in fact the instigator. Pemberton had come up with a colossal red herring, or as an early nineteenth-century legal commentator put it, 'an artifice to prejudice the jury against the prosecution'.[16]

The jury were out for over half an hour. When they returned the foreman was asked for their verdict. Borosky, Vratz and Stern were pronounced guilty. Konigsmark was declared not guilty. Borosky was called to the bar and asked what he had to say for himself. He answered that 'he prayed to God to have mercy upon him'.[17] The same question was asked of Vratz. Vratz answered truculently that 'he had not been rightly examined nor fairly tried'. When Stern was called, he replied simply and rather pathetically that 'he did it for the captain's sake; he went as a second along with him'. Of the three replies, it is interesting that the one made by Borosky has the most dignity, and yet it was the fate of Vratz that was shortly to captivate the public imagination.

When the verdict was announced Thynn's supporters in the gallery broke out in furious uproar. It was not what they had anticipated. Konigsmark was hastily ushered from the courtroom. As silence was gradually restored, the sentences on the three men found guilty were solemnly read out. All three were to be hanged, at the same place where the crime had been committed.

The Palace of Whitehall as it was in 1681

39

WHITEHALL

... if she come again let it be by Night, or else the Tarpol-
lians at Wapping will go nigh to stick their anchors in her barge,
the scolds of Billingsgate will plague her far more than either
Drums or Thunder, the scullers will be ready to give her a thousand broadsides, so that if she escapes 999 the odd one may cool
her courage.

– *The Duchess of Portsmouth and Count Konigsmark's Farewell to England*[1]

It was five in the afternoon when the crowd spilled out of the
Sessions House onto the wet and muddy street of Old Bailey.
Thynn's friends were loud in their amazement and discontent,
but Konigsmark had his supporters. According to Lord Longford, the
Count had 'defended himself so well in his pertinent and quick answers,
that the auditors were generally very favourably inclined to him'.[2] Later
in the same letter Longford added that 'when the jury brought in their
verdict not guilty, the rabble shouted with joy'. But the rabble was

notoriously fickle in its affections. Today's hero was tomorrow's devil.

Sir John Reresby, who had been in court all day, immediately took a cab and went straight to Whitehall. He wanted to be the first to deliver the hot news to Charles. He was confident the verdict was going to be to Charles's liking. 'I carried the King the news the first of this matter, who was not displeased to hear that it had passed in this manner.'[3] But Reresby was well aware that not everyone was of the same opinion: 'the party of the Duke of Monmouth . . . were extremely concerned that the Count did escape.'

There was a widespread feeling among the better-informed public that Konigsmark had only got off through the bribing of the jury. Narcissus Luttrell remarked: ''Tis more than probable good store of guineas went amongst them.'[4] He noted that Konigsmark had challenged no fewer than eighteen members of the proposed jury. 'The Count had in a paper who he should challenge and who not, and he knew his friends.' Luttrell mentions in particular 'one Mr B—, a woollen draper in Covent Garden, who . . . was askt if 500 guinies would doe him any harm, if he would acquit the Count, but there being jury men besides enough, he was not called; yet this he has attested'.[5] One can't help but wonder whether Mr B would have come forward with this story if he had been one of those selected for the trial.

That widespread bribery undoubtedly took place is confirmed by no less an authority than Sir John Reresby. Monsieur Foubert, the owner of the riding academy where Philip Konigsmark was a pupil, was at the centre of the scandal:

A gentleman that kept the French Academy in London, one Monsieur Faubert, came and desired me to direct him (if ther was any method to be followed) for the saveing of Count Conismarkes life, insinuating at the same time that as he [Konigsmark] was a gentleman of a vast estate he was sensible he could not lay it out to greater advantage then to support his innocencie, and to secure him against the danger of the law in a strange country.[6]

Reresby's response to this overture, reported by himself, was bluff and forthright: 'I tould him [Foubert] that if he [Konigsmark] was innocent the law would acquit him, though he was a forraigner, as well as if he were a native; but that he ought to be carefull how he made any offers of that kind, it being rather the way to make a man of honour his enemy then to gain him for his friend.'[7] There is no reason to doubt Reresby's word on this. He is rather full of his own self-importance but he comes across as a blunt and truthful man. His final aside on this business of bribery has an endearing frankness:

> This is one of the first bribes of value that ever was offered me, which I might safely have gotten without discovery and without doing much for itt; but I always believed that money soe gotten was noe addition to what we possess, but rather the cause of its wast . . . and therefore I denyed it, as I ever did and I hope I shall be able to resist temptations of that nature.

John Evelyn, who was no scourge of the Royalist party, and was not a great admirer of Thomas Thynn, certainly had no time for Count Konigsmark, nor the jury that acquitted him. He speaks very harshly of 'that base Coward C. Konigsmark, who had hopes to marry his [Thynn's] widow the rich Lady Ogle [Lady Bette]; & was quitted by a Corrupt Jury, & so got away'.[8]

There were some hotheads among Monmouth's supporters who were not prepared to let Konigsmark get away if they could possibly prevent it. Lords Cavendish and Mordaunt were foremost among those determined to challenge Konigsmark to a duel. Mordaunt called several times at Sir Nathaniel Johnson's house, where Konigsmark had taken temporary refuge after being acquitted. He brought a challenge from Cavendish. Konigsmark refused to come to the door or accept the challenge.

Measures were being taken to get Konigsmark quietly out of the country as speedily as possible. But there was a problem with this. Before his discharge from prison Konigsmark had been 'oblidged to give security for his appearance the first day of next term at the King's bench bar'.[9] The sum that had been asked for was a colossal £5,000. Konigsmark put up £2,000 himself. Monsieur Foubert, Major Oglethorpe and Sir Nathaniel Johnson put up a further £1,000 each. If Konigsmark left the country before he was due to reappear before the court they would all lose their money.

Despite the huge financial penalty involved, the general rumour was that Konigsmark had slipped across the Channel early on the morning of 4 March 1682, in company with Louise de Kérouaille, Duchess of Portsmouth, the most loathed of Charles's current mistresses. She was hated because she was openly Catholic, had originated from the Court of Louis XIV and was widely considered to be a French spy, whose sole purpose was to warp English politics in favour of French ambitions. A broadside was published describing their departure together in lurid terms: 'The discourse of the town is various, some say a plotter and a murderer are gone hand in hand ... they need not balance [ballast] their ship for their sins are so weighty.'[10] The pamphlet is full of the most curious, blood-curdling and bizarrely coded threats, but despite the wild rhetoric it is certainly true that the Duchess departed from England on a royal yacht early on the morning of 4 March 1682 en route to Dieppe, and it was just around this same time that Konigsmark was also spirited out of the country.

It wasn't just in anonymous pamphlets that this news was broadcast. In a letter written from London on 4 March, the respectable Lord Longford also has Louise and Konigsmark travelling together: 'The Duchess of Portsmouth went on board last night and this day her farewell has been cried and sung about the streets. Count Konigsmark is said to have accompanied her which will more open the mouths of the rabble against her.'[11] Luttrell must have picked up on the same story, for he makes the following entry in his diary for 4 March: 'notwithstanding [the considerable sum pledged by the sureties] the Count is gone into France, and 'tis much doubted whether he will return to save his bail.'

A few days later, however, Longford corrects what he has previously written: 'I misinformed your Grace in my last when I told your Grace Count Konigsmark went on board the yacht with the Duchess of Portsmouth, for in truth he went in another yacht which was sent to fetch Colonel Sidney out of Holland.'[12] It was this second report that turned out to be the true one, and it offered an even more alluring prospect for the gossips. The conclusion was that Konigsmark was on his way to meet with Lady Bette.

On 4 March Konigsmark had been smuggled aboard the yacht *Mary*, captained by Christopher Gunman, which was under Admiralty instruction to make directly for Holland. Gunman had some difficulty sailing out of the Thames, for although in the early morning he had the tide with him, by 9 a.m. there was a flat calm and he could not progress beyond the Nore buoy. A couple of hours later there was a small breeze from the west and Gunman crammed on all the sail he could, but it wasn't long before the yacht was drifting helplessly again in another calm, this time with a flood tide, forcing him to anchor on the back of Spell Sand in the Thames Estuary. The yacht remained there for the rest of that afternoon and all through the early part of the night. At 2 a.m. the following morning, Sunday 5 March, a new breeze sprang up from the west-south-west, and this time it proved more enduring. 'Handsome weather' noted Gunman in his journal.[13] By 11 a.m. he was on the other side of the Channel and could see the steeple of Dunkirk Church to the south-east. Meanwhile Bette had readied herself to travel directly to Rotterdam to meet the *Mary*, the minute news came that the yacht had arrived there.

Back in England Cavendish and Mordaunt, together with a mysterious Captain Parker, were more determined than ever to pursue Konigsmark and bring him to combat. All three were preparing to travel overseas to put their challenge into effect. The Earl of Ailesbury, who held the title of Deputy Earl Marshal, and who was responsible for preventing this kind of lawlessness, was informed of their plans on 8 March. He promptly told Secretary of State Jenkins what was afoot, and sent messages to both Cavendish and Mordaunt that they were to meet with himself and Jenkins at four that same afternoon at Jenkins's office in Whitehall. Cavendish showed up, Mordaunt did not. Cavendish gave his word to Ailesbury that he would neither receive nor issue any challenges to Konigsmark. He also agreed that he would bring Mordaunt in person at eight that evening to Lord Ailesbury's house to make a similar undertaking. Clearly Ailesbury and Jenkins between them had read Cavendish the riot act. Captain Parker was taken temporarily into custody. Considerable effort was being made at the highest possible level to nip in the bud any further repercussions of the Thynn murder.[14]

Secretary Jenkins wrote to Secretary Conway on the evening of 8 March detailing what had taken place in London. Lord Conway was with the King at Newmarket where the racing season had just started, even though the weather was bitterly cold. The Earl of Ailesbury also wrote to the King requesting that an injunction should be taken out against Mordaunt and Cavendish preventing them from going overseas to fight with Konigsmark. Charles declined the suggestion. In his usual hands-off manner, he instructed Conway to inform Jenkins and via him Ailesbury that he thought the word of the two noblemen to be a stronger bond for their future good behaviour than the imposition of a legal impediment. In this he was mistaken.

On 20 March, at noon, Jenkins received a copy of a letter from Konigsmark addressed to Lord Mordaunt. It had been forwarded to him by the Swedish envoy Leinberg, who had received it two hours earlier from the 'carrier of foreign letters'. Written on 17 March, the letter was full of bombast and bravado:

> I regret you had the useless trouble of coming 5 or 6 times after I had left. Mr
> Cavendish's eagerness to fight is very agreeable news to me. The accusation

of Mr Thynn's death does not deserve an answer from me. A pen and ink war does not suit my quality, my inclination or my profession. Therefore I reserve my answer, arms in hand. I beg you to inform Mr Cavendish that I have been waiting for some days here, and will wait here three weeks more. It is a very proper place but, if Mr Cavendish finds no opportunity of coming over, he shall know my address and I will always very willingly post 500 leagues to meet him out of England in a neutral country which he has only to name. I leave him the right to choose the weapons and shall be very glad to know the number of his seconds, in order to satisfy the eagerness of my friends.[15]

Jenkins sent a copy of the Konigsmark letter to Conway, who acknowledged receipt of it on 22 March, commenting that he had seen an earlier letter from Konigsmark dated 6 March which he had directly from Captain Parker, but that he did not have the one that Jenkins had sent him. The next day Conway wrote again to Jenkins. He had now received two more letters from Konigsmark via Captain Parker. There was clearly something in the latest batch of letters that alarmed Conway more than in the correspondence he had read the day before, because he now sent urgently for Captain Parker to attend him and was informed that Parker 'had gone away post for London'. The King was consulted a second time as to what should be done and he now responded in a slightly less laissez-faire manner than before. 'His Majesty's commands are that you should advise with the Lord Chancellor about it and do what he thinks fit,' wrote Conway to Jenkins. The upshot of this was that writs of '*ne exeat regnum*' were now issued against Cavendish, Mordaunt and Parker, which was what Ailesbury had asked for in the first place. A watch was to be organised at all 'ports leading into Flanders, Holland, Calais, and neighbouring landing places and any other ports that the said Lords and Captain may be suspected to go to in order their transport to Flanders [be stopped], the ports in the Thames being in the first place intended to be narrowly watched and stopped'.[16]

The measures seem to have been effective. Cavendish, Mordaunt and Parker remained on English soil. In mid-April a rumour briefly circulated that Konigsmark had been seen in London, but nothing came of it and the Swedish envoy gave an assurance that there was no truth in it.

On 18 May 1682, when the dust was beginning to settle on the Thynn affair, the shadowy Duke of Albemarle, one of Charles's most trusted administrators, sent Konigsmark the following private letter. 'I have received those thanks you are pleased to give me. I should be very glad to meet an opportunity of rendering you any service within my power which is due to your person and quality, for which I have all respect imaginable, and was very much concerned for your late misfortune, out [of] which I did rejoice at your happy deliverance.'[17]

It comes as no great surprise to learn then that on 19 May 'on the petition of Sir Nathaniel Johnson, Col Oglethorpe and Mr Foubert praying his Majesty to pardon the forfeiture of the recognizance of 2000 l. entered into by Count Konigsmark and of 1000 l. entered into by each of the petitioners as his sureties at the sessions lately held at the Old Bailey . . . his Majesty granted them their request'.[18] Konigsmark may have pretended to the jury that he was a good Protestant. The truth was he was in the pay of Louis XIV and given succour by Nathaniel Johnson, a devout Catholic and supporter of James, Duke of York. He was also a member of a highly secretive society dedicated to the resurgence of Catholicism throughout Europe. But none of that precluded the immediate possibility he might elope with Bette, and it was the outcome of that affair that was most eagerly awaited.

The Condemned Cell at Newgate

40

VRATZ'S CELL

Honour and bravery was the Idol he adored, a piece of preposterous devotion he maintained to the last.

– Anthony Horneck on Captain Vratz[1]

After the sentences had been read, the three condemned men, Borosky, Lieutenant Stern and Captain Vratz, were escorted under armed guard the short distance from the Sessions House back to Newgate Gaol. Their ankles were shackled but they were not subjected to the further indignity of wrist manacles and iron collars. Vratz was in an ugly mood. As they left the courtroom he turned on Stern, abusing him and calling him a 'murderer'.[2] He was not referring to the killing of Thynn. In Vratz's opinion it was the loose words from Stern in his original statement to the Justices that had incriminated him and led to his own death sentence. Stern was visibly upset that his mentor and master, the man he had looked up to, almost at times worshipped, should now treat him in this unkind manner. After all, as Stern saw it, it was Vratz who had led him astray and not the other way around. But before the quarrel could develop, all three men were led to their separate cells. Now that the drama of the trial was over they had nothing to distract them from their imminent death. It was Tuesday, 28 February 1682. They were due to be hanged on the following Wednesday, 8 March.

Vratz's cell was relatively luxurious. It was furnished with a table and possessed a chimney and a hearth where a fire burned in the grate. He had books and writing implements at his disposal and could command whatever wine and food he wished for. On Sunday, 5 March, he received an unsolicited visit from Gilbert Burnet. There had been snow the previous night, but it was a pleasant and frosty day. Burnet had hoped to find Vratz in a more penitent and accessible state of mind than on their previous encounter. The proximity of death was well known to bring about miraculous changes in a man's demeanour. But in Vratz he was disappointed. The Captain continued to rant in a mood of anger and recrimination, most of which he directed towards Stern. He accused Stern of having told lies 'in spite to him that he might not be pardoned'.[3] Burnet told Vratz bluntly that 'it was in vain for him to dream of a pardon' and added that if he was receiving visitors 'that kept him up with the hopes of it they deceived him'.

Vratz had his private reasons for remaining optimistic which he did not care to discuss with Burnet. Within a day or so of the trial, before Charles left for the racing at Newmarket, a young woman dressed all in white paid a visit to the aging King in his rooms in Whitehall.[4] She went to beg the life of Captain Vratz. A virginal white shift was the traditional apparel for such missions of mercy. According to Luttrell she was unsuccessful, but he was in the habit of writing up his diary some weeks after the event, and when he made this entry he probably already knew that Vratz had been hanged. It would have been uncharacteristic of Charles to give the young woman a blunt refusal. It is much more likely that his answer was vague, and it was this vagueness that perhaps kept Vratz believing that a pardon would come through, albeit at the last minute. The identity of the young woman is not known. She may have been a lover of Vratz, but the only women mentioned in connection with the Captain are street whores, and it seems unlikely they would have gone out of their way to beg his life or even been admitted into Charles's presence. It seems more probable that this mystery woman was a member of Konigsmark's retinue.

Burnet made no better progress on spiritual issues with Vratz than he did on temporal ones. Vratz made it clear that he regarded any confession as a private business between himself and his God and he did not require a priest as an intermediary. He also remarked that he did not believe in hell, other than as a state in which a man was 'excluded from the presence of God'.[5] So far as Burnet was concerned it was a most unsatisfactory interview: 'I left him when I saw that nothing I could say had any good effect on him, and resolved to have gone no more to him.'[6]

Horneck's style was more fire and brimstone than the psychologically insidious Burnet, but he fared no better in his attempts to extract from Vratz a confession. He tried reminding the Captain, with a flourish of his black robes, of 'the all seeing Eye above, who knew his crimes'.[7] Vratz was not to be intimidated by any all-seeing eye. Instead, he responded with the interesting theological doctrine that he 'was confident God would consider [him] a gentleman, and deal with him suitably to the condition and profession he had placed him in, and would not take it ill if a soldier who lived by his sword, revenged the affront offered to him by another'. This attitude was abhorrent to Horneck, who answered him that revenge in a gentleman was as much a sin as it was in a peasant. But Vratz was unbowed. He assured Horneck that as long as he lived he would 'give anyone as good as he brings', with some expressions that the fastidious Horneck was 'loth to repeat, for they made me so melancholick, that I was forced to leave him'.

If the priests were getting nowhere with Vratz, at least they had the comfort that they were making marvellous progress with the soul of Lieutenant Stern, who relished every opportunity he could come by of confessing the error of his ways. Stern was enraptured by the way in which the course of his own life appeared to provide a moral that the entire world could benefit from. He felt that God had 'suffered him to be thrown down, that through that loss he might rebound the higher', and 'that though he had walked in the dark he doubted not that God would draw light from that darkness'.[8] He realised now that the Devil would never have entered into him if only he had continued to read *Dilheren's Way* and said his prayers regularly. Horneck was particularly admiring of the way Stern was given to 'holy ejaculations fit for a true penitent', a welcome change, no doubt, from Vratz's surly oaths.

During these uplifting spiritual exchanges with Stern, Horneck still took the opportunity of slipping in the odd sly question of a less obviously religious nature. He asked Stern at one point, 'whether he had been seduced by the Count or the Captain'.[9] Stern's answer was confusing: 'he had been in the Count's company twice, but the Captain would not let him know that it was the Count, yet he believed it was he, having formerly seen him, and that the Captain still told him that he had a quarrel with such a gentleman'. If Horneck had been hoping to pin something on Konigsmark from what Stern told him, he must have been disappointed.

Stern may have been flushed with the excitement of religious rebirth, but the Captain's harsh words still troubled him greatly. 'He often asked news of him,' states Burnet.[10] He wanted to know whether Vratz had yet been 'touched with a sense of his sin or not'. When Burnet told him that the Captain was still in denial, Stern asked whether 'he might be suffered to go to him and speak with him; for he said, though others might speak much better, yet he hoped he might say somewhat that would be more effectual'. Burnet warned Stern that the Captain 'would perhaps use him roughly'. He told Stern that Vratz was forever 'upbraiding him for his ingratitude, and for having accused him falsely'. But a missionary zeal glowed strongly inside the Lieutenant and he insisted on going 'to see if he could by any means do him any good'.

Vratz meanwhile had successfully petitioned for the day of execution to be delayed. 'The Captain having petitioned for longer time to prepare himself for another world, they have the liberty of a reprieve til Friday ... hoping they will make good use of it.'[11] It seems most unlikely that Vratz really wanted the extra time to prepare his soul. It is more probable that he was still being told by his friends that endeavours to obtain his release were progressing and a few more days should clinch it.

The meeting between Vratz and Stern was arranged for Wednesday, 8 March. It was another bright frosty day. There had been a succession of them. There had also been some more snow overnight. The route from Stern's cell to the room where the Captain lay involved climbing some stone stairs and passing through the prison chapel. As he left his own cell, Stern turned back to Burnet and said 'he was going up to the House of God, but he should go higher within two dayes, to a house not made with hands'.[12] Burnet related how he was moved by this touching display of faith. Stern gives the impression that he was not just enjoying the sense of being forgiven for his sins. He was also basking in all the attention he was getting from the famous author and theologian and was saying whatever he thought it would most please him to hear.

The same cannot be said for Vratz. Horneck, being the more fluent in German, was to be present at the proposed meeting between the Lieutenant and the Captain. He arrived at Vratz's cell some time before Stern and greeted Vratz in his customary sanctimonious style. 'I told him I hoped he had taken his dangerous condition into consideration, and wrought himself into a greater sense of his sins than I could observe in him, when I was last with him.'[13] Vratz answered 'that he knew not what [Horneck] meant by this address'. Horneck then explained that he 'spake it with relation to the late great sin he had been engaged in, and that [he] hoped his approaching death had made him more penitent'. Vratz answered that if Horneck expected him to say that 'Count Konigsmark had been the contriver of the murder, and had been in consultation with him about compassing his design and prompted and bribed him for that end', then he would be disappointed, for it was a 'falsehood he would never be guilty of, if he had never so many lives to lose'. He then added for good measure that he believed 'the Lieutenant had been tampered with by promises of a decent burial ... to confess things notoriously false'.

Horneck was undeterred by Vratz's intransigent attitude. He launched into a long sermon, the substance of which was that Vratz owed it to society at large and to Thynn's relations to make a full confession, 'and that it was an injustice to the publick, not to betray the complices, and assistants, and occasions in such heinous offences'. But Vratz was not to be beguiled or intimidated. He replied 'that he feared no Hell ... He was not such a fool as to believe, that souls could fry in material fire; or be roasted as meat in a great hearth', and here he pointed at his own chimney piece and sneered with derision.

After this outburst Vratz fell silent for a while. He turned his attention to some books that were open on his table and pretended to occupy himself reading them. Then he mentioned to Horneck, as it were casually, 'that he understood the Lieutenant's papers were to be printed'.[14] When Horneck confirmed the truth of this, the Captain countered that 'if they were printed, he would print his own story too'. He then went on to say that 'as for the Lieutenant, he was a fellow that was poor and wretched ... and sometimes he was not well in his wits'. He claimed that if it hadn't been for his own generosity the Lieutenant would have starved to death, 'and if the Lieutenant persisted with his falsities he would die with a lie in his mouth'.

Horneck then announced that the prison governor, Mr Richardson, would soon be bringing Stern to Vratz's cell so the two men could 'speak together'[15] and resolve their differences. At this news Vratz 'grew angry, and reply'd, He had nothing to say to him, nor did he care for seeing him, nor for being troubled with any English Divines; they being men too inquisitive and meddling with things that belonged not unto them'. With this he turned back to the book that lay on the table before him.

When Stern entered Vratz's cell shortly afterwards 'with a penitent countenance'[16] Vratz angrily stalked off into a far corner of the room. He then turned and asked Stern what he had come for and added: 'he did not care for the sight of him'. Stern 'very meekly' answered him, 'that they had not long to live, and therefore he was come to admonish him to repent of what he had done'. He went on to add that 'he freely forgave him the wrong he had done him'. This infuriated Vratz. He called Stern a liar and demanded of him 'how he durst vent such abominable lyes concerning him and Count Konigsmark . . . one would think you are distracted or had a soft place in your head; is this your gratitude to a person that has relieved you and done you kindnesses'.

The abuse continued to flow from Vratz, but Stern stood his ground. He mentioned again the letter that Vratz had once showed him from the Count and the various sums of dollars that had been promised for disposing of Thynn. 'You know and your conscience knows the truth of these things,' said Stern. 'You know you made me these offers; God forgive you, and I forgive you.'[17] Even Horneck was impressed by Stern's self-control. 'The Lieutenant stood before him, talking with great meekness and humility, and for the most part with his hat off,' observed Horneck. Stern was still very attached to that three-cornered hat of his. But this interview, which Stern had hoped would bring Vratz to his knees, with much mutual weeping and forgiveness, was fruitless. 'When the Lieutenant saw, that his speaking did but enrage him more, he took his leave.'

Horneck remained behind, still hoping for some small show of remorse. But Vratz crossed back to his table and sat down and once again began reading his book, refusing to answer anything Horneck said. Eventually Horneck, 'left him too, wishing him a better mind'.

On his return to his own cell, Stern told Burnet what had occurred and how 'sorry he was to see the Captain in such a condition'.[18] He explained that in the past he would not have been able to control his own behaviour when abused in such a manner, but today he was able to endure the Captain's reproaches calmly, and how he hoped his fortitude 'had got [him] two steps higher in his way to heaven'. Burnet answered that it was a 'good sign, that he had learned to be like his saviour, who when he was reviled, revil'd not again'. Stern promptly demurred: 'Ah! Such a miserable criminal as I am, must not be in any thing compared to my blessed Redeemer.'

It was now that Stern asked if Borosky could spend the day with him in his cell. Permission was immediately granted. Stern 'found he [Borosky] had a mind well disposed, but was ignorant. So he took great pains to instruct him.'[19] Borosky proved more fertile ground than Vratz. Like Stern he made a full confession. It was much shorter than Stern's and did not say much more than he had already told the Justices. He stressed how, when he had first been told of the plan to murder Thynn, he had not been happy about it, and had gone into a separate room and prayed to God, but he had then allowed himself to be persuaded that it was God's will that he should do it. He explained that from the moment he was first introduced to Vratz 'he was never alone, nor had any opportunity of recollecting himself but was hurried into it blindly'.[20]

Borosky also told Burnet the story of how a couple of days after his imprisonment he had been lying awake at night in his cell and the door had opened. At first he thought it was the prison keeper checking on him, but afterwards he realised it was a woman who had appeared on occasions before to him when he was in Germany. She looked at him but said nothing and then vanished. He believed she was sent from God to touch his heart, for 'she had certainly a very good effect on him'.[21] From that time onwards he was 'wonderfully changed'. He had no fear of death. 'He said he was ready for it and longed for it more than he did anything in his life.' According to Stern, Borosky 'had an excellent soul, and though he had not much knowledge, yet he himself learned much from him; for he had the simplicity of a little child'.[22]

On the evening of 9 March Burnet paid a final solemn visit to Stern. He found the Lieutenant in a weakened and overwrought state. The former mercenary had worked himself up into such a frenzy of religious transport he had become quite faint and was at times incoherent. In his more lucid moments he told Burnet that he fully accepted that he was going to die and he spoke about his desire to be united with God. 'He never once asked me if I thought a pardon might be obtained,'[23] remarked Burnet, obviously surprised and impressed. 'On the contrary he said that he deserved to die and desired it as much as he deserved it.' Stern's only request was that he might be beheaded rather than hanged, but this had no chance of being granted. Beheadings were for high-ranking aristocrats only.

Stern did not argue. Instead he rambled on in semi-delirium about how he thought of this last night 'as the Eve of his Wedding and therefore it would seem tedious to him'.[24] He asked that Borosky might stay with him in the same cell during the long hours of darkness. Stern was anxious that one of them should be continuously praying. 'It was not fit that both should be together asleep that night.'[25] He took the sacrament and murmured: 'Now I have got my passport and I long to be gone.'

Stern's mood on that last evening was greatly cheered when a message came from the Captain that the latter had, after all, made arrangements for Stern to receive a decent burial. Stern sent a message back 'full of great affection'.[26] A German minister had visited Vratz earlier in the day, Horneck having given up on him. This minister told Stern, in front of Burnet, that Vratz had confessed to him that he had led both Stern and Borosky into the murder plot. Nothing was said about the role of Konigsmark. Stern had been planning to make a final speech from the scaffold. Now he changed his mind in case what he had to say might upset the Captain: 'it would perhaps put him in some disorder and he [Stern] would not venture [the Captain] being discomposed in the last moment of his life.'[27] He continued, however, to fuss about his *Last Confession*. He had not quite finished it. He told Burnet he would hand it to him at the place of execution.

At midnight, long after Burnet had departed, a servant of the gaol walked with slow menace along the narrow and low-ceilinged corridors of Newgate, ringing a handbell. He paused outside the cells of the three condemned men and recited a poem the opening lines of which were:

All you that in the condemned hole do lie,
Prepare you, for tomorrow you shall die ...[28]

The Execution of the murtherers of S.[r] E.B.Godfrey

Public Hanging 1679

41

THE HAYMARKET

The vilest rogues, and most despicable villains, may own a thousand crimes, and often brag of the most abominable actions; but there is scarce one, who will confess he has no courage ... The further a man is removed from repentance, nay, the more void he seems to be of all religion, and the less concern he discovers for futurity, the more he is admired by our sprightly people.

– B. Mandeville, *An Enquiry into the Causes of the Frequent Executions at Tyburn*, 1725[1]

O n the following morning, Friday 10 March, Burnet arrived at the prison early. The bells of the church of St Sepulchre, situated opposite Newgate, had already begun their loud and repetitive tolling, signifying to the doomed prisoners that the day of their execution had finally arrived. Burnet found Stern a little stronger than he had been the night before. He had had three hours' sleep. He and Borosky were singing Psalm 51 together. They sang it right through from beginning to end three times in succession. Burnet noted that Stern appeared visibly affected when he came to the lines: 'Deliver me from blood guiltiness oh God, thou God of my salvation'.[2]

When a warder came in and asked him 'how he did', Stern answered 'a friend had sent to call him to come dine with him, and he was ready to go'.[3] He then added: 'he longed much for the officers that should carry him away'. He was still undecided, however, whether or not he would make that last speech from the scaffold. He was now thinking he might say something after all, 'chiefly to have warned the people not to cast off the sense of God'. In these last days Stern was as anxious to impress Burnet of his devotion, as he had previously been to convince Vratz of his loyalty.

Burnet also took the opportunity of paying a last visit to the Captain. He had originally determined to have nothing further to do with Vratz, but having heard from the German priest that he had finally confessed, Burnet clearly thought that a further visit would be worthwhile. He certainly found Vratz in a more agreeable frame of mind than before, but all he wanted to talk about was whether Burnet could procure him a coach for his journey to the scaffold, so he could avoid travelling on the back of a common cart. When Burnet 'prayed him to consider that which concerned him more', Vratz answered him complacently 'that was already done'.[4] Undeterred, Burnet pressed on and asked him if he was now ready for the 'confessing [of] his sin'. Vratz replied: 'he had written it, and it would be published to all Europe.' This was, of course, a lie. He had written nothing.

The three condemned prisoners were taken from their cells and stood in chains upon the backs of individual carts in the Press Yard. The tolling of the bells was louder now, causing the very air to vibrate with a sense of their doom. From the Press Yard they were driven slowly, but with grinding inevitability, to their place of execution. They passed by the Conduit and over the bridge across the Fleet and along by Holborn. The crowds that lined the route were vast. It was as if the entire world had turned out to see them go to their death and cheer them on their way. It was a bitterly cold morning. There had been a fierce frost overnight and the gullies of the roofs where the sun had not yet reached were still brilliantly white. Even the stink of the Fleet River had been rendered less noxious by a seal of ice. The people stood in doorways, clung to parapets, walked upon the leads of the rooftops, and clambered on boxes to get a better view.

The hanging was scheduled to take place at noon at the southerly end of the Haymarket, close by where the shooting had occurred. That the murderers should be put to death in the same place that they had committed their crime was all part of the elaborate ritual of atonement. Jack Ketch the hangman was overseeing the final preparations, making certain the gibbet was strong enough to support three men, at least two of whom, Vratz and Borosky, were larger than average. Appropriate lengths of good-quality hemp had been provided. Ketch was confident that the three assassins would very shortly be 'dangling in the air ... like a bunch of fat thrushes'.[5] These were busy times for Ketch, 'so many horrid murders and Duels about this time being committed'.[6] But this was a much bigger occasion than most that he attended to, and he was hoping for lucrative pickings. He was entitled to any clothes or personal possessions that were unclaimed by relatives.

The business of hanging had its own mystique and rituals. It was suggested by some medical men that it was best to adjust the knot of the noose to a position beneath the left ear, as this would constrict the flow of blood to the brain and so bring about death by apoplexy. This was considered preferable to allowing the rope to constrict the windpipe, which would result in suffocation, an altogether more protracted business. Whatever the relative merits, it usually took the condemned person between ten and fifteen minutes to die. Sometimes friends and relations attempted to speed up the process by pulling on the victim's legs or beating their breast with sticks. After about half an hour the corpse would be cut down by the hangman and, except in special cases where further humiliations had been ordered, it would be handed over to family members for disposal.

A corpse after hanging displayed much lividity and swelling of the face, particularly of the ears and lips. The eyelids turned deep blue and the eyes themselves, crimson with the effect of burst blood vessels, were frequently left bulging half out of their sockets, staring maniacally into space. A frothy mucus ran from lips and nostrils, fingers were clenched into tight fists, while faeces and urine, involuntarily expelled, soiled their breeches. Despite the grotesque horror there was always a renewed surge forward by the crowd when the bodies were cut down. Some simply wanted a closer look, but others were impelled by the widespread belief that the touch of the hand of someone who had been publicly hanged could cure a variety of diseases, skin complaints and tumours. Young women were seen pressing their bare breasts against the corpse in order to transfer its supposed magical powers.[7]

England was widely known throughout Europe for the comparative decency of its executions. Misson observed how in England there 'was no tearing of the flesh with red hot pincers' or 'pulling to pieces [the body] with four horses',[8] both favourite forms of capital punishment on the Continent. Indeed, Sir William Petty, a well-known writer on economic and social issues in the second half of the seventeenth century, was highly critical of the 'clemency and mildness of simple hanging'[9] and argued for the introduction of more painful forms of death 'as a deterrent to evil doers'.

As the raucous and winding procession approached Charing Cross the crowd became ever denser. The murder had received so much publicity that everyone wanted to catch a glimpse of the monstrous perpetrators of the crime. Even more, they wanted to see how these notorious killers conducted themselves at the moment of their own deaths, the final moment when their courage would be tested to breaking point. It was a gruesome and riveting entertainment. The mood was festive and there was much cheering and jeering. Young girls with long silk scarves trailing from their necks, and carrying baskets of flowers, danced before the carts. Orange-sellers, pie-sellers, oyster-sellers, all cried their wares, creating a great cacophony of sound. Fops paraded with their periwigs well drudged with the barber's powdering puff. Maids hung out of upstairs windows instead of tending to their duties. The gentry observed proceedings from the aloof privacy of their coaches.

The Haymarket was a wide and open arena, originally used for the purpose that its name suggests, and so it was well suited for a great spectacle like a public hanging. It led down into Piccadilly and from there to the Great Western Road. The houses on its east side were very grand and luxurious, their windows packed with gawpers. Strype describes it as a 'spacious street of great resort full of inns and places of entertainment'. One of those inns was the Black Horse, and they no doubt did a brisk trade that morning selling bottles of Cock Ale and jugs of true Nantz Brandy. The King's Head was another popular hostelry with ample room for stabling and coaches, and Paulet's Ordinary was a favourite eating house, especially among the gentry. What better than a nice dish of calves' heads, after watching a man twitch at the end of a rope.

Vratz might have been refused his request for a coach, but that didn't stop him going to some considerable trouble with his appearance. Such preening was not unusual. Misson observed: 'He that is to be hanged, or otherwise executed, first takes care to get himself shaved and handsomely dressed, either in mourning or the dress of a bridegroom.'[10] Vratz chose to wear a black suit with elaborately embroidered slippers. His silk cravat was offset by a scarlet bobbin. On his head he wore a feathered cap of the latest fashion. *The Impartial Protestant Mercury* of 14 March reported that he had paid two guineas to a coffin maker, joking with him en route that he should be sure to make it long enough, for his neck was likely to be stretched a couple of inches. He paid a further four guineas to Mr Russell the embalmer for his body to be properly prepared for sending overseas for burial.[11]

He went cheerfully on the back of his cart and continued in that posture until he reached the gallows, refusing right to the end to make any final speech or last-minute confession. The crowd, of course, loved every minute of such a show of bravado. It was a marvellous way of subverting not just authority but death itself. It was his demeanour on the scaffold more than anything that transformed Vratz into a hero in the eyes of the public.

The level-headed Sir John Reresby was no great advocate for Vratz, but he confirmed the admirable coolness of his manner. 'The Captain dyed without any expression of fear, or laying any guilt upon Count Conismarke. Seeing me in my coach as he passed by in the cart to execution, he bowed to me with a steady look, as he did to those he knew amongst the spectatours before he was turned off.'[12] For all that he admired the Captain's bravery and loyalty, Reresby had reservations about his religious humility. He concludes his remarks by stating: 'his whole carriage, from his first being apprehended to the last, relished more of gallantry than religion'.

Evelyn, who probably did not attend the hangings, perhaps regarding such an event as rather vulgar, nonetheless made the same point about Vratz's nonchalant manner, remarking that he 'went to Execution like an undaunted hero . . . dying he did not value a rush, and hoped and believed God would deale with him like a Gentleman: never man went so gallant, & so unconcern'd to his fate'.[13] Given these plaudits it is hardly surprising that almost forty years after his death Vratz was still being written of as a legendary hero, as for instance in Smith's *History of Highwaymen*.

Burnet, who was standing right by the gallows, provides a similar description of Vratz's deportment during the last moments of his life:

> It is certain that never man died with more resolution and less signs of fear, or the least disorder. His carriage in the cart, both as he was led along, and at the place of execution was astonishing, he was not only undaunted, but looked cheerful, and smiled often. When the rope was put about his neck, he did not change colour, nor tremble, his legs were firm under him: he looked often about on those that stood in Balconies and Windows, and seemed to fix his eyes on some persons; three or four times he smiled; he would not

cover his face as the rest did, but continued in that state, often looking up to Heaven, with a cheerfulness in his countenance, and a little motion of his hands.[14]

Burnet had previously warned Vratz of 'the danger of affecting to be a counterfeit bravo'.[15] The first thing Vratz said to him when they met at the scaffold was that Burnet would now see, 'it was not a false bravery, but that he was fearless to the last'. Burnet asked him if he had anything 'to say to the people'. Vratz's answer was blunt. 'He said no.'

After Vratz had refused to make a final speech, he signalled to one of the attendants that 'he was willing the rope should be tyed to the gibbet'.[16] He then called for the German minister to come to him, perhaps as a snub to Burnet. However, the crowd was now pressing in such numbers and so thickly around the base of the scaffold that the German minister was unable to approach. So Vratz asked Burnet to pray with him in French. Burnet pleaded that his French was not adequate, which was somewhat strange for a man who was a noted linguist, but since Vratz also understood English, Burnet suggested he would pray in English. Burnet probably insisted on English so that Vratz's last words might be understood by all who heard them. If this was the case he was once again to be frustrated.

Burnet concluded his account:

After I prayed he said nothing, but that he was now going to be happy with God, so I left him. He continued in his undaunted manner, looking up often to Heaven, and sometimes round about him to the Spectators: after they had stood about a quarter of an hour under the gibbet, they were asked when they would give the signal for their being turned off, they answered that they were ready, and that the cart might be driven away when it pleased the Sheriff to order it; so a little while after it was driven away, and thus they all ended their lives.[17]

All the attention at the hanging was on Vratz. Very little notice was taken of either Borosky or Stern. It was the Captain who cut the glamorous figure, proud and defiant to the last. According to the *Impartial Protestant Mercury* 'the other two were extraordinarily pensive and read all the way'[18] while being transported from prison to scaffold. Luttrell remarks that while 'The Captain died with a very undaunted temper; the other two were much dejected'.[19]

Stern decided at the last moment that he would like, after all, to make a speech from the scaffold. However, he found the noise of the crowd was so great he could not make himself heard. Frustrated and burbling incoherently he thrust his *Last Confession* to Burnet, realising that this was all he would have to rely on for his posthumous fame. It was full of crossings out and difficult to decipher. Finally, he threw his beloved copy of *Dilheren's Way* to Burnet also and asked him 'to give it to some good soul'.[20] He said a few final words to Vratz, but once again the uproar was so overwhelming, Burnet could not hear what these words were, nor make out the Captain's reply. As to exactly how Stern conducted himself during his last moments of life, Burnet draws a veil over the detail.

Torchlit Burial Procession late seventeenth century

42

THE NEW EXCHANGE

Mr. Sidney, our ambassador, is said to have a design on his return hither to court the Lady Ogle.

– Letter from Joshua Bowes to Sir Francis Radclyffe,
London, 16 March 1682[1]

The evening before the hangings Thomas Thynn had been buried in Westminster Abbey. Torchlit nocturnal burials were popular among the fashionable and Thynn had never relinquished his pretensions to fashion. It was a grand occasion involving a long procession of coaches, but it did not draw anything like the same crowds as the hangings.

There survives no official listing of the mourners but it can be assumed that Monmouth was there, in a place of honour, as also the two hotheads Cavendish and Mordaunt, still busily plotting their revenge. Arnold Quillan, the young Dutch stonemason who had just been commissioned to create Thynn's tomb, would have been present, out of simple courtesy. He had already started work on the controversial memorial. It was only right and proper that he should pay his respects. John Hall, Thynn's executor, was there of course, as was Thynn's cousin Sir Thomas Thynn, who was to inherit Longleat. Major Brett must have been there. He was said to bitterly regret his part in arranging the calamitous marriage that had ended in the death of his friend.

Mrs Potter was experiencing no such scruples of conscience. If she was weeping it was because she was perplexed as to how she was ever going to collect the £500 that Thynn still owed her for her part in promoting the marriage. And there were, no doubt, numerous other creditors traipsing along behind the solemn cortege, hoping to get a quick word in John Hall's ear to register their interest. By the time Thynn died, for all his much vaunted riches, he was hopelessly in debt. It took Hall the next seven years to sell off various farms, houses and pieces of land to raise the necessary monies, £12,260 in total, to pay off the more urgent of the claims.[2]

Some of the young gallants rode horses and were adorned with black cloaks, and black spurs and black feathers in their hats. Mourning gloves were worn, as well as black scarves and black hat bands. Mourning rings were distributed among close relatives and friends. The open coffin was trundled slowly on a large metal hearse set with lighted candles. The candles sputtered in the blustering wind that had sprung up as the sun went down. Several of them were snuffed out as heavy gouts of rain began to fall. The body, freshly washed and shaved, was wrapped in a white shroud embroidered along its edges in black thread. Shrouds by law were required to be made of wool, to support the British wool industry. As the rain fell and the wool became soaked it exuded a dark animal smell that contrasted with the scent of oil of roses and almonds with which the dead man's flesh had been anointed.

Not very many of the Court Party were present, to toast Thynn's memory with port wine. They were all at Newmarket, attending the races with Charles, and anxiously awaiting the arrival of James, Duke of York, who was now the clear favourite to succeed to the throne. Lady Bette most certainly was not present, but there was much public speculation as to just where she was and what were her intentions. A newsletter of 16 March sent from London relayed information supposedly received from The Hague claiming that 'Count Konigsmark is arrived there, where Lady Ogle still is, who does not intend to come for England so soon as was reported'.[3] The implication was obvious. Bette had delayed her return to England deliberately so she could see her lover, the Count. Now Thynn was dead and Konigsmark had been acquitted of his murder, what was there to stand in his way? Surely not Lady Bette herself, who must at the very least have been full of gratitude that Konigsmark had rid her of such a loathed husband. London was both aghast and thrilled at the thought of them running off together.

The newsletter was not entirely accurate. Konigsmark had certainly set off in the royal yacht *Mary* bound for Rotterdam, but he did not go the full distance. He had requested to be put ashore at Ostend, from where he had travelled to Nieuport in the southern Netherlands. The advantage of Nieuport was twofold. It was in territory held by Louis XIV's army and therefore it offered him protection. It was also near enough to The Hague that he could still reach it easily and quickly should the need arise. It is possible that he was waiting for an encouraging word from Bette before risking this final part of the journey. If this was so he was to be disappointed. Konigsmark was still languishing in Nieuport over a week later, occupying himself with writing bombastic letters to Mordaunt and Cavendish.

As for Bette, the suggestion that she was deliberately delaying her departure in the hopes of meeting up with her supposed lover proved to be the very opposite of the truth. The *Impartial Protestant Mercury* carried the following authoritative account of her return:

Colonel Sidney on Friday last arrived here [London], in company with Lady Ogle, who we are told, understanding that Count Konigsmark had some intentions to wait upon her Ladyship, would not in the least entertain any thoughts of seeing him, since he was suspected to have been the original contriver of the barbarous murder of Thomas Thynn Esq., and therefore to avoid all occasions of opportunity of that kind immediately desired to leave Holland and to come to her native country in which place she thinks that the Count dare not adventure again to show his face to trouble her with his unwelcome Importunities.[4]

If Bette had been complicit in the murder plot she wasted no time in disowning all those who were tainted by it.

On 7 March, the day after Konigsmark had gone ashore at Ostend, Gunman anchored the *Mary* yacht in Rotterdam Harbour. It was 'filthy gusting weather with drifts of snow and showers of haile'.[5] Colonel Sidney, Lady Temple and Lady Bette were all waiting in The Hague, anxious to depart, but there was no point in travelling to Rotterdam until the wind changed direction, for with these south-westerlies blowing they would never escape from the River Meuse. Their accommodation in The Hague was more comfortable than any that could be obtained in Rotterdam.

They waited with growing impatience for an entire week. Then, on the night of 14 March, 'came a gale at North East by East'. Gunman at once dispatched a letter to Colonel Sidney informing him that he was now ready to weigh anchor. On the fifteenth the passengers boarded and on the following morning they set sail. It was 'just 3 days and 1 hour after the full moon', noted Gunman. At five thirty in the afternoon of 17 March he landed his passengers safely at Deptford.

From Deptford, Bette went by coach straight to Northumberland House, and according to the newspapers shut herself away there with only her servants for company. A succession of relatives and friends, 'persons of quality', now took the opportunity of visiting her. They found her 'very much dejected in the unfortunate death of esquire Thynn'.[6] She told the world 'that she was altogether surprised upon the news she read of that unhappy accident, as not imagining that such barbarity could be enacted by man, much more in England'. She was probably in a state of understandable shock concerning the violence of Thynn's death, although feeling the way she did about him she can hardly have been grieving about the loss of the man himself. Nor did she pretend that she was. According to the *Daily Intelligencer* of 23 March she declared she would 'not appear in publick until the Court comes from Newmarket'. Since that was only a couple of weeks away, she was not envisaging a prolonged period of seclusion.

There was still much speculation as to whether Konigsmark would slip back into the country and renew his courtship. There were numerous sightings of his long blonde hair in London's fog-blurred and overcrowded streets, all of which turned out to be false. Bette, for her part, continued to tell the world she had no intention of admitting him into her presence.

But if it wasn't going to be Konigsmark, who was it going to be, for the world would not leave her unmarried for long – that much was certain. Just as the recent experiments of Robert Boyle had proved that nature abhorred a vacuum, so society could not tolerate an unwed heiress. There were those who believed that Henry Sidney was the new front runner, but in most respects Sidney could not be considered a serious contender. He had no money, was even older than Thynn had been, and was just as debauched in his habits. On the other hand, he was tolerably handsome and he had been the gallant knight who had both rescued her and brought her safely home. What made tongues wag even faster was that the day after Bette and Sidney had arrived together in London, Sidney had set out for Newmarket to speak with the King on urgent business.

Bette may have made the decision not to appear in public, but by public she clearly meant the halls of Whitehall or the salons of the fashionable gentry. A little shopping was another matter. She had not been back in England more than a few days before she was tempted to pay a visit to the New Exchange, a smart shopping centre at the top end of the Strand, situated handily close to Northumberland House. It had two long double galleries of shops and was particularly renowned for its drapers and mercers. The Hague offered nothing like the same enormous range of fabrics, and Bette was probably feeling the need to replenish her wardrobe with some new pigskin gloves or silk scarves, or perhaps a fine new satin dress.

The extravagance of her spending soon began to draw attention, and it wasn't long before she was recognised. The word went quickly round that Lady Bette was at large, and within minutes an angry mob had gathered and was hurling abuse at her and accusing her of being responsible for the death of her husband. 'The Mobile cry'd out that she was a Murderer etc. and what not; adding, Let us pull her to pieces.'[7] It must have been a terrifying moment. The streets of London at this time could quickly turn ugly and brutal. A contemporary pamphlet entitled *A true relation of all the bloody Murthers that hath been committed in and about the suburbs of London since the 4th of this instant June 1677* remarked that it was 'a dangerous adventure for an honest person to walk along the streets'[8] because of the risk of a random and violent attack. Bette was doubly vulnerable, not just because of her obvious wealth, but now also because she was seen as a legitimate target. She was an intriguer with foreign powers, a husband murderer and even a witch. On this occasion she was lucky. Her servants immediately closed in around her and rushed her to safety. According to the report in *The Loyal Protestant*, she was forced to leave her purchases behind and escape by jumping into a hackney cab.

It was perhaps this upsetting experience that prompted the publication, in the form of a broadsheet, of a letter purporting to be written by Count Konigsmark to Lady Bette, 'faithfully translated from the original French'.[9] In it Konigsmark remarked that he had heard how 'some malicious people do accuse you as privy to the death of Mr Thynn, and that some Audacious libellers have Exposed you in their pamphlets'. He apologised that it was because of his own actions that Bette should have suffered in this way. 'I am sorry my respects for you should expose you to that unjust Censure.' He then went on to assert her innocence. 'I do declare before God and the World, you knew nothing of it, nor was any way ayding, consenting or abetting in it.' His whole avowed purpose in writing the letter was to 'do you that right in clearing you of those aspersions which the world has cast upon you on my behalf'. For this assertion of Bette's innocence to carry any weight, it was necessary that Konigsmark should admit to his own guilt, which he did. 'I should have gone the Honourable way of my Accomplices and a halter put a period to my passion. But hanging goes by Destiny not desert.' He concluded the letter by abandoning any hope that he might once have had that Bette might marry him and begging her forgiveness, 'since all other hopes and future pretentions are laid aside, let me only Intreat this one favour (which is the last I shall ever beg) that you will allow me at this distance to bear the Title of Your Servant Konigsmark'.

It seems unlikely that this letter was genuine, although it is possible that parts of it were and Bette's supporters had chosen to adapt it. It did serve the useful purpose of absolving Bette of any blame, while also perpetuating the romantic myth that Konigsmark had acted purely out of passion: 'That I lov'd you is a sufficient proof, that I could venture so far as to be hang'd for you.' The letter was printed and published by a 'J.S.', working in London. The initials J.S. are common enough. It could have been anyone, but it may have been Jonathan Swift, who was working as William Temple's secretary at the time.

Dorothy Temple, William's wife, had been the person who had done more than anyone to rescue Bette from Thynn and whisk her out of the country. She had subsequently stayed with Bette during her period of exile in The Hague. William Temple was one of the first to visit Bette at Northumberland House after her return. He was regarded by the wider world as an important adviser and mentor to Bette, and it was to him that Sir Thomas Thynn wrote, just as soon as his cousin had been decently buried, regarding the delicate matter of any claims Bette might now have upon the late Thomas Thynn's estate. Longleat and its surrounding lands passed to Sir Thomas, but the question of whether Lady Bette had legally been married had never been decided by the courts. If Bette now chose to change her original position and assert that the marriage was after all genuine, as Thynn had always argued, then she would be entitled to £1,500 a year jointure under the terms of the original contract.

After his meeting with Bette, William Temple was able to send Sir Thomas a letter, postmarked Sheen, 29 March 1682, with some welcome news. The Lady Bette 'assures me that she never intended to make any

use or advantage of any such deeds ... unless it should be to defend herself of any claims of Mr Thynn's executors and since you can assure there
can be nothing of that kind I am confident you may reckon there will be
nothing of the other from my Lady Ogle'.[10] It is difficult to conceive what
claims the executors would have had against Bette's property, but perhaps
William Temple was just playing safe. The knowledge that Bette was not
interested in adding to her already ample fortune must have come as an
enormous relief to Thynn's beneficiaries.

William Temple's letter shows him to be the accomplished professional
diplomat. But more interestingly, it also reveals him as being by this time
heartily sick and tired of the whole Lady Bette business. He claimed that
he had helped broker this agreement purely because of a prior promise to
Sir Thomas and that apart from this he did 'keep my resolution of having
nothing more to do with her affairs'. Does this suggest he was wavering
in his support of her? Did he believe she was indeed tainted by murder?
Or was it simply out of a general fatigue with the whole business that he
now wished to distance himself? He certainly went out of his way to style
himself as 'a private country gentleman', and complained that the recent
demands that had been made upon him were 'too hard for a man that has
quite forgot all past employments'. But then he was very preoccupied with
his garden at Sheen, and had declared publicly in his writings that a man
over fifty should not involve himself in commerce or have sex.

Sir Thomas Thynn had not restricted himself to approaching William
Temple in the matter of Lady Bette's possible claims on the estate of the
deceased. He had also lobbied George Savile, the Earl of Halifax, and
Charles's foremost minister. Halifax's reply, also dated 29 March, is both
blunt and cynical: 'I told my opinion in my last letter, that it was advisable for you to come up, and fix my Lady [Bette's] generosity whilst it is
warme; it is a virtue that often cooleth upon second thoughts, and you
will hereafter be thought wanting to yourself, if by losing this critical time,
you should hereafter pay 1500 a year.'[11] Halifax thought Bette's claim was
a good one and her offer very unselfish, and one that should therefore be
seized upon immediately.

Halifax concluded his letter with a reference to the marriage merry-
go-round, which Bette once again found herself on. She 'liveth alone in
Northumberland House, where I believe she will be as much courted by
her several friends to have the selling of her, as she can be by her most
passionate pretenders of another kind'. Halifax did not think that the dis-
astrous outcome of the last attempt to sell Bette into marriage would in

any way put off new fortune hunters from coming forward in their droves. Perhaps he was basing his opinion on the letter he had just received from Sir William Coventry, his first secretary, who had described, 'the rush of suitors by which the ill fated young lady was already besieged'.[12]

Hanging in Chains

43

MILE END ROAD

Who knows the fate of his bones, or how often he is to be bury'd?
Who has the Oracle of his ashes, or where they are to be scattered?
– Sir Thomas Browne, *Hydriotaphia*[1]

O n 25 March the indefatigably curious John Evelyn went to view
Vratz's corpse.

I went hence to see the Corps of that obstinate creature Coll. Vratz the
German murderer of Mr Thynn (set on by the Principal Count Konigsmark)
the King permitting his body should be transported to his owne Country,
(being it seemes a person of a good family) it being one of the first, which
was embaulmed by a Particular art invented by one Will: Russell a Coffin
Maker; which presser[v]ed the body without disboweling or using to any
appearance any bituminous matter; The flesh florid, soft and full, as if the
person were Onely sleeping: The Cap: having now ben dead nere 15 daies:
He lay exposed in a very rich Coffin, lined with lead.[2]

There was much interest at this time in the art of embalming without disembowelling. The same edition of *The Impartial Protestant Mercury* that had reported on the murder of Thomas Thynn also had an advertisement placed in it by the enterprising John Maddox, who operated out of a shop called The Coffin, situated in Old Jewry, London. He claimed to have invented a method of preserving that enabled him:

> far beyond the pretence of any person, [to] secure the corpse of men women or children, from any ill scent or annoyance to the place where the same is kept without embalming, disembowelling, or wrapping in seacloth, so that the same may be kept above ground as long as desired, although seven years or more ... And although a corpse smell ever so bad by reason of purging, hot weather, or the unskilful doings of others, he taketh it away immediately, so soon as put into a coffin of his own preparing, he having practised and performed the same for above twenty years last past to great satisfaction and on reasonable terms.[3]

Evelyn was clearly impressed by the work that had been done on Vratz's corpse, but he was also disapproving that such a notorious criminal should be accorded such magnificence. It was indeed most unusual that a convicted murderer's remains should be permitted to be transported abroad, particularly in such an expensive and ostentatious manner. Lord Justice Pemberton was summoned by the Privy Council 'to attend to explain why Captain Vratz body not disposed of in the usual manner in such cases'.[4] They were informed that it was already out of Pemberton's hands. The King himself had given his permission. The Privy Council had apparently not bothered to check with the King first.

When the bodies were cut down, Stern's corpse was handed over to his 'friends' for them to dispose of as best they could. It is difficult to think who these friends might have been, for he seems to have been a lonely figure, Vratz being his only known intimate. It is possible that Vratz did arrange for him to have a decent burial as a last-minute gesture of comradeship. Alternatively Stern's corpse may have been taken possession of by those whose business it was to strip the dead of their last saleable items – clothes, rings, teeth, hair.

The fate of Borosky's remains provided a gruesome contrast to the care accorded to Vratz. An 'express writ'[5] came from Newmarket on the morning of the executions that Borosky's body was to be hung up as a public exhibit until it rotted, as a deterrent to others tempted to commit similar crimes. In accordance with this diktat, after his corpse was cut down it was unceremoniously thrown back on the cart and returned to Newgate. The next day about two in the afternoon it 'was carried through the City ... to Mile End Green and there hanged in chains'.[6] The choice of Mile End Green was significant, it 'being the road from the seaports where most of the Northern nations doe land'.[7] So Borosky's body was bound in tight iron hoops that resembled a close-fitting cage. Afterwards it was hoisted aloft, and then left to swing and be pecked at by crows until it turned into a skeleton. There came lashing rain and a brisk wind and the following night there was a full moon and more wild gusts of wind. As Borosky's blotched skin began to shrivel and his flesh fall away, and the iron hoops of his macabre corset creaked and groaned, he must have become an object of terror and awe for all those who passed that way. Pepys, who was not particularly squeamish about such gruesome spectacles, records how he 'rode under the man that hangs upon Shooter's Hill, and a filthy sight it was to see how his flesh was shrunk to his bones'.[8]

Petworth, after the alterations carried out by Charles, 6th Duke of Somerset

44 ≋

THE HOUSE ON THE HILL

**Had he not been a Duke he would have made an admirable master
of ceremonies, or keeper of the puppets.**

– Jonathan Swift on Charles Seymour, 6th Duke of Somerset[1]

Some time in April, Bette went down to Petworth. After her
unpleasant experience at the New Exchange it probably seemed
like a safe haven. It was while she was there, no doubt enjoying
the pleasures of the cherry orchard as it came into blossom, that Charles
Seymour, 6th Duke of Somerset, went to pay his respects and renew his
previous courtship. It was Seymour who had been the main contender
for Bette's hand the previous time around, before Thynn had managed
to intrude his suit. He was clearly not daunted by previous failure, nor by
Bette's increasing reputation for being something of a poisoned chalice.

It was entirely in character that Seymour should make his first visit in
great state, accompanied by a vast number of retainers. He loved nothing better than the pomp and theatre of grand ceremonial occasions. His

effort to impress was wasted on Bette. She simply refused to see him. Undeterred, he followed up with a second visit, this time with only one servant in attendance. On this occasion Bette did grant him an audience, but he was told by her that he 'should think no more of it'.[2] Seymour made the standard gallant response, that this command was 'impossible' for him to comply with, 'let the obstacles be ever so great'. He then enlisted the assistance of both his aunts in a lobbying exercise.

It seems the aunts must have succeeded where Seymour himself had failed. On 30 May 1682, Bette and the Duke of Somerset were married in Montagu House. Ralph Montagu had finally topped off his resplendent cupolas and chimneys, and his magnificent new palace was placed at the young couple's disposal. It provided him with an admirable occasion for showing it off. The choice of venue suggests that Bette had finally patched up her difficult relationship with her mother, Elizabeth Wriothesley. Bette had just turned fifteen years of age and it was her third marriage in the space of just three years.

Had Bette in the end been genuinely moved by Seymour's attentions? It is more probable that she was simply pressurised by the weight of family opinion in his favour. She had little choice but to get married again. If she didn't marry she would once more come under the control of her grandmother. She would also run the constant risk of being abducted. Even if she managed to escape capture and rape, she couldn't avoid the queues of suitors forever pestering her.

In many ways Charles Seymour was a suitable choice for husband. He was twenty years of age, and like Bette came from a family with a long and distinguished pedigree. He did not have the financial resources that Bette possessed, but, unlike most of his peers, he also did not have a reputation for dissolute habits. His portraits at this time show him to have been reasonably good-looking in a rather baby-faced, petulant-mouthed kind of way. His main drawback seems to have been that he was unbelievably dull and pompous, obsessed with his own rank and importance, and devoted to the niceties of Court protocols above everything else. Lord Hardwicke referred to him as 'proud' and 'capricious'.[3] Lord Dartmouth said that 'he . . . had a very low education, [and] showed it in a very indecent manner . . . His high title came by one man's misfortune and his great estate by another's, for he was born to neither but elated with both to a ridiculousness.'[4] Not exactly an outstanding character reference. Lord Stanhope's verdict was only slightly more charitable: 'a well meaning man, but of shy and proud habits and slender understanding'.[5]

Unlike her first two marriages, Bette's third foray into the conjugal state was consummated with speed. By the middle of August she was pregnant. Unfortunately, she then contracted smallpox. According to the gossips, 'her recovery [was] much doubted'.[6] In the event the baby miscarried, but Bette survived.

The marriage was reputed by some to be unhappy. According to William Legge, 1st Earl of Dartmouth, Somerset 'treated her [Bette] with little affection though he owed all he had, except an empty title, to her'.[7] But one of the few private letters of Bette's to survive suggests otherwise. There is only one to her husband, undated, but most probably written some time in the early 1690s, and it suggests that there was between the two of them a tenderness and warmth that was not perhaps immediately evident to her contemporaries.[8] She is writing from London, where she is on Court duty. Seymour has remained at Petworth. She starts off by remarking that she is pleased that he is happy with 'his house on the hill', as she calls the Palladian mansion that Charles is busy converting Petworth into. She expresses herself bored with the political intrigues of London: 'Lord Arlington dined with me yesterday and stopd til 5 oclock which made me very peevish.' But she uses Arlington overstaying his welcome as a neat lead-in to a small wifely compliment: '. . . til your letter came which I was so well pleased to read that it put me quite out of my ill humor'. Equally affectionate is her manner of signing off: 'I believe you will think it time for me to end this which I will doe with telling my dearest that I am unalterably yours, Thursday night 10 oclock.'

Bette, as Duchess of Somerset

POSTSCRIPT

Beware of Carrots from Northumberlond
Carrots sown Thyn a deep root may get
If so be they are in Sommer set
Their Conyngs mark thou, for I have been told,
They Assassine when young, and Poison when old.

– Jonathan Swift, *The Windsor Prophecy*[1]

B ette appears to have been a model wife. After the miscarriage, she was to give birth to thirteen children, five of whom died in infancy and five more during her own lifetime. Despite the usual maternal tribulations, she still found the time to lead a full and active political life. Unlike her husband, she was highly regarded for both her intelligence and the subtlety with which she manoeuvred her way around the treacherous Courts of Queen Mary and Queen Anne. Anne may have had an intense and passionate relationship with Sarah Churchill, wife of the Duke of Marlborough, but it was in the company of Bette that she felt most comfortable. Burnet observed that Bette 'was by much the greatest favourite when the queen died'.[2] Hamilton recorded in his diary how 'the

Soft courteous way of the Duchess's speaking' always had a calming effect on Anne.[3] He considered the secret of Bette's success was that she 'never press'd the Queen Hard, nothing makes the Queen more Uneasie than that'. Bette's political acumen is probably best summed up in the words of the Earl of Oxford, Queen Anne's First Minister, who, when his ministry was in deep trouble, wrote: 'Send for the Duchess of Somerset. Nobody else can save us.'[4]

Almost everyone who knew Bette remarked on her tact and decency. One of the few dissenting voices was that of Jonathan Swift. He seemed to harbour a particular dislike of her that possibly went back to his early days as Secretary to William Temple. He frequently accused her of being practised at underhand plotting for the sake of self-aggrandisement, and suggested that her facility in this dark art originated from her experience of the Thynn affair. 'The danger of losing power, favour, profit, and a shelter from domestic tyranny, were strong inclinations [in her] to stir up a working brain, early practised in all sorts of intriguing,' he wrote in his pamphlet *Some advice humbly offer'd to the Members of the October Club.*[5] It is noticeable that he doesn't just accuse her of intrigue for the sake of personal enrichment. He also suggests that she particularly welcomed the favour of the Court because it provided her with some protection against her husband, whom Swift regarded as oppressive and domineering. But Somerset had by this stage already been politically marginalised and now largely devoted his energies to remodelling Petworth to reflect his perception of his own grandeur. It was Bette who was the true source of power and influence.

The truth is that Swift saw in Bette a formidable political opponent to his Tory masters and he was determined to try and destroy her through the satiric power of his pen. To this end he dredged up the old rumours of Bette's complicity in the Thynn murder in his poem *The Windsor Prophecy.* He wrote it on 23 December 1711 and sent it off to his printers the next day, enclosing a copy for his great friend Mrs Masham. On Christmas day, at lunchtime, he called on Mrs Masham, obviously expecting to bask in her praise of his wicked wit. Mrs Masham, however, clearly felt that his references to Bette overstepped the mark.[6] She 'desired me not to let the Prophecy be published, for fear of angering the Queen about the Duchess of Somerset', recorded a crestfallen Swift in his *Journal to Stella.* After his meeting with Mrs Masham, Swift too began to get cold feet. He immediately 'writ the printers to stop them'. It was, however, too late. The poem had already gone to press and was being distributed. It had taken just three days between the author sitting down to pen his masterpiece and printed copies going on general sale. But for Swift such instant publication was to backfire horribly. Bette, predictably, was not amused by this raking over of old scandals. She quietly and unostentatiously spoke to the Queen and had her block the bishopric that Swift had recently been promised. It was to put an end to his clerical career.

Bette died some ten years later, on 23 November 1722, aged fifty-five. She had been complaining for the previous few weeks of a pain in her cheek. She was buried in the Somerset family tomb in Salisbury Cathedral.

The Duke of Somerset soon married again, this time to the daughter of the 2nd Earl of Nottingham, but his reputation for ridiculous pride did not diminish with old age. He was said to have deducted £20,000 from the inheritance of one of his own daughters because she dared to sit down in his presence while he was dozing. His absurd pomposity did, however, result in him making a belated and unintentional compliment to Bette after she was dead and buried. When his new wife tapped him playfully on the shoulder with a fan, he turned and remarked to her: 'Madam, my first Duchess was a Percy and she never took such a liberty.'[7]

On 11 March 1705, Evelyn noted in his diary that the Dowager Countess Howard had died, 'a most excellent religious lady'. The passage of time and her longevity had it seemed done something to heal her reputation. She was eighty-three years old and left most of her property to the Duke of Somerset. Bette, who was of a generally forgiving nature, had reconciled with her grandmother many years earlier. The old Countess doted on her great-grandchildren, causing Bette to remark to her husband: 'You never saw anything so fond as she is of Percy'[8] (at the time Percy was Bette's youngest son).

Elizabeth Wriothesley, Bette's mother, had died in 1690, after many years of illness. Her husband, the irrepressible Ralph Montagu, promptly married a second wealthy wife, the Duchess of Albemarle, the Duke of Newcastle's daughter and Henry Ogle's sister. She was very rich and very mad and had declared publicly that she would only ever wed the Emperor of China. Most of her suitors were put off by this demand, but not the enterprising and unscrupulous Montagu, who had the audacity to dress up and woo her in that guise. After the marriage had been formally concluded, he had her locked up as being insane and happily proceeded to fritter away her money.

Count Konigsmark spent most of his remaining few years of life either in France or fighting in the Venetian army led by his uncle Otto, against the Turks in Greece. He took with him, disguised as his page, a beautiful young English girl. The details are given in the *Mémoires de la Comtesse d'Orléans*: 'The English ladies are said to be much given to running away with their lovers. I knew a Count Konigsmark, whom a young English lady followed in the dress of a page. He had her with him at Chambord, and as there was no room for her in the Castle, he lodged her under a tent which he had put up in the forest.'[9] It was to this romantic setting that the Comtesse d'Orléans asked to be taken so that she could meet Konigsmark's mistress in person. She was suitably impressed: 'Never in my life did I see anything prettier than this girl ... She had large and beautiful eyes, a charming little nose, and an elegant mouth and teeth ... her hair was a beautiful chestnut colour and hung about her neck in large curls.' As Konigsmark never returned to England after his departure in such haste in early March 1682, it seems that this girl may have travelled with him in the royal yacht. She may even have been the young woman in white who went on an unsuccessful errand to King Charles to solicit the life of Captain Vratz. While Konigsmark lived he apparently took good care of this paragon of beauty, and when she gave birth to his baby he placed her and the child in a convent, Fontevrault Abbey, where the abbess was the aunt of his close friend the Comte de Thianges, nephew of Louis XIV's influential mistress, Madame de Montespan. Konigsmark died while fighting against the Turks, at the battle of Argos in the Morea on 29 August 1686.[10] The unnamed young woman with the chestnut hair died shortly afterwards. The orphaned baby was brought up by the nuns at Fontevrault.

Acknowledgments

I owe an immense debt of gratitude to all those archivists and scholars, both past and present, who have helped conserve and catalogue the wonderfully rich source material that still exists for the seventeenth century, which makes books such as this possible.

I would particularly like to thank the Archbishop of Canterbury for access to the Lambeth Palace Library manuscripts, the Dean and Chapter of Westminster for access to Westminster Abbey Library, Lord Egremont for permission to consult the Petworth archive, the Duke of Northumberland for permission to consult the Northumberland archive; the Marquess of Bath for permission to consult the Longleat papers; the Jarvis family for access to the Gunman papers, and the University of Nottingham for copies of relevant letters from the Newcastle (Clumber) Collection. I would also like to thank the staff of the British Library, the National Archives, the Guildhall Library London, the West Sussex Record Office, and Cambridge University Library, for their impressive efficiency in the production of such a diverse wealth of material.

A special thank you must go to my agent, Barbara Levy, and my publisher, Alan Samson, for their enthusiasm and commitment, and many thanks also to Lucinda McNeile and everyone else at Orion who has been involved in the editing, indexing, design and production of this book.

Finally, but most importantly, I would like to thank my family and friends who have given support, encouragement and helpful comment along the way.

Notes

Prologue

1 From *Captain Vrats Ghost*, printed in London, Fleet Street, for J.V., 1682, British Library Cup.21.g.41/27.

2 Arnold Quillan, 1653–86, was the son of Artus Quillan, a Dutch stone carver. The family had workshops in Antwerp and Amsterdam. Arnold was married to Frances Siberechts, daughter of the famous Dutch artist Jan Siberechts, who had been working in England since 1672. Siberechts had painted a view of Longleat House. After Quillan's death at the age of 33 his wife married his former assistant, Jan Ost.

  See Vertue, George, *The Notebooks*, vol. 4 (Oxford 1930–55); Beard, Geoffrey, *Grinling Gibbons* (London 1989).

3 For the full text of the original Latin inscription see Krull, J., *The Antiquities of St Peter's of the Abbey Church of Westminster* (London 1715).

4 Grinling Gibbons also came from Holland, having arrived in England in 1667. His work was discovered and promoted by the diarist John Evelyn, and he was to become the most celebrated of British woodcarvers. In 1681 Gibbons and Quillan went into partnership, but their association was not a success and the partnership was dissolved in May 1683. The document of severance refers to Quillan having achieved 'very little' and to there having been 'severall controversies and differences' between them. See National Archives, C9/415/250.

5 Hatred of Catholics and paranoia about popish plots was rife during the late 1670s and early 1680s and the literature on the subject is vast. See Harris, T., *Restoration* (London 2005) and *London Crowds in the Reign of Charles II* (Cambridge 1987); Hinds, P., *The Horrid Popish Plot* (Oxford 2009); Elliot, A., *A Modest Vindication of Titus Oates, the Salamanca Doctor* (London 1682).

1 The Amsterdam Ordinary

1 Ward, p. 16.

2 Stern, p. 22.

3 For population growth see Earle, P., *A City Full of People* (London 1994); Anon., *A Foreigner's Guide to London* (London 1729).

4 Topographical details are largely taken from Strype, J., *An Atlas of London*, 2 vols (London 1720). See also Morris, D. and Cozens, K., *Wapping 1600–1800* (Brentwood 2009); Morgan, W., *London Actually Surveyed* (London 1682).

5 Stern, p. 22.

6 High Dutch in this period was close to what is now known as German.

7 Stern, p. 24.

8 Stern, p. 24.

9 Stern, p. 24.

10 Stern, p. 24.

11 Reresby, J. and Bridgeman, W., 'Examination of Lieutenant John Stern, Feb 17th 1682 and

Feb 19th 1682', Printed for Richard Chiswell at The Rose and Crown, 1682, published as part of Stern, p. 27.

2 The Royal Exchange

1 The Countess of Rutland was a cousin of Lady Bette. The letter is printed in Historical MSS Commission, Duke of Rutland II, Appendix Part V, 24.2, p. 57.

2 For details on the marriage and subsequent breakdown of relations between Lady Bette and Thynn see the following: Lambeth Palace Library, London, MS, 49 VB 1/4/200 1682 Ogle Somerset; 50 VB 1/4/200 1682 Ogle Somerset; Arches E 7/24, 7/26, 7/108, 7/109; Act Book 23 Oct. 1680–21 Oct. 1682, MS Film 76. Also National Archives, London, Equity Pleadings Chancery, C 6/239/55 Percy v Thynn 1681; and Longleat Archive, copies of MS held at British Library, London, on microfilm, Cavendish, Lady Elizabeth, née Percy. Papers relating to her marriage with Thomas Thynn, vol. XI (Micro 904/21).

3 Major Brett's suggestion regarding immediate bedding and Lady Bette's refusal is detailed in Lambeth Palace Archive, Arches E 7/108. Richard Brett was an MP, held several lucrative sinecures and monopolies and was a notorious gambler. See Calendar of State Papers Domestic various; Calendar of Treasury Books various; Henning, B. D., *House of Commons 1660–1690* (London 1983).

4 Northumberland House was demolished in the 19th century. See Gater, G. H. and Wheeler, E. P., *Survey of London*, vol. 18 (London 1937).

5 For details of Bette's escape see Letter of the Duke of Newcastle to the Duke of Albemarle, 10 Nov. 1681, Historical MSS Commission, Duke of Buccleuch, vol. 1 – 45.1, pp. 334–5. Also Letter of the Earl of Longford to Ormonde, 12 Nov. 1681, Historical MSS Commission, Ormonde, new series vol. 6, p. 223.

6 Details of weather and wind direction have been taken from the logbook of the *Pearl*, National Archives London, ADM 51 3932.

7 The Royal Exchange was more commonly called the Old Exchange to differentiate it from the New Exchange that had recently been built in the Strand. See Strype, J., *An Atlas of London*, 2 vols (London 1720). Also Delaune, T., *The Present State of London* (London 1681).

8 Turkey had been a source of highly prized and glittery mosaic stone for many centuries.

9 Defoe, D., *Conjugal Lewdness or Matrimonial Whoredom* (London 1727). The 1753 Hardwicke Marriage Act was largely introduced as a result of pressure from the aristocracy and was an attempt to put an end to clandestine or forced marriages. See also Outhwaite.

10 There is evidence of Countess Howard's shortness of temper in Rachel Russell's letter to her husband, London, 23 Sept. 1672 – see Russell. There is supporting evidence in Lady Bette's testimony to various courts listed in note 9 chapter 22. Brenan refers to the Countess Howard's fondness for using corporal punishment on her servants. Such punishment was commonplace in seventeenth-century England. See Cliffe, chapter 6, 'Servants and Masters'.

11 The plan to marry off Bette to George Fitzroy had been several years in the making – see Ralph Montagu's letter to Danby, 1 March 1677, Browning, p. 259.

12 See letter of Earl of Longford to Ormonde, 12 Nov. 1681, for details of conversation between Brett and Charles II, published in Ormonde, Historical MSS Commission, new series vol. 6.

13 Letter of the Duke of Newcastle to the Duke of Albemarle, 10 Nov. 1681, Historical MSS Commission, Duke of Buccleuch, vol. 1 – 45.1, pp. 334–5.

14 Duke of Newcastle to Duke of Albemarle, see note 5 above.

15 Charles Bertie to his niece the Countess of Rutland, 18 Nov. 1681, Historical MSS

Commission, Duke of Rutland II, Appendix Part V, 24.2, p. 59.

16 Chaloner Chute to the Countess of Rutland, 15 Nov. 1681, Historical MSS Commission, Duke of Rutland II, Appendix Part V, 24.2, p. 58.

17 Viscountess Campden to her daughter, the Countess of Rutland, 16 Nov. 1681, Historical MSS Commission, Duke of Rutland II, Appendix Part V, 24.2, p. 59.

18 Charles Bertie to his niece the Countess of Rutland, 10 Nov. 1681, Historical MSS Commission, Duke of Rutland II, Appendix Part V, 24.2, p. 58.

19 Duke of Newcastle to Duke of Albemarle, see note 5 above.

3 The Dutch Lutheran Church, Broad Street

1 Luttrell, 5 Aug. 1681.

2 Anon., *Foreigner's Guide to London* (London 1729).

3 See Strype, J., *An Atlas of London*, 2 vols (London 1720).

4 Stern, p. 24.

5 Smith, pp. 269–72.

6 Stern p. 22.

7 Luttrell, entry for 8 Nov. 1681.

4 The *Cleveland* Yacht

1 Osborne, pp. 181–2.

2 Portrait of Lady Temple by Gaspar Netscher, 1671, National Portrait Gallery, London.

3 See the Introduction to the 2001 edition of Osborne's *Letters*, ed. K. Parker.

4 Pepys, *Diary*, 10 March 1660.

5 Strype, J., *An Atlas of London*, 2 vols (London 1720).

6 For a brief résumé of Sidney's life and character, see Fraser, *The Weaker Vessel*, pp. 395–6.

7 National Archives, ADM 2/1726.

8 For details of Royal Yachts see Cowburn, pp. 253–62.

9 National Archives, ADM 2/1726.

10 Ormonde, Historical MSS Commission, New Series, vol. 6, Letter from Earl of Longford to Ormonde, 12 Nov. 1681.

11 Logbook of the *Pearl*, National Archives London, ADM 51 3932.

12 Sidney, pp. 222–4.

13 C.S.P.D. 1680–1682, 16 March 1682, Joshua Bowles to Sir Francis Radclyffe.

14 Ormonde, Historical MSS Commission, New Series, vol. 6, Letter from Earl of Longford to Ormonde, 15 Nov. 1681.

5 Peter's Coffee House

1 Hinds, p. 319, quoting from *The Character of a Coffee House* (London s.n., 1665), p. 2.

2 C.S.P.D. 15 Oct. 1681, Thomas Venn to Richard Newcourt.

3 C.S.P.D. 11 July 1681, Colonel Ralph Stanell to Sir Leoline Jenkins.

4 C.S.P.D. 23 Apr. 1681; 11 May 1681; 19 Nov. 1681.

5 In parliamentary terms the Protestants were the Whigs and the Court Party or Loyalists were the Tories. Not all Tories were Catholics, but they were often smeared with the label Papist.

6 C.S.P.D. 24 Sept. 1681, Sir James Hayes to Sir Leoline Jenkins.

7 C.S.P.D. 7 Oct. 1681, Lord Conway to Sir Leoline Jenkins.

8 See Knights, p. 109.

9 See Peerbooms; also Sutherland, for details of Thompson's character and career.

10 Sutherland, pp. 250–3.

11 Evelyn, J., *Particular Friends*, entry for 28 April 1682.

12 Hinds, pp. 322–5, for an account of this episode.

13 See Hinds, pp. 318–21, for description of coffee houses in this period.

14 *Loyal Protestant and True Domestick Intelligence*, 19 Nov. 1681.

15 Aubrey, *Letters*, p. 480, vol. 2, part 2.

16 Peerbooms, p. 71, quoting *Loyal Protestant and True Domestick Intelligence*.

17 *Observator*, newspaper printed by Roger L'Estrange, edition 30 Nov. 1681.

18 See Harris, T., *London Crowds in the Reign of Charles II* (Cambridge 1987).

19 Anon. poem quoted in Hinds.

6 The Road from Strasbourg to Metz

1 Butler, Samuel, *Characters and Passages from Notebooks*, ed. A. R. Waller (Cambridge 1908), p. 227; quoted in Durston, p. 104.

2 Hargrave, p. 540.

3 C.S.P.D. 17 Aug. 1680.

4 See Chapter 14, note 7.

5 Godley, pp. 69, 84.

6 *Loyal Protestant Mercury*, 14 Feb. 1682. A pistole was a gold coin widely used throughout France and Spain, approximately equivalent in value to one golden guinea.

7 The details of this route are taken from *Carte générale de Postes de France . . . mise au jour par les Héritiers de Homann*, 1745.

8 Published in the *Loyal Protestant Mercury*, 14 Feb. 1682.

9 *True Protestant Mercury*, 9–12 Nov. 1682.

7 Petworth Manor

1 Recipe Book of Anne Glyd, Brockman Papers, BL Add. Ms. 45196 f. 57, quoted in Crawford.

2 For an example of Turner's Petworth see *Dewy Morning, 1810*, in the White Library. For Petworth see National Trust, *Petworth House*, 1997; Jerrome; Hussey.

3 For advice during pregnancy, see Sharp; Woolley; Gelis.

4 See Locke's correspondence with Mapletoft for the latter's views and outlook.

5 For furnishings of Elizabeth Wriothesley's chamber at Petworth see Inventory Petworth 1671, Micro no. 351, Northumberland Archive, Alnwick.

8 Hôtel de la Bazinière

1 Evelyn, *Memoirs*, ed. Bray, p. 611.

2 For character of Algernon, see Temple, p. 123.

3 Anon., *The Character of a Town Gallant* (London 1675), p. 4.

4 Evelyn, *Memoirs*, ed. Bray, p. 611.

5 For Lord Percy's feelings towards his betrothed, see Letter of Lord Percy to Dr Mapletoft, 6 July 1662, quoted in Fonblanque, vol. 2, part 2, p. 479.

6 Joscelyn Percy to Dr Mapletoft, Petworth 5 Oct. 1663, Letters, Micro no. 287, Northumberland Archive, Alnwick.

7 Lord Percy to Dr Mapletoft, 6 July 1662, as above.

8 Lord Percy to Dr Mapletoft, 16 Nov. 1663, as above.

9 Lord Percy to Dr Mapletoft, 22 Oct. 1663, as above.

10 PHA 5809.

11 Fonblanque, vol. II, part 2, p. 482.

12 National Trust, p. 68.

13 Inventory Petworth 1671, as above.

14 For Montagu's general deviousness, see Browning.

15 Gady.

16 Ferrier, pp. 25–6.

17 Wren, p. 105.

18 A *rouillons* was a light carriage for just two persons.

19 Lister.

20 Hist. Ms. Comm. Buccleuch, vol. I, p. 459.

21 Perwich, p. 59.

9 Palazzo Colonna

1 *Avvisi di Roma*, 15 Feb. 1670, quoted in Rancini.

2 C.S.P.D. 1670, 23 April. Whitehall, C. Perrott to Williamson, p. 179.

3 Evelyn, 11 June 1699, *Memoirs*, pp. 573–4.

4 Mancini, p. 125.

5 C.S.P.D. 1670, 3 May, p. 196, Whitehall, H. Muddiman to John Gauntlett, Sarum Newsletter.

6 Fonblanque, II 2, p. 485.

7 Perwich, p. 92. Paris, 10 June 1670.

8 See Houlbrooke, *Death*; Gittings; Misson; Greenhill.

9 Clutterbuck to Williamson, Fleming MSS p. 79, quoted in Hartmann, *Clifford of the Cabal*.

10 The *droit d'aubaine* permitted the monarch to confiscate the property of any deceased foreigner.

11 C.S.P.D. 1670, 9 June, p. 264, Whitehall, H. Muddiman to Thomas Bond.

12 C.S.P.D. 1670, 21 June, p. 287, Dover, J. Carlile to Williamson.

13 Macky, p. 44.

14 Gramont, p. 209.

15 C.S.P.D. 1670, 12 July, p. 329, Portsmouth, Hugh Salisbury to Williamson.

16 Northumberland Archive, Inventory Petworth 1671.

17 Mancini.

18 Locke, vol. I, p. 344.

19 Locke, vol. I, p. 341.

20 Northumberland Archive, Inventory Petworth 1671.

21 The picture is now in Pepys Library, Magdalene College, Cambridge.

22 The original painting by Lely can be viewed at Syon House.

10 Whetstone Park

1 Longleat Papers, vol. X, 15 July 1669, Thomas Thynn to his uncle Sir James Thynn, referred to in Burnett.

2 See Longleat Archive, Tradesman's and other bills, 1671–1681.

3 Wilmot, *Complete Poems*, 'Coxcombs in Place'.

4 Pepys, *Diary*, entry 26 July 1665.

5 Magalotti, *Court of Charles II*, p. 41.

6 See Arnold, pp. 108–9; Spur; Watson.

7 See Hinds.

8 Wilmot, *Complete Poems*, 'Regime de Vivre'.
9 Lord, vol. I, p. 175.
10 Lord, vol. I, pp. 172–4.
11 C.S.P.D. Newsletter, 4 Jan. 1671.
12 Dryden, vol. XI, p. 281.
13 Lord, vol. I, p. 173.
14 Quoted in Goldsworthy, p. 147, 'The Disabled Debauchee'.
15 Lord, vol. I, p. 174.
16 Lord, vol. I, p. 174.

11 Althorp

1 Wilmot, *Letters*.
2 Savile, *Letters to and from*, 14 Feb. 1673, p. 37.
3 Quoted in the Introduction to Savile, *Letters to and from*.
4 Referred to in Dalrymple, *Memoirs*, vol. II, p. 298.
5 See Dibdin for Althorp at this period.
6 Dalrymple.
7 C.S.P.D. 28 Aug. 1671.
8 Quoted in Dibdin, p. xxxviii, referencing James II, *Memoir of his Own Life*.
9 Quoted in Goldsworthy, p. 91.
10 Finch provided a detailed account of what occurred in a letter to his son, 12 Sept. 1671, HMC, Finch, ii, pp. 3–4.
11 Quoted in Goldsworthy, pp. 176–7.
12 Muddiman's letter is quoted in Treglown pp. 68–70.

12 Numéro 50, rue de Vaugirard

1 Sévigné.
2 Locke describes an audace as 'a piece of ordinary loop lace made use of to support the overgrown brim of a flapping hat'.
3 Locke.
4 Sévigné, Paris, 30 Dec. 1672.
5 Sévigné, Paris, 15 Apr. 1673.
6 Sévigné, Paris, 19 May 1673.

13 St James's Park

1 Quoted in Berry, p. 270 (Rachel Wriothesley became Lady Vaughan on her first marriage, and later Lady Russell). The date given by Berry of 2 Feb. 1670 cannot be correct.
2 For St James's Park see Misson, Pepys, Porter, Boulton and Picard.
3 Williamson, Letter from Henry Ball, Whitehall, 13 June 1673.
4 *Rochester Savile Letters*, ed. J. Wilson, note on p. 81.
5 Williamson, Letter from Henry Ball, Whitehall, 15 Aug. 1673.
6 Williamson, Letter from James Vernon, Whitehall, 22 Aug. 1673.
7 Williamson, Letter from James Vernon, Whitehall, 29 Aug. 1673.
8 Williamson, Letter from Sir Robert Southwell, Whitehall, 31 Aug. 1673.
9 Russell, Letter from Lady Vaughan to Mr Russell, London, 23 Sept. 1672.
10 Russell, Letter from Lady Vaughan to Mr Russell, London, 23 Sept. 1672.
11 Quoted in Fonblanque, vol. II, part 2, p. 490.
12 Williamson, Letter from T. Derham, London, 5 Nov. 1673.

13 Williamson, Letter from Sir Gilbert Talbot, Whitehall, 13 Nov. 1673.
14 Quoted in Fonblanque, vol. II, part 2, p. 490.

14 Northumberland House

1 Gouge, treatise 5, on the duties of children.
2 For feminine cosmetics and fashion generally see Evelyn, Mary; Woolley; Picard; and PHA 258 and 259 for Bette's personal predilections.
3 Mrs Stanhope is frequently mentioned as accompanying Bette on her travels to France, and had her own bedchamber at Petworth, the furnishings of which are itemised, suggesting that she was a lady of some social standing. See PHA 6261, Inventory of everything at Petworth, 1680.
4 Evelyn, *Fumifugium*, pp. 7–8.
5 For details of the Dowager Countess, Elizabeth Howard's love of pomp, see Fonblanque, vol. II, part 2, p. 491.
6 Batten, pp. 93–6.
7 Hooke, *Diary*, pp. 115, 133.
8 Browning, vol. II, p. 259, quoting Montagu's letter to Danby, Paris, 1 March 1677.
9 Browning as above.
10 Fonblanque, vol. II, part 2, p. 493, quoting 'Saccharissa' Lady Sunderland's letter to Algernon Sidney, State Papers, 12 March 1679.
11 Evelyn, *Diary*, 18 Dec. 1684.
12 Russell, Lady Northumberland to Lady Russell, 11 Feb. 1676.
13 Russell, as above.

15 St James's Park at Night

1 Wilmot, *Complete Poems*.
2 Courtin to Louis XIV, 9 July 1676, Corr. Angleterre, CXXA, f. 143, quoted in Andrews.
3 Courtin to Marquis de Pomponne, 20 July 1676, quoted in Hartmann.
4 Rochester, from the poem 'Cullen with his flock of misses', 1679.
5 H.M.C., Rutland MSS, vol. II, pp. 34–6; Rutland II, appendix Part V, pp. 44–6; also Hartmann.
6 Montagu to Danby, Paris, 1 March 1677, quoted in Browning, vol. II, p. 259.
7 H.M.C. Ormonde MSS, vol. IV, pp. 443–4.
8 Hawkins, entries for years 1676, 1677.
9 Barbara Palmer to Charles II, Paris, Tuesday 28 June 1678, BL Harleian MSS 7006 ff. 171–6, quoted in full in Andrews, Appendix, p. 202.
10 Barbara Palmer to Charles II, Paris, July 1678, BL Harleian MSS 7006 ff. 171–6, quoted in full in Andrews, Appendix, p. 210.
11 Barbara Palmer to Charles II, Paris, Tuesday 28 June 1678, BL Harleian MSS 7006 ff. 171–6, quoted in full in Andrews, Appendix, pp. 202–3.
12 H.M.C. Ormonde MSS, vol. IV, p. 443.
13 Browning, vol. II, pp. 566–7, n. 6.
14 Sidney, Dowager Countess of Sunderland to Mr Sidney, 23 Jan. 1679.

16 The Studio of Peter Lely

1 North, p. 237.
2 Porter, quoting the Earl of Bedford, p. 7. See also Sheppard, F. H.W., *Survey of London* (1970), vol. 36, p. 323.

3 For Lely's studio and life, see Kirby Talley; Hendriks; Baker; Barber.

4 Vertue, vol. IV, p. 169.

5 Horace Walpole, *Anecdotes of Painting in England*, p. 92, vol. II, 3rd edition, London 1876, quoted in Kirby Talley, p. 748.

6 Gérard de Lairesse, *The Art of Painting*, trans. J. F. Fritsch (London 1738), p. 345, quoted in Kirby Talley, p. 748.

7 General term of abuse quoted in Hendriks.

8 British Library, Add. Ms. 32506, fol. 176v, Autobiography of the Hon. Richard North.

9 Temple, Dorothy, Chicksands 1653, p. 173 (ed. Parry, 1858 edition).

10 Letter from the Marquess of Ormonde to the Earl of Ossory, 10 Dec. 1678, H.M.C. Ormonde, New Series 5.

11 Brenan, p. 377, quoting a holograph letter in the possession of Lord Leconfield.

17 Syon House

1 Allestree, p. 177.

2 Nottingham University, Dept. of Manuscripts, Pw1/410.

3 Sidney, letter from the Countess of Sunderland to Henry Sidney, 12 March 1679.

4 Nottingham University, Dept. of Manuscripts, Pw1/410.

5 Evelyn, *Diary*, p. 392, vol. IV, entry for 23 Oct. 1684.

6 Nottingham University, Dept. of Manuscripts, Pw1/410.

7 Quoted in Watson, pp. 12–13.

8 Russell, letter of Lady Russell to the Countess of Ogle, 1 April 1679.

18 Petworth Manor Revisited

1 Charles Sedley, *The Mulberry-Garden*, Act I, scene I, *The Works of the Hon. Sir Charles Sedley*, vol. II (London 1722).

2 Petworth Archive PHA 258.

3 Nottingham University, Dept. of Manuscripts, Pw1/75.

4 Petworth Archive PHA 258, and PHA 259.

5 Makin, p. 22.

6 Makin, p. 11.

7 Makin, p. 36.

8 Makin, p. 23.

9 Bickley, p. 137.

19 Longleat

1 Lord, vol. II, p. 273.

2 H.M.C. Rutland MSS, vol. II, 12th Report, Appendix Part V, pp. 49–50, Lady Chaworth to her brother Lord Roos, at Belvoir Castle, London, 16 Apr. 1678.

3 As above.

4 C.S.P.D. 1679–80, p. 377, newsletter to Christopher Bowman at Newcastle, 22 Jan. 1680, London.

5 C.S.P.D. 1681, p. 515, Thomas Venn to Richard Newcourt, 15 Oct. 1681, Ham.

6 For details of Thynn's wardrobe see Longleat Archive, Tradesman's and other bills.

7 From Dryden's poem *Absalom and Achitophel* (London 1681).

20 The Plaza Mayor, Madrid

1 Aulnoy, *The Ingenious and Diverting Letters*.

2 C.S.P.D. 17 August 1680. The confusion over Konigsmark's military rank was understandable. His uncle, Otto, was a general in Louis XIV's army.

3 For Charles II of Spain see Nada, also the painting by Coello in the Prado Gallery, Madrid.

4 For bullfights and Madrid in this period see, Salgado; Dunlop; Villars, Madame de; Villars, Pierre; and Anon., *An Exact Relation*.

5 Aulnoy, *The Ingenious and Diverting Letters*, Letter X.

6 As above.

21 The Wilderness

1 Evelyn, *Elysium*, p. 133.

2 Gadbury, John.

3 See PHA 5807 for typical Petworth Estate activity at this period.

4 Evelyn, *Diary*, vol. II, p. 81.

5 Lambeth, Arches, E 7/108.

6 As above.

7 As above.

8 See Brenan, pp. 398–400, for the early life of Charles, Duke of Somerset, and his elder brother.

9 Lambeth, Arches, E 7/108.

22 The House of Mr Brouncker

1 Pepys, *Diary*, 29 Apr. 1667.

2 See Henning, p. 729, for Evelyn quote and brief life history.

3 See Allen for details of this abduction.

4 The original painting is in the National Portrait Gallery.

5 Allen.

6 Quoted in Lasch, p. 97.

7 C.S.P.D. 1714–1719, p. 323.

8 Lambeth, Arches, E 7/108.

9 Lambeth as above.

23 Welbeck

1 Quoted in Savile, George.

2 Nottingham University MS, Pw1/410. The quotations throughout this chapter are all taken from this document unless otherwise indicated.

3 Nottingham University MS, Henry Ogle's debts, 1 Nov. 1684, Pw1/402.

24 Major Brett's House, Richmond

1 This is the only known surviving portrait of the Dowager Countess. The flower in her hand suggests it was painted just before her marriage to Algernon, 10th Earl of Northumberland, in 1642 as his second wife. A noted beauty, she was one of several daughters of Theophilus Howard, 2nd Earl of Suffolk.

2 Anon., *The Compleat Gamester*.

3 Russell, Elizabeth Wriothesley's letter to Lady Russell, 18 Feb. 1676.

4 See Delpech, p. 81.

5 Lambeth Palace Library, Arches E 7/108.

6 Henning, vol. I, see entry for Richard Brett.

7 Lambeth Palace Library, Arches E 7/108.

8 National Archives, PROB 5/646, Thomas Thynn of Longleat. Miscellaneous Inventories, Accounts, and Associated Documents, 1689.

9 Salmon, p. 446, quoting Echard, *History of England*.

10 H.M.C. Rutland, vol. II; Chaloner Chute to the Countess of Rutland, 15 Nov. 1681, pp. 58–9.

11 Lambeth Palace Library, Arches E 7/108.

12 Lambeth Palace Library, Arches E 7/108.

13 Longleat Archive, vol. XI, Affidavit etc. deposing to the particulars of his marriage with Lady Ogle 1681, ff. 108–19.

14 Longleat Archive, vol. XI, Affidavit.

15 Lambeth Palace Library, Arches E 7/108.

25 Lady Katherine's Bedchamber

1 Longleat Archive, vol. XI, f. 64, Singer, Anne wife of R. Singer, letter to her husband.

2 Longleat Archive, vol. XI, Affidavit.

3 Longleat Archive, vol. XI, Affidavit.

4 Longleat Archive, vol. XI, Affadavit.

5 Lambeth Palace Library, Arches E 7/108.

6 Lambeth Palace Library, Arches E 7/108.

7 Lambeth Palace Library, Arches E 7/108.

8 Chaloner Chute to the Countess of Rutland, 15 Nov. 1681, pp. 58–9, H.M.C. Duke of Rutland MSS vol. II.

9 Lambeth Palace Library, Arches E 7/108.

10 Lambeth Palace Library, Arches E 7/108.

11 Lambeth Palace Library, Arches E 7/108.

12 Hall and Keane v Jane Potter, *Journal of the House of Lords*, vol. 15, 11 January 1695/6.

13 Lambeth Palace Library, Arches E 7/108.

14 Lambeth Palace Library, Arches E 7/108.

15 Lambeth Palace Library, Arches E 7/108.

16 Longleat Archive, vol. XI, Affidavit.

17 *The Reports of Sir Cresswell Levinz*, vol. 3, p. 411, (Dublin 1793–97).

26 Madame Fourcard's House, Leather Lane

1 Quoted in Goldsworthy, pp. 129–30.

2 Blanchard, p. 18.

3 Blanchard, p. 24.

4 Savile, *Rochester Savile Letters*, 2 July 1678.

5 Savile, *Rochester Savile Letters*, July 1678, p. 65.

6 Wilmot, *Complete Poems*.

7 Savile, *Rochester Savile Letters*, July 1678.

8 For a general history of syphilis, see Brown, Kevin.

9 Earl of Longford to Ormonde, 12 Nov. 1681, London, H.M.C. MSS Marquess of Ormonde, vol. VI.

10 Quoted in Brenan, p. 385.

11 C.S.P.D. 1682, Jan., p. 48.

12 *Impartial Protestant Mercury*, Issue 86, 14–17 Feb. 1681.

27 The Royal Palace in The Hague

1 British Library Add. Ms. 37979.
2 Osborne, *The Letters*.
3 British Library Add. Ms. 37979, Thomas Plott to Mr Blathwayt, 28 Nov. 1681.
4 British Library Add. Ms. 37979, Thomas Plott to Mr Blathwayt, 28 Nov. 1681.
5 British Library Add. Ms. 37979, Thomas Plott to Mr Blathwayt, 2 Dec. 1681.
6 For Holland at this time see Ward, *A Trip*; Temple, *Observations*.
7 British Library Add. Ms. 37979, Thomas Plott to Mr Blathwayt, 2 Dec. 1681.
8 British Library Add. Ms. 37979, Thomas Plott to Mr Blathwayt, 9 Dec. 1681.
9 British Library Add. Ms. 37979, Thomas Plott to Mr Blathwayt, 9 Dec. 1681.
10 Earl of Longford to Ormonde, 18 Feb. 1682, H.M.C. Ormonde MS N.S VI, p. 315.
11 National Archives, C 6/239/55, 17 Dec. 1681.
12 Burney Collection of Newspapers, British Library.
13 William Montagu to Lord Montagu, 15 Dec. 1681, H.M.C. Duke of Buccleuch, vol. I, p. 335.
14 C.S.P.D. 1682, Jan., p. 48.
15 Evelyn, *Diary*, entry for 15 Nov. 1681.
16 Evelyn, *Diary*, entry for 15 Nov. 1681.

28 Lodgings, King Street, Westminster

1 Burney Collection of Newspapers, British Library.
2 *Loyal Protestant* no. 109, 28 Jan. 1682.
3 Luttrell, entry for 13 Jan. 1682.
4 Anon., *Tryal and Condemnation*, for details of Konigsmark's and Vratz's return to London.
5 Stern, *Last Confession*, p. 26.
6 Quoted in Porter, illustration 26. Defoe was well placed to know the attractions or otherwise of King Street. In 1696 he became a tenant of Lord Weymouth, and took a lease on the house in Canon Row where Thomas Thynn had previously lived. It may explain part of his interest in the Captain Vratz legend. Longleat Archive, vol. XXIV, f. 311.
7 Stern, *Last Confession*, pp. 24–7.
8 Stern, *Last Confession*, p. 25.
9 Stern, *Last Confession*, p. 28.
10 Anon., *Tryal and Condemnation*, p. 30.
11 Reresby, *Memoirs*, p. 253.
12 Anon., *Tryal and Condemnation*, p. 30.
13 Stern, *Last Confession*; Anon., *Tryal and Condemnation*; Godley.

29 The House of the Swedish Envoy

1 Godley, p. 85.
2 Anon., *Tryal and Condemnation*, p. 42.
3 Defoe, *A Tour thro' the Whole Island of Great Britain*.
4 For Nicholas Barbon's extraordinary career as a developer see Elizabeth McKellar, *The Birth of Modern London: The Development and Design of the City 1660–1720*, particularly p. 51.
5 Godley, pp. 84–5.
6 Godley, p. 156.
7 Godley, pp. 82–3.
8 Godley, p. 82.

30 Monsieur Foubert's Academy

1 Lord, vol. II, p. 19.
2 Vizetelly.
3 Evelyn, *Diary*, 18 Dec. 1684.
4 For example, '100 l to Mons. Foubert as Royal Bounty, July 19th 1679', Calendar of Treasury Books 1679–1680, p. 140.
5 Stern, *Last Confession*, p. 26.
6 Godley, pp. 88–92; Anon., *Tryal and Condemnation*, pp. 26–8.
7 *Tryal and Condemnation*, pp. 26–8.
8 Godley, p. 90.
9 Godley, p. 90.
10 Godley, p. 90.
11 Godley, p. 91.
12 See Roberts for further details.
13 Evelyn, *Diary*, entry for 20 June 1671.
14 Anon., *Tryal and Condemnation*, p. 23.
15 Stern, *Last Confession*, p. 27.
16 Stern, *Last Confession*, p. 27.
17 Stern, *Last Confession*, p. 26.
18 Stern, *Last Confession*, p. 26.

31 The Black Bull

1 Stern, *Last Confession*, p. 24.
2 Strype.
3 Stern, *Last Confession*, p. 28.
4 Stern, *Last Confession*, p. 28.
5 Anon., *Tryal and Condemnation*, p. 9.
6 The Wren Temple Bar Gateway has been moved more than once in its lifetime. It is now situated close by St Paul's Cathedral.
7 C.S.P.D. 14 Feb. 1682, p. 78.
8 Anon., *Tryal and Condemnation*, pp. 11–12.
9 Anon., *Tryal and Condemnation*, p. 12.
10 Godley, p. 65; see also Godley, p. 198; Stern, *Last Confession*, p. 8.
11 Stern, *Last Confession*, p. 1.
12 Burney Collection of Newspapers, British Library.
13 Stern, *Last Confession*, p. 3.
14 Anon., *Tryal and Condemnation*, p. 17.
15 Stern, *Last Confession*, p. 3.
16 Godley, p. 61.
17 Anon., *Tryal and Condemnation*, p. 11.
18 Anon., *Tryal and Condemnation*, p. 12.
19 Anon., *Tryal and Condemnation*, p. 12.
20 *Impartial Protestant Mercury*, 14–17 Feb. 1682, Burney Collection of Newspapers, British Library.
21 Quoted in Sutherland, p. 61.

32 Sir John Reresby's House

1 John Gay, *Dramatic Works*, ed. Fuller, 2 vols (Oxford 1983), II, pp. 7–8.

2 See *Dictionary of National Biography*, entry for Sir John Reresby (Oxford 2004).

3 Reresby, *Memoirs*, p. 249.

4 Reresby, *Memoirs*, p. 243.

5 Reresby, *Memoirs*, p. 243.

6 Reresby, *Memoirs*, p. 249.

7 Reresby, *Memoirs*, pp. 249–50.

8 Reresby, *Memoirs*, p. 250.

9 Reresby, *Memoirs*, p. 250.

10 Reresby, *Memoirs*, p. 250.

11 Reresby, *Memoirs*, p. 250.

12 Reresby, *Memoirs*, p. 250.

13 See Sutherland, pp. 59–67, for an excellent account of how the story of the murder was variously treated in the press of the day.

14 *Impartial Protestant Mercury*, 14–17 Feb. 1682, Burney Collection of Newspapers, British Library.

15 Reresby, *Memoirs*, p. 251.

16 Reresby, *Memoirs*, p. 252.

17 Reresby, *Memoirs*, p. 252.

18 Reresby, *Memoirs*, pp. 252–3.

33 Next the Cross Keys, Fetter Lane

1 Quoted in Hinds, p. 70.

2 Quoted in Lord, vol. II, p. 300.

3 Quoted in Lord, vol. II, p. 300.

4 *Observator in Dialogue*, Monday, 20 Feb. 1682, Burney Collection of Newspapers, British Library.

5 *Impartial Protestant Mercury*, 14–17 Feb. 1682, Burney Collection of Newspapers, British Library.

6 See Bamford, also article by D. F. Allen published in *European History Quarterly*, vol. 20, No. 3, July 1990. For Vendôme's presence in London and hasty departure see *Impartial Protestant Mercury*, 14–17 Feb. 1682, Burney Collection of Newspapers, British Library.

7 See Vizetelly.

8 Godley, p. 162.

9 Quoted in Sutherland, p. 62.

10 Quoted in Sutherland, p. 62.

11 Quoted in Sutherland, p. 63.

12 Quoted in Sutherland, p. 63.

13 *True Protestant Mercury*, 9–12 Nov. 1681, Burney Collection of Newspapers, British Library.

14 Jeudi 10 janvier 1686, *Journal du Marquis de Dangeau*, ed. Saint-Simon, vol. I, p. 280 (Paris 1854).

15 H.M.C. MS Marquess of Ormonde, vol. IV, p. 315.

34 The House of Derek Raynes at Rotherhithe

1 Quoted in Earle, p. 13.

2 For Watts's testimony see Godley, pp. 109–23.

3 Godley, p. 152.

4 Godley, p. 95.

5 Godley, p. 121.

6 H.M.C. MS Marquess of Ormonde, vol. IV, p. 319.
7 Godley, p. 127.
8 Quoted in Godley, p. 130.
9 Luttrell, entry for 19 Feb. 1682.

35 The Red Lyon at Gravesend

1 *Impartial Protestant Mercury*, 21–24 Feb. 1682, Burney Collection of Newspapers, British
   Library.
2 *Impartial Protestant Mercury*, 17–21 Feb. 1682, Burney Collection of Newspapers, British
   Library.
3 Weather details throughout are taken from Gadbury and also supplemented by Locke's
   weather diary and the logbooks of the *Pearl* and the yacht *Mary*.
4 This account of Konigsmark's arrest is taken largely from Godley, supplemented by Ormonde and various newspaper articles.
5 Godley, p. 136.
6 Godley, p. 137.
7 Godley, p. 137.
8 Godley, p. 137.
9 Anon., *A True Account of the Apprehending and Taking of Count Konigsmark*.
10 Godley, p. 138.
11 Godley, p. 139.
12 Godley, p. 139.
13 Godley, p. 140.
14 Godley, pp. 134–5.
15 Godley, pp. 139, 140.
16 *The Loyal Protestant and True Domestick Intelligence*, 21 Feb. 1682, quoted in Sutherland,
   p. 64.
17 Reresby, *Memoirs*, p. 253.
18 H.M.C. MS Marquess of Ormonde, vol. IV, p. 320.
19 H.M.C. MS Marquess of Ormonde, vol. IV, p. 320.
20 Luttrell, entry for 19 Feb. 1682.
21 Reresby, *Memoirs*, p. 254.

36 Newgate

1 Quoted in Rumbelow, p. 161.
2 See Durston for a fuller discussion of judicial punishment during this period.
3 Defoe, *Moll Flanders*, pp. 273–4.
4 Defoe, *Moll Flanders*, pp. 277–8.
5 Stern, p. 1.
6 Stern, p. 1.
7 Stern, p. 1.
8 Stern, p. 1.
9 Stern, pp. 1–2.
10 Stern, p. 2.
11 Stern, p. 2.
12 Stern, p. 3.
13 Stern, p. 2.
14 Defoe, *Moll Flanders*, p. 288.

15 Defoe, *Moll Flanders*, p. 325.

37 The Sessions House I

1 See 'Sir John Hawes upon the Trial of Count Konigsmark, 1689', in *Cobbett's Complete Collection of State Trials*, by William Cobbett (London 1809–1826).

2 See Halliday, Beattie, Griffiths, Sharpe, and Mandeville for Newgate and broader issues of crime and punishment in this period.

3 Godley, p. 50.

4 Anon., *Tryal and Condemnation*, p. 4.

5 Godley, p. 53.

6 Godley, p. 56.

7 Godley, pp. 57–8.

8 Godley, p. 60.

9 Anon., *Tryal and Condemnation*, pp. 12–13.

10 Godley, p. 64.

11 See 'Sir John Hawes upon the Trial of Count Konigsmark, 1689', in *Cobbett's Complete Collection of State Trials*, by William Cobbett (London 1809–1826).

12 Godley, p. 64.

13 Godley, p. 72.

14 Godley, pp. 72–3.

15 Godley, p. 73.

38 The Sessions House II

1 C.S.P.D. 1680–1681, p. 270.

2 Godley, pp. 74–96.

3 Godley, p. 97.

4 Godley, pp. 99–118.

5 Godley, pp. 108–9.

6 Godley, pp. 150–1.

7 Godley, p. 152.

8 Godley, p. 152.

9 Godley, p. 153.

10 Godley, p. 155.

11 Godley, p. 156.

12 Godley, p. 156.

13 Godley, p. 162.

14 Godley, p. 164.

15 Godley, p. 173.

16 Craik, G. L., ed., *English Causes Célèbres* (London 1840), vol. I, p. 59.

17 Godley, p. 177.

39 Whitehall

1 Printed by J. Bayley, London 1682.

2 Earl of Longford to Ormonde, 1 March 1682, London, p. 325, H.M.C. MSS Marquess of Ormonde, vol. VI.

3 Reresby, *Memoirs*, p. 255, entry for 28 Feb. 1682.

4 Luttrell, entry for 28 Feb. 1682.

5 Luttrell, entry for 4 March 1682.

6 Reresby, *Memoirs*, pp. 254–5, entry for 26 Feb. 1682.

7 Reresby, *Memoirs*, pp. 254–5, entry for 26 Feb. 1682.

8 Evelyn, *Diary*, entry for 9 March 1682.

9 Luttrell, entry for 4 March 1682.

10 Pamphlet, printed by J. Bayley, London 1682.

11 Earl of Longford to Ormonde, 4 March 1682, London, p. 331, H.M.C. MSS Marquess of Ormonde, vol. VI.

12 Earl of Longford to Ormonde, 7 March 1682, London, p. 336, H.M.C. MSS Marquess of Ormonde, vol. VI.

13 Gunman's handwritten journals, part of the Jarvis collection on loan to Lincolnshire Archives, provide a wonderful insight into the life of a captain of this period in command of a royal yacht. A few weeks after this voyage to Holland he was part of the small fleet escorting James to Scotland to fetch back his pregnant wife, Mary of Modena, to London. James's ship was wrecked en route, and although James himself was saved, many seamen and members of the nobility lost their lives. Gunman was to be court-martialled for his role in the disaster and was put in Marshalsea prison.

14 This whole business of this duel is best followed in C.S.P.D. 1682, pp. 116–38, entries between 10 and 24 March.

15 C.S.P.D. 1682, p. 129.

16 C.S.P.D. 1682, p. 138, Secretary Jenkins, Whitehall, 24 March.

17 H.M.C. MSS Duke of Buccleuch, vol. I, p. 336, The Duke of Albemarle to the Count de Konigsmarke, 18 May 1682, Albemarle House.

18 C.S.P.D. 1682, p. 212, 19 May, Windsor.

40 Vratz's Cell

1 Stern, p. 12.

2 Stern, p. 3.

3 Stern, p. 7.

4 Luttrell, entry for 4 March 1682.

5 Stern, p. 7.

6 Stern, p. 7.

7 Stern, p. 8.

8 Stern, p. 9.

9 Stern, p. 9.

10 Stern, p. 3.

11 *The Loyal Protestant and True Domestick Intelligence*, 4–6 March 1682.

12 Stern, p. 3.

13 Stern, pp. 9–10.

14 Stern, p. 11.

15 Stern, p. 11.

16 Stern, p. 11.

17 Stern, p. 11.

18 Stern, p. 4.

19 Stern, p. 4.

20 Stern, p. 6.

21 Stern, p. 6.

22 Stern, p. 6.

23 Stern, p. 4.

24 Stern, p. 4.

25 Stern, p. 4.

26 Stern, p. 4.

27 Stern, p. 4.

28 The bell and the poem are on display in St Sepulchre Church, Newgate, the custom orig-
inating from a bequest by Robert Dowe in 1605 of £50, 'the bellman to give 12 sobarre
towels [tolls] with double strokes'.

41 The Haymarket

1 Mandeville, p. 28.

2 Stern, p. 5.

3 Stern, p. 5.

4 Stern, p. 7.

5 The phrase comes from *The Journals of Two Travellers, Thomas Platter and Horatio Busino*,
p. 149 (London 1995).

6 Evelyn, *Diary*, vol. IV, p. 401.

7 Gittings, *Death, Burial and the Individual*, p. 67.

8 Misson, p. 266.

9 *The Petty Papers, Some Unpublished Writings, Edited from the Bowood Papers by the Marquis
of Lansdowne* (London 1927), vol. II, *Crime and Punishment*, p. 211.

10 Misson, quoted in Gittings, *Death, Burial and the Individual*, p. 69.

11 *Impartial Protestant Mercury*, 10–14 March 1682, Burney Collection of Newspapers, British Library.

12 Reresby, *Memoirs*, 4 March 1682, p. 257.

13 Evelyn, *Diary*, entry for 10 March 1682.

14 Stern, p. 6.

15 Stern, p. 7.

16 Stern, p. 7.

17 Stern, p. 7.

18 *Impartial Protestant Mercury*, 10–14 March 1682, Burney Collection of Newspapers, British Library.

19 Luttrell, entry for 10 March 1682.

20 Stern, p. 5.

42 The New Exchange

1 C.S.P.D. 16 March 1682, p. 128.

2 National Archives, PROB 5/646, Thomas Thynn of Longleat. Miscellaneous Inventories,
Accounts, and Associated Documents, 1689.

3 C.S.P.D. 16 March 1682, newsletter to J. Squier, Newcastle, p. 127.

4 London, 20 March, in the *Impartial Protestant Mercury*, 17–21 March 1682.

5 Gunman's Journal, entry for 7 March 1682, Lincolnshire archives.

6 *Daily Intelligencer*, 23 March 1682, quoted in Brenan, p. 397.

7 *Loyal Protestant*, 23 March 1682.

8 Anon. (London 1677), p. 3.

9 *Count Conningsmark's Letter to the Lady Ogle from Flanders* (London 1682), printed for J.S.

10 Longleat Archive, vol. XII, ff. 3,17.21.33, Sir William Temple, Letters to Lord
Weymouth.

11 Savile, George, *Life and Letters*, letter dated 29 March 1682, Earl of Halifax to Sir Thomas
Thynn.

12 Savile, George, *Life and Letters*, letter dated 27 Feb. 1682, Sir Wm Coventry to Lord Halifax.

43 Mile End Road

1 Sir Thomas Browne, *Hydriotaphia and The Garden of Cyrus* (London 1658), p. 1.
2 Evelyn, *Diary*, entry for 22 March 1682.
3 *Impartial Protestant Mercury*, 10–14 February 1682, Burney Collection of Newspapers, British Library.
4 PC/2/69 p. 480, National Archives.
5 C.S.P.D. 1682, Letter from Secretary Jenkins to the Earl of Conway, Whitehall, 8 March 1682, with Conway's reply from Newmarket, 10 March 1682.
6 C.S.P.D. 1682, Newsletter from London to John Squier, Newcastle, 14 March 1682.
7 Luttrell, entry for 10 March 1682.
8 Pepys, *Diary*, ed. Latham and Mathews, entry for 11 April 1661, vol. II, pp. 72–3.

44 The House on the Hill

1 Quoted in Brenan, p. 405.
2 Letter from Charles, Duke of Somerset, to his aunt, quoted in Brenan, p. 401.
3 Quoted in Fonblanque, vol. II, part 2, p. 504.
4 Quoted in Craik, p. 82.
5 *Stanhope's History of England*, vol. I, p. 84, quoted in Brenan, p. 403.
6 Luttrell, entry for 15 Aug. 1682.
7 Quoted in Craik, p. 82.
8 P.H.A. 16, undated letter from Duchess of Somerset to her husband.

Postscript

1 Swift, *The Windsor Prophecy* (London 1711).
2 Burnet, vol. VI, pp. 34–5.
3 Hamilton, *Diary*, p. 46.
4 Quoted in Green, p. 315.
5 Printed London 1712.
6 For details of this episode see Green, pp. 261–2.
7 Quoted in Craik, p. 85.
8 P.H.A. 16, undated letter from Duchess of Somerset to her husband.
9 See *Secret Memoirs of the Court of Louis XIV by The Duchess of Orleans* (London 1895).
10 See Craik, p. 79.

List of Illustrations

Prologue. Detail from the South Aisle at Westminster Abbey by George Sidney Shepherd (1784–1862) *(Crown copyright/UK Government Art Collection)*

1. *Brothel Scene* by Frans van Mieris, c.1658–9 *(Mauritshuis Royal Gallery, The Hague)*
2. The Royal Exchange in 1681, from *Old and New London*, vol. I, by Edward Walford, 1878 *(National Maritime Museum, Greenwich)*
3. Detail from 'A True Narrative of the Horrid Hellish Popish-Plot' *(The Trustees of the British Museum)*
4. The Cleveland Yacht *(The Trustees of the British Museum)*
5. Illustration from *Vulgus Britannicus* by Ned Ward *(British Library)*
6. 'Le Tour du Monde', 1867 *(Bibliothèque nationale de France)*
7. Elizabeth Montagu (née Wriothesley), Countess of Montagu by Thomas Watson, after Sir Peter Lely *(National Portrait Gallery, London)*
8. Joceline Percy, 11th Earl of Northumberland, mezzotint after Sir Peter Lely c.1684 *(National Portrait Gallery, London)*
9. Piazza de Santi Apostoli c.1675 *(Alvaro de Alvariis/flickr)*
10. Thomas Thynn, engraving by Robert White c.1675–1700 *(National Portrait Gallery, London)*
11. Althorp in 1677 by Johannes Vostermann *(From the collection at Althorp)*
12. Ralph Montagu, 1st Duke of Montagu, engraving by William Nelson Gardiner c.1795 *(National Portrait Gallery, London)*
13. Detail from an illustration of St James's Park in *Old and New London*, vol. IV, by Edward Walford, 1878 *(British Library)*
14. Drawing of the Strand front (north) of Northumberland House by G. Vertue, 1725 *(V&A Images/Victoria and Albert Museum)*
15. John Wilmot, 2nd Earl of Rochester, engraving by William Nelson Gardiner *(National Portrait Gallery, London)*
16. Etching of Lady Bette's betrothal portrait by Van der Vaart, original by Peter Lely *(National Portrait Gallery, London)*
17. Illustration of Syon House from *The Environs of London*, vol. III, by Daniel Lysons, 1795
18. Petworth House as it was in 1679 *(from the collection at Syon Park and His Grace the Duke of Northumberland)*
19. Illustration of Longleat from *The Beauties of Wiltshire*, vol. II, by John Britton, 1801 *(British Library)*
20. Count Konigsmark from Woodburn's Portraits of 100 Illustrious Characters *(The Trustees of the British Museum)*
21. The Gardens at Syon in the late seventeenth century *(from the collection at Syon Park and His Grace the Duke of Northumberland)*

References

PRIMARY MANUSCRIPT SOURCES

British Library

Add. Ch. 65798	Percy formerly Cavendish (Henry) Earl of Ogle, Letters of Administration for his estate, 1681
Add. Ms. 4107, ff. 25–436	Sir Thomas Thynn, extracts from a diary in his possession, 1668–1688
Add. Ms. 23072	Diary of Mary Beale
Add. Ms. 27962 T, f. 149	re Murder of Peter Virnill by Monmouth and others
Add. Ms. 32328	Family Pedigree of Percy
Add. Ms. 37047, f. 244	Account of assassination of Thomas Thynn of Longleat, 1682
Add. Ms. 37979	Letters of Thomas Plott to William Blathwayt
Add. Ms. 37980	Thomas Chudleigh to Lord Conway, 1682
Add. Ms. 38855, ff. 113, 115	Papers relating to murder of Thomas Thynn, 1682
Lat 4455, f. 75.	Epitaph for Thomas Thynn, 1682
Add. Ms. 70500 ff. 69	Letter from Margaret Cavendish, Duchess of Newcastle, re Henry Ogle, 13 July 1674
Add. Ms. 70500 f. 57	Letter from Countess Howard (calling herself Elizabeth of Northumberland) to the Duke of Newcastle. The letter has been annotated 1676 by a later editorial hand but is in fact 1671.

Lambeth Palace Library

49 VB 1/4/200	1682	Ogle Somerset
50 VB 1/4/200	1682	Ogle Somerset

Act Book 23rd Oct. 1680–21st Oct. 1682, MS Film 76, Matrimonial Cases, Espousals, Case Number 9152.

Arches	E	7/24	Thynn v Ogle 1681
Arches	E	7/26	Thynn v Ogle 1681
Arches	E	7/108	Thynn v Ogle 1681
Arches	E	7/109	Thynn v Ogle 1681

Lincolnshire Archives

Jarvis 9/1/A/5   Journals of Captain Christopher Gunman, March 1682

Longleat Archive

Copies held by the British Library, London, England, on microfilm

Cavendish, Lady Elizabeth, née Percy, wife of Henry Earl of Ogle. Papers relating to her marriage with Thomas Thynn, vol. XI (Micro 904/21)

Tradesman's and other bills 1671–1681, vol. XI (Micro 904/21)

National Archives, Kew, London, England

Equity Pleadings Chancery, C 6/239/55, Percy v Thynn 1681
PROB 5/646 Thomas Thynn of Longleat. Miscellaneous Inventories, Accounts, and
    Associated Documents, 1689
C9/415/250 For dissolution of the partnership between Gibbons and Quillan
ADM 51/3932 Log Book of the *Pearl* (for weather and wind details)
ADM 2/1726 For details of yacht movements and passengers on board in 1681–82

Northumberland Archive, Alnwick

Copies held by the British Library, London, England, on Microfilm. Permission required
    from Duke of Northumberland before access permitted

vol. 19, 3rd Report page No. 936, letters 1664–1684	Micro No. 287
vol. 107, 3rd Report page No. 1096, Inventory 1671	Micro No. 351
vol. 566, 3rd Report page No. 122a, Notes of Journies 1679–80	Micro No. 348

Nottingham University Library, Nottingham, England

Department of Manuscripts and Special Collections

Pw1/192–206	Letters between Dowager Countess of Northumberland and Countess Ogle (Elizabeth Wriothesley), 1674–1679 and undated
Pw1/207	Letter from Elizabeth Wriothesley, Countess of Northumberland, 26 December 1678, re marriage of her daughter
Pw1/49–50	Essex to Duke of Newcastle, 1679
Pw1/75	Henry Ogle to his father the Duke of Newcastle, 1679
Pw1/402	Henry Ogle's Debts, 1 November 1684
Pw1/410	The sadd and Miserable Case of Henry Duke of Newcastle by his wife

Petworth House Archives

Consulted at West Sussex Record Office, Chichester, England

PHA 11	Letter from Charles II to the Dowager Countess, 1679
PHA 16	Letters from the Duchess of Somerset to her husband
PHA 144	Accounts of J. Weekes, servant and paymaster to the Countess of Ogle, for year ending 25 December 1681
PHA 147	Accounts of Orlando Gee, servant to the Countess of Ogle and one of the trustees of Josceline, Earl of Northumberland, deceased
PHA 258	Accounts of Countess of Ogle, 1679–1681
PHA 259	As above
PHA 304–306	Household Accounts London and Petworth, 1675–1678
PHA 316	Accounts for purchases of small articles of clothing, haircutting, cleaning of guns and pistols, pocket money, etc., on behalf of Lord Percy, 1659
PHA 683	Correspondence various, 1680–1699
PHA 5243	Weekly accounts of household expenses with monthly summary of servant and personal expenses by Henry Barnard of Petworth, gentleman, Jan. 1666/7–Dec. 1667
PHA 5807	Accounts, works at Petworth, 1666
PHA 5809	Accounts of Orlando Gee, re Josceline, apparel, 1666
PHA 5820	Accounts of John Weekes, Petworth, 1667
PHA 6261	Inventory of everything at Petworth under charge of Barwick, 1680

PHA 6346   Miscellaneous Accounts of Duke and Duchess of Somerset, 1682–1700

PRIMARY PRINTED SOURCES

Allestree, Richard   *The Ladies Calling* (Oxford 1693, 6th impression)

Anonymous   *Captain Vrats Ghost* (printed in London Fleet Street for J.V. 1682, British Library Cup.21.g.41/27)

— *The Complete Gamester* (London 1680)

— *Confession and Manner of Execution* (London 1682, Cup.21.g.27/52, BL)

— *An Exact Relation of the Marriage of Charles II* (London 1679) (Sel.2.121, Cambridge University Library)

— *A Foreigner's Guide to London* (London 1729)

— *Great and Bloody News from Turnham Green* (London 1680, British Library pamphlet 816.m.19 (47))

— *The Matchless Murder* (printed for J. Conyers at the Black Raven, London 1682)

— *A True Account of the Apprehending and taking of Count Konigsmark* (London 1682, Cup. 21.g.33/23, BL)

— *A True Account of the Murder* (London 1682, 515.1.2 (63) BL)

— *The Tryal and Condemnation of George Borosky* (printed for Thomas Basset, London 1682, British Library pamphlet 6485.h.1)

— *Tryal of Philip Earl of Pembroke for the Murder of N. Cony 4th April 1678* (London 1679, British Library pamphlet Mic. A. 11300 (1))

Aubrey, John   *Letters Written by Eminent Persons . . . and Lives of Eminent Men* (London 1813)

— *Memoir*, ed. John Britton (London 1845)

Aulnoy, M. C.   *Memoirs of the Court of England in 1675*, ed. G. A. Gilbert (London 1927)

— *The Ingenious and Diverting letters of the Lady d'Aulnoy's Travels into Spain* (London 1692)

Blanchard, Monsieur   *Method of Curing the French Pox, annotations by William Salmon* (London 1690)

Borodzycz, George   *The Confession of George Borodzycz the Polonian, Signed with His Own Hand in Prison, before his Execution* (printed for Richard Chiswell at The Rose and Crown, 1682)

Bulstrode Papers   *A Series of Newsletters Addressed to Sir Richard Bulstrode* (London 1897)

Burnet, Gilbert   *History of His Own Time* (London 1850)

— *Some Passages of the Life and Death of John Earl of Rochester* (London 1680)

— *An Account of the Deportment of Captain Vratz, Lieutenant Stern, and George Borosky, the Murtherers of Tho. Thynn, Esq; both in the Prison, and at their Execution* (printed for Richard Chiswell at The Rose and Crown, 1682)

C.S.P.D   *Calendar of State Papers Domestic, Charles II*, various, 1660–1685, 28 vols (London 1860–1947)

Dalrymple, John   *Memoirs* (London 1773)

Defoe, Daniel   *Religious and Didactic Writings of Daniel Defoe*, ed. W. R. Owens and P. R. Furbank, 10 vols (London 2006)

— *Conjugal Lewdness of Matrimonial Whoredom* (London 1727)

— *Moll Flanders* (Oxford 2009)

— *A Tour thro' the Whole Island of Great Britain* (London 1724)

Delaune, T.   *The Present State of London* (London 1681)

Dryden, John   *Absalom and Achitophel* (London 1681)

— *Complete Works in 18 vols* (London 1808)

Dunlop, John   *Memoirs of Spain 1621–1700* (London 1834)

Elliot, A.   *A Modest Vindication of Titus Oates, the Salamanca Doctor* (London 1682)

Evelyn, John   *Diary of John Evelyn*, ed. E. S. de Beer, 6 vols (Oxford, 1955)

— *Diary and Correspondence of John Evelyn*, ed. William Bray, 4 vols (London 1859)

— *Memoirs of John Evelyn*, ed. William Bray (London 1871)

— *Particular Friends: The Correspondence of Samuel Pepys and John Evelyn*, ed. Guy de la Bedoyere (Woodbridge 1997)

— *Fumifugium* (London 1661)

— *Elysium Britannicum*, ed. Therese O'Malley (Harvard 1998)

Evelyn, Mary   *Mundus Muliebris* or *The Ladies Dressing Room Unlocked* (London 1690)

Ferrier, Richard   *Journal*, Camden Miscellany, 5th Series, vol. 9 (London 1895)

Foxcroft, H. C.   *Life and Letters of Sir George Savile, First Marquis of Halifax* (London 1898)

Gadbury, John   *The Astrological Seaman unto Which is Added a Diary of the Weather for XXI Years Exactly Observed in London* (London 1710)

Godley, E., ed.   *The Trial of Count Koningsmarck* (London 1929)

Gouge, William   *Domestical Duties* (London 1634)

Gramont, Count   *Memoirs, by Anthony Hamilton* (London 1809)

Green M. A. E., ed.   *Calendar of State Papers Domestic 1660–1685*, 28 vols (London 1860–1938)

Greenhill, Thomas   *The Art of Embalming* (London 1705)

Hamilton, Anthony   *Memoirs of the Count de Grammont*, trans. and ed. Horace Walpole (London 1911)

Hamilton, David   *The Diary of, 1709–1714*, ed. P. Roberts (Oxford 1975)

Hargrave, Francis, ed.   *A Complete Collection of State Trials*, 5th Edition, vol. III (London 1797)

Hatton, Christopher   *Correspondence Family of Hatton*, ed. E. M. Thompson, 2 vols (Camden Society Publications no. 22, London 1878)

Hawkins, Susan   *The Diary of The Blue Nuns*, ed. Joseph Gillow (London 1910)

Hawes, Sir John   *Remarks upon the Trial* (London 1689)

Hist. Ms. Comm.   *Buccleuch*, 2 vols (London 1897, 1903)

— *Rutland*, 4 vols (London 1888–1905)

— *Ormonde*, 3 vols (London 1895–1909)

— *Hastings*, 4 vols (London 1928–1947)

— *Portland*, 10 vols (London 1891–1931)

— *Belvoir*, 4 vols (London 1888–1905)

— *Finch*, 5 vols (London 1913–2004)

Hooke, Robert   *Diary*, ed. H. W. Robinson and W. Adams (London 1935)

— *Micrographia* (London 1665)

Horneck, Anthony   *Account of What Himself Observed in the Carriage of the Late Prisoners* (printed for Richard Chiswell at The Rose and Crown, 1682)

Howell, T. B., ed.   *A Complete Collection of State Trials*, 34 vols (London 1816–1828)

Konigsmark, K.   *Count Conningsmark's Letter to the Lady Ogle* (London 1682, University Library, Cambridge, pamphlet Sel.2.121.14)

Krull, J.   *The Antiquities of St Peter's of the Abbey Church of Westminster* (London 1715)

Lister, M.   *A Journey to Paris in the Year 1698* (London 1823)

Locke, John   *The Correspondence*, ed. E. S. de Beer, 8 vols (Oxford 1976–86)

Lord, George, ed.   *Poems on Affairs of State*, 7 vols (London 1963)

Luttrell, Narcissus   *A Brief Historical Relation of State Affairs, 1678–1714*, 6 vols (Oxford 1857)

Macky, John   *Memoir of the Secret Services of John Macky* (London 1733)

Magalotti, Lorenzo   *Lorenzo Magalotti at the Court of Charles II*, ed. W. E. Knowles Middleton (Canada 1980)

— *Travels of Cosmo 3rd* (London 1821)

Makin, Basua   *An essay to revive the antient education . . .* (London 1673)

Mancini, H. and M.   *Memoirs*, ed. and trans. Susan Nelson (London 2008)

Mandeville, B.   *An Enquiry into the Causes of the Frequent Executions at Tyburn* (London 1725)

Misson, Henri   *Memoirs and Observations*, trans. Mr Ozell (London 1719)

Montagu, Ralph   *The Montagu Arlington Letters*, Calendared by R. E. G. Kirk, H.M.C. no. 45 (London 1899)

— *The Court in Mourning* (London 1709)

Morgan, W. and J. Ogilby   *London Actually Surveyed* (London 1682)

Morrice, Roger   *The Entring Book: being an Historical Register of Occurrences 1677–1691*, ed. Mark Goldie, 7 vols (Woodbridge 2007–2009)

North, Roger   *Notes of Me*, ed. Peter Millard (Toronto 2000)

Osborne, Dorothy   *The Letters from Dorothy Osborne to Sir William Temple*, ed. E. A. Parry (London 1914)

Pepys, Samuel   *The Diary*, ed. R. Latham and W. Mathews, 11 vols (London 1970–1983)

Pepys Library   *Catalogue of the Pepys Library at Magdalene College Cambridge*, ed. Robert Latham, vol. 3, Prints and Drawings (Part One, Woodbridge 1981; Part Two, Cambridge 1994)

Perwich, William   *The Despatches*, ed. M. B. Curran, Royal Historical Society, Camden, 3rd Series, vol. V (London 1903)

Philips, Katherine   *Poems* (London 1667)

Reresby, John   *Memoirs of Sir John Reresby 1634–1689*, ed. A. Browning (Glasgow 1936)

— *Examination of Lieutenant John Stern, Feb 17th 1682 and Feb 19th 1682* (printed for Richard Chiswell at The Rose and Crown, London 1682)

— *Examination of George Boroski, Feb 17th 1682* (printed for Richard Chiswell at The Rose and Crown, London 1682)

Russell, Rachel   *The Letters*, ed. Lord John Russell, 2 vols (London 1853)

Salgado, James   *Impartial and Brief Description of the Plaza . . . and the Bull Baiting There* (1680)

Savile, George   *Life and Letters of Sir George Savile*, ed. H. C. Foxcroft (London 1898)

Savile, Henry   *Letters to and from Henry Savile*, ed. W. D. Cooper (London 1858)

— *The Rochester Savile Letters*, ed. J. Wilson (Ohio 1941)

Sévigné, Madame de   *Lettres de Madame de Sévigné*, ed. A. Edward Newton, 7 vols (London 1928)

Sharp, Jane   *The Midwives Book* (1671)

Sidney, Henry   *Diary of the Time of Charles II, Including His Correspondence with the Countess of Sunderland and Other Distinguished Persons*, ed. R. Blencowe (London 1843)

Stern, John   *The Last Confession, Prayers and Meditations of Lieuten. John Stern, together with the Last Confession of George Borosky, to which is added an account of their Deportment both in the prison and at the place of their execution, written by Gilbert Burnet and Anthony Horneck. Together with a postscript of the Examinations of John Stern and George Borosky before Sir John Reresby and William Bridgman* (London 1682)

— *Letter to Dr Burnet written in prison, 1682* (printed for Richard Chiswell at The Rose and Crown, London 1682)

Strype, J.   *Survey of London* (London 1720)

Swift, Jonathan   *Journal to Stella*, ed. H. Williams (Oxford 1948)

— *The Windsor Prophecy* (London 1711)

— *Some advice humbly offer'd to the Members of the October Club* (London 1712)

Temple, William   *Works* (London 1814)

— *Observations upon the United Provinces of the Netherlands* (London 1705)

Vertue, George   *The Notebooks* (Oxford 1930–55)

Villars, Pierre   *Mémoires de la Cour d'Espagne 1679–1681* (Paris 1893)

Villars, Madame de   *Lettres de Madame de Villars à Madame de Coulanges 1679–1681* (Paris 1868)

Vincent, Thomas   *Funeral Sermon of Abraham Janeway* (London 1667)

Waller, R.   *Posthumous Works* (London 1705)

Ward, Ned   *London Spy*, ed. Paul Hyland (East Lansing 1993)

— *A Trip to Holland* (London 1699)

Williamson, Joseph   *Letters to Sir Joseph Williamson*, Camden Society Publications, 2 vols (London 1874)

Wilmot, John   *The Letters of John Wilmot, Earl of Rochester*, ed. Jeremy Treglown (Oxford 1980)

— *The Complete Poems*, ed. David Vieth (Yale 1962)

Woolley, Hannah   *The Gentlewoman's Companion* (London 1682)

— *The Lady's Delight* (London 1672)

Wren, C.   *Parentalia, or Memoirs of the Family of the Wrens*, ed. E. S. Enthoven (London 1903)

Newspapers

The Impartial Protestant Mercury, ed. Langley Curtis and Henry Care, printed Richard Janeway (London 1661–1682)

The London Gazette

The True Protestant Mercury

The Loyal Protestant and True Domestic Intelligence, ed. and printed Nathaniel Thompson (London 1681–1683)

The Observator in Dialogue, ed. Roger L'Estrange, printed Joanna Brome (London 1681–1687)

La Gazette (Paris 1631–1761)

SECONDARY SOURCES PRINTED

Allen, David   *Bridget Hyde*, essay in Guildhall Studies in London History, vol. 2 (London 1980)

Andrews, Allen   *Royal Whore* (London 1671)

Arnold, Catharine   *City of Sin* (London 2010)

Baker, Henry   *Lely and the Stuart Portrait Painters* (London 2012)

Bamford, P. W.   'The Knights of Malta and the King of France 1665–1700' (*French Historical Studies* 3:429–53, 1964)

Barber, Tabitha   *Mary Beale* (London 1999)

Batten, M. I.   *The Architecture of Dr Robert Hooke F.R.S.*, Walpole Society, 25, 93–96 (London 1936–37)

Beard, Geoffrey   *Grinling Gibbons* (London 1989)

Beattie, J.   *Crime and the Courts of England 1660–1800* (Cambridge 1986)

Berry, Mary   *Some Account of the Life of Rachel Wriothesley* (London 1819)

Bickley, Francis   *The Cavendish Family* (London 1911)

Boulton, William   *The Amusements of Old London* (London 1901)

Brenan, Gerald   *A History of the House of Percy*, 2 vols (London 1902)

Brown, K. M.   'Gentlemen and Thugs in Seventeenth Century Britain', *History Today* XL (London 1990)

Brown, Kevin   *The Pox* (Stroud 2006)

Browning, Andrew   *Earl of Danby*, 3 vols (Glasgow 1951)

Burnett, David   *Longleat* (London 1978)

Cartwright, Julia   *Sacharissa* (London 1901)

Cliffe, J. T.   *The World of the Country House in Seventeenth Century England* (London 1999)

Cowburn, Philip   'Charles II's Yachts', *History Today*, April 1962, pp. 253–62 (London 1962)

Craik, George   *English Causes Célèbres* (London 1840)

Crawford, P. and L. Gowing, eds   *Women's Worlds in 17th Century England* (London 2000)

Cruickshanks, E., ed.   *The Stuart Courts* (Stroud 2000)

Davis, Ralph   *The Rise of the English Shipping Industry in the Seventeenth and Eighteenth Centuries* (London 1962)

Delpech, Jeanine   *The Life and Times of the Duchess of Portsmouth* (London 1953)

Dethloff, Diana   'The Executor's Account Book and the Dispersal of Sir Peter Lely's Collection', *Journal of the History of Collections* 8, No. 1, pp. 15–51 (London 1996)

Dibdin, Thomas   *Aedes Althorpianae* (London 1822)

Durston, Gregory   *Crime and Justice in Early Modern England* (Chichester 2004)

Earle, Peter   *Sailors, English Merchant Seamen 1650–1775* (London 2007)

— *A City full of People* (London 1994)

Falk, Bernard   *The Way of the Montagues* (London 1947)

Fonblanque, Edward B. de   *House of Percy*, 2 vols (London 1887)

Foyster, E. A   *Manhood in Early Modern England* (London 1999)

Fraser, Antonia   *Charles II His Life and Times* (London 1979)

— *The Weaker Vessel* (London 1993)

Gadbury, John   *Nauticum astrologicum . . . unto Which is Added a Diary of the Weather for XXI years Together* (London 1710)

Gady, Alexandre   *Les hôtels particuliers de Paris* (Paris 2008)

Galinou, Mireille, ed.   *City Merchants and the Arts* (London 2004)

Gater, G. H. and E. P. Wheeler   *Survey of London*, vol. 18 (London 1937)

Gatrell, V. A. C.   *Execution and the English People* (Oxford 1994)

Gelis, Jacques   *History of Childbirth* (London 1991)

Gittings, C.   *Death, Burial and the Individual in Early Modern England* (London 1984)

Gittings, C. and P. Jupp, eds   *Death . . . Illustrated* (London 2002)

Goldsworthy, Cephas   *Satyr, An Account of the Life . . . Earl of Rochester* (London 2001)

Grant, Douglas   *Margaret the First* (London 1957)

Greaves, Richard   *Secrets of the Kingdom* (Stanford 1992)

Green, David   *Queen Anne* (London 1970)

Griffiths, Arthur   *Chronicles of Newgate* (London 1884)

Grigsby, J. E.   *Royal Yachts* (1953)

Halliday, Stephen   *Newgate* (Stroud 2006)

Hardwick, J. C.   'The Thynn Affair' (*Cambridge Journal* 4, pp. 599–610, 1951)

Harris, Tim   *London Crowds in the Reign of Charles II* (Cambridge 1987)

— *Restoration* (London 2005)

Hartmann, C. H.   *The Vagabond Duchess* (London 1926)

— *Clifford of the Cabal* (London 1937)

Hendriks, Ella   'Lely's Studio Practice', *Hamilton Herr Institute Bulletin* 2, pp. 21–37
    (1994)

Henning, B. D.   *House of Commons 1660–1690* (London 1983)

Hinds, Peter   *The Horrid Popish Plot* (Oxford 2009)

Holmes, G. S.   *British Politics in the Age of Anne* (London 1987)

Houlbrooke, Ralph   *The English Family* (London 1984)

— *Death, Ritual and Bereavement* (London 1989)

Hussey, Christopher   *Petworth House* (London 1926)

Hyde, R.   *The A–Z of Restoration London* (Kent 1992)

Jardine, Lisa   *Ingenious Pursuits, Building the Scientific Revolution* (London 1999)

Jerrome, Peter   *Petworth from the Beginning to 1660* (Sussex 1990)

Jesse, John Heneage   *Memoirs of the Court of England During the Reign of the Stuarts*
    (London 1855)

Kenyon, J. P.   *Robert Spencer, Earl of Sunderland* (London 1958)

Kirby Talley, M.   'Extracts from the Executors Account Book of Sir Peter Lely 1679–
    1681', *Burlington Magazine* 120 (London Nov. 1978)

Kiernan, V. G.   *The Duel in European History* (Oxford 1988)

Knights, Mark   *Politics and Opinion in Crisis* (Cambridge 1994)

Lasch, Christopher   'The Suppression of Clandestine Marriage', essay in *Salmagundi* 26,
    pp. 91–109 (1974)

Llewellyn, Nigel   *The Art of Death* (London 1991)

Macleod, Catherine   *Painted Ladies, Women at the Court of Charles II* (London 2001)

Marshall, Alan   *Intelligence and Espionage in the Reign of Charles II* (Cambridge 1994)

McCann, Alison, ed.   *Petworth House Archives, a Catalogue* (Chichester 1997)

Metzger, E. C.   *Ralph, First Duke of Montagu* (New York 1987)

Morris, Derek and Ken Cozens   *Wapping 1600–1800* (East London History Society
    2009)

Nada, John   *Carlos the Bewitched* (London 1962)

National Trust   *Petworth House* (1997)

Outhwaite, R. B.   'Clandestine Marriage in England 1500–1850', *Economic History
    Review*, vol. 50, 1997

Peerbooms, G. M.   *Nathaniel Thompson* (Nijmegen 1983)

Petherick, Maurice   *Restoration Rogues* (London 1951)

Picard, Liza   *Restoration London* (London 1997)

Porter, Roy   *London a Social History* (London 2000)

Porter, Stephen   *Pepys's London* (Stroud 2012)

Roberts, David   *Thomas Betterton* (Cambridge 2010)

Rosvall, T. D.   *Hortense Mazarine* (London 1969)

Rumbelow, Arnold   *The Triple Tree* (London 1982)

Sabatier, Gerard   *Louis XIV Espagnol* (Paris 2009)

Salmon, R.   *State Trials, A Critical Review* (London 1735)

Schwoerer, L. G.   *Lady Rachel Russell* (Baltimore 1988)

Scott Thomson, Gladys   *The Russells in Bloomsbury 1669–1771* (London 1940)

Sharpe, J.   *Crime in Early Modern England 1550–1750* (London 1999)

Shifrin, Susan, ed.   *The Wandering Life I Led, Essays on Hortense Mancini* (Newcastle 2009)

Smith, Alexander   *A Complete History of the Lives and Robberies of the Most Notorious Highwaymen*, ed. Arthur Hayward (London 1926)

Spurr, John   *England in the 1670s* (Oxford 2000)

Stone, Lawrence   *Family and Fortune* (Oxford 1973)

— *Family, Sex and Marriage* (London 1977)

Sutherland, James   *The Restoration Newspaper* (Cambridge 1986)

Thynn, Daphne   *Longleat and the History of the Thynn Family* (1949)

Uglow, Jenny   *A Gambling Man, Charles II and the Restoration* (London 2009)

Vizetelly, Henry   *Count Konigsmark* (1890)

Watson, J. N. P.   *Captain General and Rebel Chief* (London 1979)

Whitaker, Katie   *Mad Madge, Margaret Cavendish Duchess of Newcastle* (London 2003)

Wise, Charles   *The Montagus of Boughton* (Kettering 1888)

Index